# Rethinking
# SCIENTIFIC LITERACY

The *Critical Social Thought* Series
edited by Michael W. Apple, University of Wisconsin—Madison

# Rethinking
# SCIENTIFIC
# LITERACY

Wolff-Michael Roth
Angela Calabrese Barton

ROUTLEDGEFALMER
NEW YORK AND LONDON

Published in 2004 by
RoutledgeFalmer
29 West 35th Street
New York, NY 10001
www.routledge-ny.com

Published in Great Britain by
RoutledgeFalmer
11 New Fetter Lane
London EC4P 4EE
www.routledgefalmer.com

10 9 8 7 6 5 4 3 2 1

Cataloging-in-Publication Data is available from the Library of Congress.
ISBN 0-415-948428 (hardcover)
ISBN 0-415-948436  (paperback)

# TABLE OF CONTENTS

# ACKNOWLEDGMENTS

Projects such as this book always develop in particular contexts, which provide support and encouragement but also resistance that pushes people to work harder on explaining their ideas. Projects such as this book also have histories, outside of which they cannot be understood; ideas evolve from previous writings and, at times, undergo significant changes when they reappear in a new form and context. In the following, we acknowledge all those who helped us in direct and indirect ways and we acknowledge prior publications from which emerged some of the ideas presented here.

Chapter 2 constitutes a considerable development from an article published in *Public Understanding of Science.*[1] Chapters 1 and 3 contain materials that originally had been published in the *Journal of Curriculum Studies.*[2] Chapter 5 began as a presentation at the 2002 annual meeting of the National Association for Research in Science Teaching (NARST), but subsequently underwent considerable alteration and development.[3] It received the 2003 NARST Award for the "Paper with the greatest significance and potential in the field of science education." Similarly, Chapter 7 began its life as a presentation at the annual meeting of the American Educational Research Association, but it, too, experienced considerable alteration and development before taking its current form.[4] The research reported in Chapters 2, 3, 6, and 7 was supported by two grants from the Social Sciences and Humanities Research Council of Canada. We are grateful to Sylvie Boutonné, G. Michael Bowen, and Stuart H. Lee for their contributions during the teaching and data collection. Furthermore, we are grateful to those individuals who have read and critiqued the ideas that were budding in these original papers. Among these individuals Ken Tobin and Margaret Eisenhart figure most prominently. Stuart H. Lee, too, has given his time to discuss ideas with Michael Roth; a special thanks is owed to him.

Some parts of Chapter 4 have previously been published in *Theory into Practice*.[5] The Spencer Foundation Postdoctoral Fellows Program and the National Science Foundation (REC 0096032) made possible the research reported in Chapters 4 and 5. For the research conducted in Chapter 4, we are grateful to Kimberley Yang for her contribution to the data collection. For Chapter 5, we are grateful to Courtney St. Prix, Dana Fusco, and Sumi Hagiwara for their contributions to running the after-school science program and for the data collection. We appreciate the support that Angie received from Teachers College Columbia University and to the shelters—the administrators and families—where the research was conducted. The research in Chapter 8 was funded by the Spencer Foundation, support that is acknowledged with gratitude. This chapter is based on a paper delivered at the annual meeting of the American Educational Research Association;[6] one portion of one of the three case studies (Haleema) presented has previously featured in an article that appeared in the *International Journal of Science Education*.[7] All ideas expressed in these chapters are the opinions and sole responsibilities of the authors and not that of the Spencer Foundation. We are grateful for the support of the University of Texas at Austin and the Ali Institute of Education in Lahore, Pakistan.

Angela Calabrese Barton is also indebted for the ongoing support provided to some of the members of her research team and who have contributed their ideas and critiques to the research represented here: Jason Ermer, Gustavo Perez, Erin Turner, Tanahia Burkett, and Kathleen St. Louis. She would also like to thank her husband, Scott, for his enduring support.

# SERIES EDITOR'S INTRODUCTION

We live in a time when there is more and more to know. Unfortunately, all too often, sufficient time and resources are not devoted to actually learning what is considered essential in ways that might make a difference in our collective lives. At a time when a socially, ethically, and intellectually challenging critical education has never been more important, we treat education as a commodity to be placed on a market to be bought and sold like cars and television sets, or we standardize it through national or state testing and national or state curricula. Of course, the goals of these "reforms" are supposedly to create a more competitive and rigorous school system; yet, in the process, the results are often exactly the opposite of such meritorious intentions. These policies have often created even more inequalities (Apple 2001; McNeil 2000) and have cut us off from practices that have been demonstrated to be even more effective (Apple, et al. 2003; Apple and Beane 1995).

Part of the problem is the inadequacy of the ways we think about education and the knowledge that is important to know. In this society, as in so many others, education does not stand alone, a neutral instrumentality somehow above the ideological conflicts and inequalities of the larger society. Rather, it is deeply implicated in the formation of and action against the forms of differential cultural, economic, and political power that dominate a society like our own. Thus, to think seriously about education is also to think just as seriously about power, about the mechanisms in which certain groups assert their visions, beliefs, and practices. While education is not totally reducible to the political, not to deal with the ideological and structural sources of differential power and the role that education may play in reproducing and contesting such power is not to deal with education as a cultural and social act at all.

After decades of cogent analyses, these general arguments are irrefutable. Yet, even given the increasingly wide acceptance of such critical points, there are at least two problems with these arguments. First, much of the content of such arguments is exactly that—general. The arguments have not been as consistently located and developed within specific areas of expertise such as science and mathematics as they have been in, say, literacy and history, although that is changing now. Second, even if the critical arguments have been developed, what one is to do about them in terms of educational policy and practice remains a thorny issue. This is where *Rethinking Scientific Literacy* enters.

Roth and Barton make a significant contribution to our understanding of these issues and to what can be done to deal with them in critical and yet still practical ways. The authors begin with a "hard" but absolutely crucial question. What place does "school science" now have in relations of differential power? Their answer is provocative and telling, since they are clearly not at all satisfied with the roles that science and scientific literacy now play both in the larger society and schools. They then go on to do, and do well, what very few others have even attempted. They ask, and answer, the following question. How might scientific literacy be reconstructed so that it is overtly connected to the real lives of people and to the struggles for social justice that must play such a large role in these lives if such differential power is to be contested?

In formulating their response, the authors recognize that concepts such as literacy are what might be called "sliding signifiers." They have multiple meanings, depending on which group is using them for what purposes. Literacy itself is a socially constructed form, shaped by and reflecting wider social practices, relations, values, goals, and interests; however, increasingly, the meaning has become fixed around functional definitions and viewed as a set of skills that would lead to economic progress, discipline, and achievement on internationally comparative tests. Yet, as I argue in an earlier book of my own, our aim in education should not be to create "functional literacy," but *critical* literacy, *powerful* literacy, *political* literacy that enables the growth of genuine understanding and control of all spheres of social life in which we participate (Apple 2000). This more substantive vision of literacy is exactly what underpins this important new book.

Roth and Barton prove to be excellent storytellers as well. They provide richly detailed and powerfully evocative examples of children and adults engaged in practices of critical scientific literacy. From children who are "living" in homeless shelters, to those who are labeled "intellectually challenged," to schools in other nations, to adults in local communities—each group is shown in action as it engages in a rich practice of serious scientific literacy that, when reconstructed, enables individual and collective action to make the world in which they live a better place. I know of no book in science education that does this better.

But this is a book that is not "only" for those in science and science education. *Rethinking Scientific Literacy* deserves a wide readership both from all those who are concerned about creating more socially, ethically, and intellectually responsive educational institutions and from all citizens who are, justifiably, worried that our definitions of literacy have become so truncated, so limited, that education is in danger of becoming simply memorization of facts for tests or reduced to work skills for an increasingly unequal labor market. In a time of conservative reconstruction of our schools and society, we need good arguments for and good examples of an education that is worthy of its name. Roth and Barton provide us with these arguments and examples.

Michael W. Apple
John Bascom Professor of
Curriculum and Instruction
and
Educational Policy Studies
University of Wisconsin, Madison

## REFERENCES

Apple, Michael W. (2000) *Official Knowledge.* New York: Routledge.

Apple, Michael W. (2001) *Educating the "Right" Way: Markets, Standards, God, and Inequality.* New York: RoutledgeFalmer.

Apple, Michael W. et al. (2003) *The State and the Politics of Knowledge.* New York: RoutledgeFalmer.

Apple, Michael W. and Beane, James A. (1995) *Democratic Schools.* Alexandria, VA: Association for Supervision and Curriculum Development.

McNeil, Linda (2000) *The Contradictions of School Reform.* New York: Routledge.

# 1

## SCIENCE AS COLLECTIVE PRAXIS, LITERACY, POWER, AND STRUGGLE FOR A BETTER WORLD

Time is out of joint. We cannot avoid remembering September 11, 2001—on that day we were forced to experience the negative results that the work of science educators can bring forth. By means of technology enabled by science, enabled by science education, we watched an act of horror—perpetrated by technology enabled by science, enabled by science education—as the Twin Towers of the World Trade Center were destroyed and thousands working there were killed. Watching the news a few weeks later, we were forced to experience the response. Again live, we saw more acts of horror as B-52 bombers, developed by engineers and built by technicians, who had been trained by science educators, destroyed Afghan villages and maimed more innocent people, mostly women and children. There were, of course, other responses in the wake of these events, the redirecting of funding from humanistic programs, increased efforts in the areas of science that feed the technologies of "star wars," of "exoatmospheric kill vehicles" and other "hit to kill" technologies, and of bomblets of the type that littered Afghanistan and functioned as antipersonnel landmines.

Speaking at the Centennial Nobel Peace Prize Symposium on December 6, 2001, the Chairperson of Amnesty International thought that the government's response to the horrific human rights abuses of September 11, would be a restriction of civil liberties and human rights, ostensibly to promote security. The means of restricting civil liberties and human rights were again linked to technologies that automatically record and recognize ordinary citizens'[1] faces as they pass

1

airport security, which, once implemented broadly, is a means of tracking frequent travelers in every move they make. Again, scientists and scientifically trained engineers and technicians are involved in designing and developing these technologies. Further development of weapons and "security systems" that destroy human lives and restrict human freedoms are in the making, if we believe the U.S. Secretary of Energy Spencer Abraham when he spoke on homeland security:

> Our world-class scientific and engineering facilities and creative researchers have helped make our nation more secure for over 50 years. These same resources have been trained on the threats posed by terrorism for some time, and because of this foresight, technologies such as these are in deployment today.[1]

And again, scientists were at the forefront of the development as the Lawrence Berkeley National Laboratory offered its expertise and program experience to the US leaders charged with "strengthening homeland security" and "countering terrorist activities." That is, the causes, results, perceptions of, and responses to the horrors of terrorism, war, and resistance are deeply about science and technology as well as people, culture, mores, and ethics. Science is deeply enmeshed with all aspects of our world—in both good and bad ways—and events like the attack on the World Trade Center, the subsequent anthrax scare in the United States, the mass killings of livestock in Britain, the fears concerning genetically modified organisms (GMOs) and economic globalization make this apparent. They make imperative an articulation of scientific literacy that is deeper and more critical than that espoused in current science education initiatives.

Every night, science- and scientist-related images flash across the television screen. A drug is pulled off the shelves after thirty years on the market because it has now proven to be cancerous. Geneticists manufacture plants whose seeds are infertile and cannot be used to plant for a crop during subsequent years. Few other than those in the anti-GMO and anti-globalization efforts seem to be concerned and challenge scientists to account for their actions. Time and again, industry, which often uses scientists as their mouthpieces, tells television audiences to leave them with all decisions because, so they say, they know best. Looking at the history of scientific "advances" (nuclear arms, GMOs, drugs), we doubt that scientists individually or as a community know best what is good for society. Unbridled support for development-happy science that lacks parallel development of ethical-moral dimensions will not keep in check the technoscientific advances made. As citizens and science educators we ask ourselves before, during, and after the nightly news, "How and where do we provide opportunities for this and future generations to engage scientists in a dialogue about what they do and what they produce?" "How and where do we currently allow scientific literacy to emerge?" The traditional answer to the question about scientific literacy is to expose children and older students to a faint and distorted image of scientists' science. This science is claimed to be a pure subject, often taught in special, physically separated rooms, unsullied by common sense, aesthetics, economics, politics or other characteristics of everyday life. Science education often is a form of indoctrination to a particular worldview so that young people do *not* question the very presuppositions that underlie science. Scientific literacy currently means to question nature in ways such that do *not*, reflexively, also question science and scientists. The worst is the other part of the current rhetoric about scientific literacy—it is to be for *all*. All individuals (e.g., Americans), so goes the idealist rhetoric, have to learn and exhibit certain basic facts and skills. Just imagine, every individual taking the same ("scientific") perspective on GMOs, genetic manipulation of the human genome, or use of drugs (such as those used to dope certain kinds of children, labeled with Attention Deficit Hyperactivity Disorder to make them compliant). Conventional approaches to scientific literacy, knowing, and learning are based on an untenable, individualistic (neo-liberal) ideology that does not account for the fundamental relationships between individual and society, knowledge and power, or science, economics, and politics. There is a need to rethink some of our educational goals in terms of society. Scientific literacy cannot be prepackaged in books or delivered to students away from the lived-in world. It must be understood as community practice, undergirded by a *collective* responsibility and a social consciousness with respect to the issues that threaten our planet. We need to treat scientific literacy as a recognizable and analyzable feature that emerges from the (improvised) choreography of human interaction, which is always a collectively achieved, indeterminate process.

## SCIENCE AND LITERACY

There is no doubt that since its introduction, the notion of scientific literacy has played an important role in defining the science education reform agendas. In response to specific events—for Americans, the launching of Sputnik by their arch rivals; for Germans, the outcomes of the PISA test results; for Canadians, the poor showing on the TIMMS tests—efforts are mounted to do something about what are perceived to be national concerns. Usually, the concerns are framed in terms of the lack of knowledge and skills by students of all ages. Even at the time of this writing, we have overheard science educators mocking the responses by Harvard graduates who did not know that the sun was closer to the Earth in winter than in the summer. Reform projects and conceptual change research in science education consistently define science and scientific knowledge in terms of models, theories, concepts, and principles that all students ought to know, understand, and use. The different agendas insist that any reform, if it is to be significant and lasting must be comprehensive and long-term. The rhetoric also insists that reform must center on all children, all grades, and all subjects. Despite this apparent inclusiveness, little has changed over time in the reform rhetoric: the emphasis remains on what each individual needs to know or be able to do independent of the physical and social setting. The knowledge and skills listed are often highly technical and distinct from daily living. Take the following samples from the *Benchmarks* established by the American Association for the Advancement of Science.[2]

> Neutrons have a mass that is nearly identical to that of protons, but neutrons have no electric charge. Although neutrons have little effect on how an atom interacts with others, they do affect the mass and stability of the nucleus. Isotopes of the same element have the same number of protons (and therefore of electrons) but differ in the number of neutrons. (Physical Setting, Structure of Matter, Grades 9–12)

> A living cell is composed of a small number of chemical elements, mainly carbon, hydrogen, nitrogen, oxygen, phosphorous, and sulfur. Carbon atoms can easily bond to several other carbon atoms in chains and rings to form large and complex molecules. (Living Environment, Cells, Grades 9–12)

> Communication between cells is required to coordinate their diverse activities. Some cells secrete substances that spread only to nearby cells. Others secrete hormones, molecules that are carried in the bloodstream to widely distributed cells that have special receptor sites to which they attach. Along nerve cells, electrical impulses carry information much more rapidly than is possible by diffusion or blood flow. Some drugs mimic or block the molecules involved in transmitting nerve or hormone signals and therefore disturb normal operations of the brain and body. (Human Organism, Basic Functions, Grade 12)

The need for a general scientific and technological literacy is often based on the argument that an effective workforce participation in the twenty-first century requires a certain amount of scientific knowledge. But whereas (science) educators appear to accept it as perfectly normal that we do not learn about the principles underlying the functioning of a small engine (e.g., gas-powered lawn mower, electric mixer) or how to fix it, they insist that we acquire specialized knowledge about the world that is simply inaccessible to our experience. These things are not only inaccessible but also irrelevant to most of our lives. On the other hand, we do frequently encounter a broken small engine, bicycle, or appliance. As a mother living with her two high-school-aged boys in a family homeless shelter once told us:

> In my opinion, what does it teach your kids today? Unless they're gonna become mathematical geniuses or they're going to go into science, a lot of it doesn't make sense because they're not preparing them to go out into the workplace. Even college these days because they're so centered on learning from books—I understand that it's important—but they have too many different things to learn that seriously, they're never gonna use in life. I mean, to me, a good education involves bending over backwards and giving that individual child what they need to succeed in life. Not what maybe ten kids or twenty kids or the top one hundred kids are going to need. What about those other nine hundred kids? It all boils back to the way the school system is set up. They are not offering our kids any alternatives, but going to college or fail. Now that's not an alternative; that's an ultimatum.

Despite the rhetoric of scientific literacy for all students, science in schools remains virtually unchanged; students are confronted with basic facts and theories, such as those featured in the previous examples from the *Benchmarks*. The standards of warrants for science knowledge claims often differ dramatically from the standards characteristic of First Nations people, residing in the authority of the cultural historical developments of oral teachings, or of women, who may approach science with "a feeling for the organism." That is, the poor, people of color, and women may fail in school science (or be failed by school science) exactly because of the nature of science practices and forms of knowing that are stressed in teaching. Unsurprisingly, minorities (e.g., African Americans, First Nations) and women are often discouraged from studying science because its ways of knowing and its everyday practices privilege white middle-class and male standpoints or from moving into science trajectories (as if scientific literacy had no other outcomes). Students opt out of science or are counseled out of science because success in that field of study means acting white or masculine or because a science trajectory is incommensurate with their life goals or current needs. Science class has become a mechanism for controlling what it means to "know and do science" rather than an empowerment zone where students are valued for their abilities to contribute to, critique, and partake in a just society. Indeed, the pursuit of scientific literacy promoted by recent national agendas does little to address the diverse audiences, many of which have been squeezed out of science in traditional approaches.

Others, often outside the reform movement, maintain that true and lasting scientific literacy is an impossible task for all but a small fraction of the population. Thus, one critic, Norman Levitt, maintains that science is an elitist calling and that "raw intelligence and special skills that far exceed what is to be expected of the average person are required to attain it."[3] Morris Shamos, another critic, thinks that "Few responsible educators really believe that any amount of reform or tinkering with science education will ever elevate all, or even most Americans, to any reasonable state of scientific literacy, however one chooses to define it."[4] Basing his estimates on the number of scientists and engineers in society on the one hand and on the results of John Miller's benchmark studies on the other, Shamos concludes that, at best, 5 percent of American adults are sufficiently literate in science to reach independent judgments on technoscientific societal matters. Shamos concedes that the presence of one or more individuals who are scientifically literate according to his independent judgment criterion should inform and even guide the decision-making process. In this, he does not think of outside experts, who might be considered to follow agendas of some other individual, group, or agency, but they should be considered fellow group members. These experts, even if they are not asserting their knowledge and experience to others in the group, are nevertheless expected to make the real issues salient to all group members and thereby to deflect unfounded rumor and speculation. How this might occur has not been addressed—how can there be both differences in assessment and focus on the real issues?

The other often-neglected issue is that enculturation into a domain, such as science, includes appropriation of the value systems tacitly embodied in the cultural-specific ways of knowing and doing. Thus, if our goal is to allow more people (students and adults alike) to appreciate science in the way that practitioners appreciate it, there might in fact be fewer who engage science in a critical way. Learning to construct and interpret graphs may not be neutral but enculturate (in insidious ways) to the decontextualized scientific worldviews. Thus, we find problematic the request that we ought to strive for the education of an appreciative audience that supports spending on science and technology, even apart from military requirements.

## CHANGING THE DRIVERS

In recent years, new ways of thinking science and science education have emerged. In "Changing the Drivers for Science Education," Peter Fensham argues that school science has been theorized from within science and its vassal, science education.[5] For too long, science educators and scientists have proposed a model according to which science for all citizens ought to look and sound like scientists' science. Fensham proposes to rethink what the drivers for science education ought to be. To make science education a viable enterprise in our world, he suggests, it needs to be theorized from a more encompassing position: society. From this position, science, which is but one of many important human endeavors, is given its due place in the overall effort of schooling.

Whereas we agree that it is important to include social issues in the consideration of education for participation in a risk society, we believe that there are limitations to Fensham's approach because it does not critique schooling and because it rethinks science education from the position of (curriculum) theoreticians. The efforts of rethinking science education from a society perspective leave intact schooling as a mechanism for reproducing an inequitable society. It is not surprising that there are arguments for the need to find ways to deinstitutionalize science education.[6] There is not only precedence that ordinary (nonscientifically trained) people can take a stand on health, environment, or controversial issues where science comes into play, but also that there are ways in which school science can be relevant to community life.[7] Pertaining to the second limitation, our long-time practical experience teaching science in school and nonschool settings have shown us that rethinking education from outside of praxis runs afoul of the theory-practice gap. It is easy to argue that a new approach won't work because it is possible in theory but not in practice. To overcome this limitation, careful studies of concrete change efforts are needed because they show pathways along which science education can actually, rather than possibly, change.

Studies in public understanding of science construct an image of the interaction between scientists and non-scientists that is much more complex, dynamic, and interactive than the traditional opposition between "scientific expertise" and ignorance or rejection of scientific knowledge may lead us to believe.[8] In the everyday world of a community, science emerges not as a coherent, objective, and unproblematic body of knowledge and practices. Rather, science often turns out to be uncertain, contentious, and unable to answer important questions pertaining to the specific (local) issues at hand. In everyday situations, citizen thinking may offer a more comprehensive and effective basis for action than scientific thinking.

## CRITIQUE OF ALTERNATIVE REFORM AGENDAS

Science educators pursuing agendas according to which science education should be rethought from a societal perspective do not go far enough because they do not question some of the fundamental problems of schooling that lead to inequities along traditional lines of difference such as race, sex, and social status. Schooling is an activity system in which students are coaxed, urged, coerced, or forced into learning—the traditional discourse about objectives. In this activity system as it currently works, students are asked to engage with discipline-specific tasks, producing artifacts (lab reports, exams) that teachers can mark.[9] But in every production, an individual also produces and reproduces his or her identity and her or his role in society. Not only do students produce outcomes, evaluated by teachers, but also they are produced as subjects of a certain type—good and poor students, dropouts, or geeks. In these terms, we do not see that recent society-focused reform proposals provide any hope for change. Rather, replacing science experts with social experts does not change or abandon present forms of schooling, an activity system that reproduces inequitable societies. In many Western nations governed by the economic interests of a few, this means that it reproduces a society ridden with injustice and inequity. Science education has done its share to contribute to the reproduction of an inequitable and unjust society by using marks as a tool to rank students. Those on top of the scale have virtually unlimited access to future learning resources, whereas those who rank lower are denied access to these same resources.

A vicious cycle ensues. Students from all different kinds of backgrounds arrive at science class and are subject to a homogeneous body of knowledge upon which they are tested at the culmination of the school year. Science is defined not by how one manages, alone or collectively, to use or produce science by way of this knowledge at home or at school, in response to a need or concern or practically toward their own or their community's future. Rather, success takes the form of a predetermined response to a cooked-up problem, an abstract set of ideals, predicated upon an imposed ideology. Success (or lack of success) in this system is a form of social control, with the consequences most real for those who sacrifice most to achieve success (to be controlled) within the system, that is, acting white or masculine, privileging the demonstration of understanding locally useless knowledge over community action. Take the case of New York State as one typical example. Students must obtain a state-endorsed high school diploma to be eligible to receive state financial aid at state-sponsored colleges and universities. State-endorsed diplomas are based upon success on end-of-year high-stakes exams (called Regents exams) in academic areas (e.g., science). Thus, access to college for students most in need of college funding is tied to their ability to perform (to be controlled) on exams that favor, for example, one's ability to call up their knowledge of the circulatory system of a grasshopper. This cycle is becoming more and more important as federal funds also become tied to school performance or are sent to states through block grant programs.

There are other problems as well in traditional science education, the structures of which are untouched in society-focused reform proposals. For example, in school science (as in schooling more generally), the means of production and the curricular goals are under the teachers' control. There is therefore a contradiction between the motive of an activity and the motive of individual students, forced into the production of outcomes by focusing on curricular objects and by using tools that are of little interest to them. Such contradictions lead to the production of resistance that both interferes with achieving the teacher-desired outcomes and reproduces the very conditions that have led to the resistance in the first place.

There are further contradictions that haunt recent alternatives to traditional science education. We begin with the supposition that learning is the expansion of possibilities for acting in and toward the world. It is immediately evident that school science operates in a contradiction, for there exists considerable research that shows that competence in these microworlds (school-related tasks) bear little or no relation to levels of competence in everyday situations. In other words, there are fundamental problems with the assumption that school (microworld) learning transfers to other activity systems. It is not surprising that a critical analysis leads us to understand school learning as defensive learning, that is, learning to avert negative consequences, rather than expansive learning, learning that leads to increased possibilities for acting and control over one's life conditions. If reformers propose to conduct science education from a societal perspective while leaving intact traditional structures of the schooling activity system, we see very little change possible. On the other hand, legitimate peripheral participation does lead to robust learning. That is, if students engage in the "authentic" activities of their community, the question of transfer does not pose itself, for students are on a trajectory of legitimate participation and therefore do not need to engage in the "boundary crossing" as they do today.

## SCIENCE IN THE COMMUNITY: POWER, STRUGGLE

It makes sense to conceive scientific literacy in terms of citizen science, which is a "form of science that relates in reflexive ways to the concerns, interests and activities of citizens as they go about their everyday business."[10] In our own research, citizen science is related to a variety of contexts, ranging from personal matters (e.g., accessibility to safe drinking water), livelihood (e.g., best farming practices), leisure (e.g., gardening in sustainable, organic ways), to activism or organized protest. In the community, however, citizen knowledge is collective and distributed: our lives in society are fundamentally based on the division of labor. If we need advice for a backache, we go to the doctor or chiropractor; if our cars or bicycles do not work, we go to the car or bicycle shop. In the same way, science in the community is distributed; scientific literacy in everyday community life means to be competent in finding whatever one needs to know at the moment one needs to know it.

In contrast to the current ideology of scientific literacy as a property of individuals, we further propose to think about it as a characteristic of certain everyday situations in which citizen science occurs. In such a context, the notion of *learning* merely means that "some persons have achieved a particular relationship with each other, and it is in terms of these relations that information necessary to everyone's participation gets made available in ways that give people enough time on task to get good at what they do."[11] This implies that science educators no longer seek to stack educational environments to coax *individuals* into certain performances, but that they set up situations that allow a variety of participatory modes, more consistent with a democratic approach in which people make decisions about their own lives and interests. If we wish science education to be relevant to people's citizenship or everyday lives, we do well to allow the learners to participate in a diversity of these relations. Expecting one set of relations (institutional school) to prepare students for a world of many relations does not make sense.

Throughout the different case studies that we assembled in this book, we show that critical scientific literacy is inextricably linked with social and political literacy in the service of social responsibility. The children, students, and adults that feature in our accounts are, in one way or another, involved in struggles to make this a better world, not only for themselves, but for all of those in their community or sometimes, as with teachers, in their direct care. The kind of engagement that we envision includes the confrontation and elimination of injustices along the lines of race, sex, or social class, which are just a few of the existing terrains of discrimination. We advocate substantial shifts away from the uncritical consumer, often unaware that his or her (a) vegetables have been genetically modified; (b) beef and fish have been raised in part with animal meals and antibiotics; and (c) behaviors are inconsistent with environmentally sustainable lifestyles. We advocate adopting appropriate technologies: appropriate because they are consistent with our moral-ethical principles, do not exploit or disadvantage individuals from any group, and do not have adverse impacts on the environment and on our food supplies. We agree with Derek Hodson who suggests that the ultimate purpose of education for scientific literacy is "to produce activists: people who will fight for what is right, good, and just; people who will work to refashion society along more socially-just lines; people who will work vigorously in the best interests of the biosphere."[12]

Participation in collective actions in the interest of the biosphere does not have to be in the form of being and becoming a scientist, nor must it be in the form of public protest. Individuals and groups concerned with the environment may start cultivating vegetables in their backyard or in community gardens. Each garden, in fact, each vegetable or fruit grown organically with non–genetically modified plant material constitutes an act of resistance against companies like Monsanto and their scientists that populate the world with new organisms whose long-term impact on the environment they do not know; each organically raised plant is also an act against chemical companies whose scientists develop more and more powerful compounds that eradicate "noxious" animals and plants and simultaneously increase the chemical load on each local aquifer; each homegrown produce is an act of resistance against the oil industry, whose engineers rapidly exploit the last of remaining fossil fuels; and each homegrown plant is an act of resistance against multinational companies whose productions in Third World countries exploit local soils and workers. But all these acts of resistance are also acts for an environmentally sustainable form of life in the future, consistent with a saying among some Northwest coast aboriginal peoples: "We do not inherit this land from our ancestors but we borrow it from our children."

## SCIENCE: CONTESTED FIELD AND MEANS FOR STRUGGLE

Human beings are endowed with a fundamental capacity: power to act, or agency. This capacity allows us to go beyond reacting to the environment: we actively change and shape the physical and social worlds that we inhabit. We do so, however, because division of labor allows us to pursue activities that are not directly related to individual survival but to the survival of society as a whole. For example, laboratory scientists survive although most of them do not contribute to the production or gathering of food and the killing of animals. They do not need to build the laboratories, maintain and clean them, or build, install, and repair the systems that heat them. They do not need to build the bicycles and cars that take them to the university, and they do not need to know how cars and bicycles work or why they are as strong as they are. They do not need to know how the computers they use work or, in most cases, do not need to build the computers to be able to do their work. Scientists can hunt quarks, figure out the genome, or construct new macromolecules because they are, like all the construction workers, cleaners, repairpersons, computer programmers, and so on, a constitutive part of society. Scientists and all the other people contribute to the survival of society and thereby guarantee their own access to basic resources and survival. It becomes clear, then, that it is not individual knowledge and skill that is important, but knowledge and skill that are available to human endeavors at a collective level. If we accept that there are many things that scientists do not know or need to know, we should also accept that others—baker, construction worker, farmer—do not need to know that a neutron has a mass nearly identical to protons, or what neutrons and protons are in the first place. If we accept that most scientists do not know that their lawn mower has stopped working because the carburetor is clogged or how to take out and clean the carburetor, why then do we expect all to know that a living cell is composed of a small number of elements mainly carbon, hydrogen, nitrogen, oxygen, phosphorous, and sulfur?

Of course, we must balance access with how we define success, especially in societies as hierarchically organized as we find them in the industrialized world. Scientists (on the whole) have social and economic privileges not afforded to the bakers, construction workers, or repair people (on the whole). Funders of science (CEOs, major stockholders, and the wealthy) have even more privileges. While we do argue, like the homeless mother we cited earlier, that requiring (and expecting) students to learn an abstracted, highly focused body of knowledge is dangerous in how it limits the public construction of what counts as science or limits students' abilities to become scientifically literate in a powerful way, we also recognize that possessing such knowledge opens gates to economic and political privilege otherwise held from reach. In a society, like the United States, where racial minority students are disproportionately placed in "special education" classes and where white and middle-class students score disproportionately high on state and national exams, the question of success and access is of particular importance. Herein lies a fundamental paradox, and one we believe is only solvable by recasting the very essence of scientific literacy for all or for anyone.

Once we accept that education needs to focus on the individual as integral and constitutive part of the collective, and on the distributed nature of knowledge and skill, then we have to begin thinking about the modes by which individuals with different expertise coparticipate in resolving the complex problems that their communities, countries, and humanity as a whole face today. It is clear and comes out in every chapter that follows that when there are different expertise, sociohistorical and sociocultural positions, and value systems there is also the potential for conflict and struggle for power. Science itself becomes a contested field, an arena for struggle. At the same time, science is often a tool, a means to conduct the struggle. Science is therefore a dialectic entity, both the site and means for struggle.

Throughout the chapters that follow, we see people not individually but in interaction with others, always located differently within the sociopolitical field constituting the present context. In Chapters 2 and 3, we find the residents of one Canadian community engaging one another in (context) and with science (tool). For environmental activists and laypeople in Chapter 2, whose interests are aligned, the interactions are characterized by consensus and by concerns for social and collective responsibility. In the collaboration of activists, scientists, and locals (students and adults alike), science furthermore is an outcome of collective activity—the products of the work are being used to secure further funding dedicated to make the community a better place to live and to ascertain the environmental health of their watershed. For the residents in Chapter 3 who want social justice by being connected to the water main that already supplies most others in the community, the interactions are best characterized as struggle. Here it is clearly evident that science is a contested field—did the scientific consultant use appropriate method? And are his interpretations correct given other information already available? At the same time, science is also a tool, such as when the residents draw on the results of privately funded consultant studies to make counter arguments. It is also a tool in the hands of the community politicians to keep the water main away from the residents for fear that the latter will use the improvements to gain personal benefits through increases in property values. This chapter also allows a reframing of science in the community. Rather than being the pure entity and praxis that characterizes the ascetic and monastic activities in ivory towers cut off from most of public life and scrutiny, it is a living thing that comes about as people from all walks of life contribute to a collective endeavor concerned with a salient problem.

The next two chapters feature teens who live in homeless shelters in different parts of the United States, engaged in contests over science but also using science as a means for struggle. As a tool, science is a means for actions, contributing centrally to the establishment of a community garden, and therefore to making a difference in high-poverty urban communities. Rather than accepting their lot and the environment where they are forced to live, they actively engaged in transforming their environment. It is in the actions of these teens that we can see the potential of science to make a difference when it is in the service of the agency of people allowing them to make changes to their life conditions. In the stories we see how entry into and access to science-related experiences are based on the teens' need to build a better world and his or her desire to express individual and community agency in ways not sanctioned or valued by those in political power. Their enactment of science in the community stands separate from their abilities to succeed in school science. Although it remains to be seen if science can be both a context and a means for these teens to move themselves and their families out of poverty, we do learn from these teens the importance of shaking up our academic notions of success (i.e., school achievement) to also include the daily struggle of their lives. As one teen stated, his participation in after-school science was important because he wanted to make his community a place people wanted to live in rather than leave (as moving up the economic ladder in Western society often means moving out of inner-city communities, leaving family and friends behind).

Chapters 6 and 7 feature seventh-grade students engaged in science-related actions in the same community as the adults in two previous chapters. In both chapters, the nature of science as a contested field and means of struggle is much less salient but nevertheless latently present. For example, one of the students found out that the coliform counts in the creek were way up immediately below two farms. Making the results of his research public during an open house hosted by an environmental activist group, however, becomes a political statement that might have consequences. Struggle is evident in a somewhat different way in our case study of the student Davie, labeled by the school system as "learning disabled." It turns out that there are situations, such as his mathematics class, where he shows the behavior that has led to the label. On the other hand, the data we gathered shows that in other situations, Davie's participation in teaching and learning about the endangered Henderson Creek cannot be interpreted along the lines of learning disability. For Davie, then, making it through school as it is therefore constitutes a struggle, one that he, if school does not change, is not likely to win. With some support, however, science could be both a field and a means to emancipate himself from the disability that has claimed him.

Acting in contested terrain and engaging in struggle often comes with dangers. These dangers are no more clearly articulated than in our last chapter, featuring three female teachers in Pakistan. We make the case that engaging in such a practice is a dangerous activity for these women because it explicitly situates their work within social, cultural, and political tensions. It also situates the science they do with children across people, within power, and as part of social processes and institutions. Yet, we also make the case that the women manage or even remake these tensions by using science as both a context and tool for change in the enactment of power and relationships—in other words, science means interactivity, pulling people and contexts together in particular ways. Situating "working for change" in the context of science gives the practice a power and validity that the lives of women and poor children might not have otherwise.

Some readers may think that the notion of science as tool or means of struggle alone is empowering. We do not think so, particularly when science is viewed in terms of what scientists normally know and do. Rather, teaching and learning science needs to be seen in dialectical terms. As tool, science can be used both for and against a particular position over a contentious issue. But more importantly, science is only a good tool if it can be used reflexively, that is, to critique and even deconstruct itself. Science leads to empowerment only when it does not lead to the adoption of the reigning ideology (decontextualized truth) but if it can be used to interrogate its own ideology, that is, when science becomes a contested field.

Above all, science needs to align itself with other fields and become but one of the many contested fields and tools in the service of a truly democratic and equitable society. We must not continue supporting the hegemony of laboratory science by unquestioningly accepting its practices and results. Science must be consistent with social responsibility, not with the exploitation of particular sections of the social (poor, Third World) and natural (farms, fish farms) environments of powerful laboratories (Monsanto). We do not have to accept genetically modified food or cattle and salmon raised on animal meal and antibiotics. Here again, science can become the fields that we want to contest *and* the tool that we want to use as one of the means for fighting our causes.

## AGENCY, LEARNING, AND IDENTITY

Although rarely addressed in the discussion of science, scientific literacy, and learning of science, identity is closely associated with agency and learning. Identity refers us to the question of who is the agent in an activity. From a cultural-historical perspective, identity is both a product and a byproduct of activity. That is, through their agency, the people in an activity both produce material outcomes, and in the process produce and reproduce themselves and others *qua* participants in the relevant community. Therefore, the identity of an individual is not something that can be taken for granted as an a priori constituent of activity, but is something that is made and remade as activities unfold and when individuals participate in multiple activity systems.

The making and remaking of identities is particularly visible when people are involved in struggle both individually and collectively. Since struggles are especially visible when individuals enter new cultural fields, science lessons or contentious issues in the community are ideal sites for studying identity-producing interactions between participants. Throughout this book, the making and remaking of identities is present—sometimes explicitly, sometimes tacitly—as individuals of different ages engage in science as contested fields or use science as means for their struggle. Thus, when Davie attempts to cope with a graphing task posed by the teacher by avoiding engagement for much of the lesson, he becomes a "learning disabled" student (Chapter 6). On the other hand, when he tutors other seventh-grade students to conduct research in a local creek and, in the course of the task, assists them in producing a graph, he is made to be a "scientifically literate" student. Similarly, their contributions to the articulation, planning, and execution of the community garden allowed some students to become successful community activists rather than being just another group of urban kids caught up in the consequences of poverty, homelessness, and growing up in the inner-city. We can see this in our work with youth and adults because we have gotten to know them as individuals who use and produce science (a shift that requires us to move science out of the center of science education and into the world of individuals/humanity). Darkside (Chapter 4), for example, must confront on a daily basis a society that pegs him as poor, black, homeless, and the child of immigrant parents. Though he expresses and enacts scientific literacy in profound and mature ways in out-of-school settings, his access to more formal paths in science-making will no doubt be cluttered, perhaps impeded, with the baggage of traditional and narrow views of scientific literacy. That is, who we are is as much an outcome of our actions as of the changes in the social and material world that we bring forth by means of them. This is as true for individuals enacting science as it is for the identity of the science education community charged with guiding and monitoring this learning process.

As we participate in the world, we expand what we can do and therefore our room to maneuver; expanded agency is equivalent to saying that learning has occurred. Rather than getting science-related stuff into the heads of children, we want them to expand their agency, the room that they have to maneuver, and the possibilities for acting and thereby changing their life conditions. In this sense, agency is a dialectic concept because it changes agency (limiting or expanding); in the process, it produces and reproduces identity.

What we envision are science-related contexts that lead to positive formative experiences for students and adults alike, and which do not have boundaries along age or school buildings. We want students to be able to build positive identities, which for some will be related to scientific careers, for others as community activists. In any event, formal and informal science education should be liberating, allowing individuals to find, struggle for, define, and take their place in a just society. The residents involved in a struggle over access to safe drinking water are not just scientists, developers, or farmers, but they are also active citizens who engage in efforts to change their life conditions. The children who dig a hole under the fence between their shelter for the homeless and a basketball court so that they can play at night also actively engage in changing their world, and with every act of resisting the oppressive rules of their shelter, they evolve identities associated with resilience.

## SCIENCE FOR ALL

In schools, norms encapsulated in curricular objectives such as "students will be able to state that water is a basic constituent of life," because they make statements about all individuals irrespective of social location, contribute to the production of failure. Here, those students who do not produce particular statements in situations where they are cut off from all of the resources that are normally available to them are constructed as lesser or as failures in the attempt to make them scientifically literate. Equal competencies are not the norm in everyday life—furthermore, different individuals contribute in their own ways to make events recognizable for what they are. For example, in Chapter 3, we describe the interactions between scientific consultants and laypeople during a public hearing. Not all laypeople asked questions or critiqued the methods and interpretations by the consultants. Yet they still need to be considered as participants in making the public meeting just that. Some residents actively asked questions or interrogated a presenter. Others provided their perspectives and evidence from their daily lives that made salient the problematic nature of well water in the area. Yet others simply listened or provided supportive "yeas" and applause. These participants are not to be taken as scientifically illiterate but as important participants in the context that allowed scientific literacy to occur. Everyone present contributed to make this event recognizable as a public hearing, which led to the emergence of scientific literacy. It is the very context of a public hearing—which includes speakers, moderator, and audience, experts and laypeople, individuals with stakes in the outcome and "impartial" consultants—that makes visible and thereby allows the identification of scientific literacy. We might say that everyone was part of the choreography of a public hearing that produces moments for the public appearance of scientific literacy and citizenship. Potential problems in one consultant's methodology, and therefore the fact that scientific expertise can be questioned, were produced in this hearing as much as the cunning abilities attributed to individual citizens to expose these problems. The applause and supportive utterances, which contributed to making visible the problems and cunning abilities, were as much part of the production of the public hearing as the questions and responses and therefore the very phenomenon of scientific literacy and engaged citizenship that were exhibited and visible.

Citizenship is often mentioned in connection with the necessity of science, technology, and economy to live in today's society. However, almost all science and even science-technology-society courses take an approach that says what students do in the classroom *should be* applicable to their immediate and future lives rather than *being* immediately part of it. Furthermore, in actual practice, courses that are designed for students to make connections between science, technology, and society are intended for those students who have difficulties mastering technical material, that is, scientific concepts as treated in textbooks, and mathematics. We believe that this aspect of science education has to be rethought as well.

Teaching for citizenship and scientific literacy as praxis has the potential to challenge traditional separations in the school curriculum that relegate science, technology, mathematics, and social studies into separate classrooms, each concerned with the subject in a more or less pure form. Citizenship and scientific literacy as praxis require integrated approaches to be compatible with the ways in which the everyday world works, where people draw on those resources that come to hand and do the job irrespective of whether they are called science, mathematics, or social studies. Not every science educator will be comfortable with an integrated approach because treating science as but one of the many different strands of everyday life threatens existing aspirations of science, scientists, and science educators to have a privileged status in society. However, studies of science in everyday life show that it is intertwined with economics, politics, power, and values more generally. Science in society as enacted by citizens cannot be separated neatly and cleanly from the other subjects. Rather, central concerns and motives govern activities and people (scientists and non-scientists alike) draw on the resources that they deem to be most appropriate in the situation. We believe that the time is right to rethink science education and scientific literacy—we propose here to do this by positing citizenship and inclusive democracy and to teach science accordingly.

Before closing this chapter, let us return to the issues with which we began, September 11, 2001, the arms race, and war more generally. Many, especially European, scholars have pointed out that the events of September 11 need to be seen in the context of world politics and economics. Many Third World countries see the U.S. economy and foreign policy as the root causes of exploitation and poverty, often linked to corrupt regimes (Noriega, oil-rich emirs) that enrich themselves at the expense of their fellow countrymen. Scientists and engineers involved in the production of genetically modified foods, cigarettes, and weaponry exported to countries already in trouble currently seem to be little concerned with the ethico-moral contexts that shape the use of their productions. From our perspective, such scientists are not acting in socially responsible ways but support the status quo of exploitation, inequitable (geographic and social) distribution of benefits and costs that come with development, and non-democratic distribution of political power. The kind of science that we envision is in the service of a socially conscious democratic society. It opens itself up to be both contested terrain and means to conduct such contest. Science and science education must advocate a free democratic society where all, rather than only a few, have access to basic necessities and resources. Our own ideological commitments include improving and extending social justice and democratic practices, especially how these play out across traditional difference markers such as race, class, gender, age, and so on.

# 2

## SCIENTIFIC LITERACY AS EMERGENT FEATURE OF COLLECTIVE PRAXIS

The means of pursuing scientific literacy suggested by current reforms do not seem to anticipate diverse groups of people who put science to use in broader, different, or socially responsible ways.[1]

As science educators we (the authors) are interested in ways of understanding scientific literacy and public understanding of science that allows us to conceive of development as trajectories of legitimate peripheral participation. That is, we are not interested in what scientific literacy looks like *just* in individual adults, or what science education looks like *just* in schools. Rather, we are interested in understanding and theorizing ways of participating in science and scientific literacy that do not have boundaries coincident with formal education and life thereafter. In this effort, we do not believe that models from life after school, such as the concept of "authentic science" derived from studies of scientific practice, ought to be imposed on school activity. Equally, we do not believe that the often narrowly conceived ideas of science and scientific literacy that predominate in science education today ought to be imposed on what and how people should know about science once they have left formal education. Both our research agendas are in part concerned with science and science education in the community, including in schools, where the boundaries dissolve to the point that students and ordinary people can participate reciprocally in activities that previously have been created for their respective age group.

The concept of scientific literacy has played a central role in recent reform efforts in science education. Science educators and curriculum reformers agree that general scientific literacy should be an important outcome of schooling. But despite the nearly fifty-year history of "scientific literacy," science educators have not been able to arrive at a precise or agreed-upon definition. For many science educators, efforts to promote greater scientific literacy have been shaped by the image of laboratory science. Science courses are often a means of pushing students into the world of scientists rather than a way of helping them cope with their own life worlds. Few within science education have dared to question the definitions of science and scientific literacy, which are regularly used as templates for science in everyday life.

In this chapter, we intend to shift the discourse about science and scientific literacy by considering three (radical?) propositions. First, we propose that scientific literacy is a property of collective situations and characterizes interactions irreducible to characteristics of individuals. Second, we propose to think of science not as a single normative framework for rationality but merely as one of many resources that people can draw on in everyday collective decision-making processes. Third, we propose that people learn by participating in activities that are meaningful because they serve general (common) interests and, in this, contribute to the community at large rather than making learning a goal of its own.

## OCEANSIDE

For a period of three years, Michael and his graduate students have done ethnographic research in the Henderson Creek watershed and in Oceanside, the community that lies within this small coastal watershed in the Pacific Northwest. The research generally focused on the role of science in a variety of settings within the community. Specifically, the focus of the research was science as it related to the precarious water situation that has, as recurrent articles in the local media show, plagued Oceanside for many years. Henderson Creek has become a focal point because of the pressures on its ecological health from both farming and industrial production. Henderson Creek drains the north end of the watershed, Gordon Creek the south, and they meet in a valley, forming the main stem of Henderson Creek, which then flows west, into the Pacific Ocean (Figure 2.1). The watershed is located about twenty-five kilometers from the center of a continuously expanding mid-sized city, pushing suburbia into the rural, agricultural landscape.

In Oceanside, the climate has long favored hot, dry summers and wet winters, with concomitant shortages and excesses of water avail-

**Fig. 2.1** The Henderson Creek watershed, viewed from east to west toward the inlet, which lies between the peninsula (foreground) and the mountains in the background.

able to the community. During many summers, an insufficient water supply requires the community to limit the amount available to residents. Other residents, with individual wells that draw on the local aquifers, have found their water biologically and chemically contaminated and sometimes have to get their water from gas stations about five kilometers from their homes. An indigenous community is also located in the watershed, but to date, its inhabitants have shown little interest in participating with the activists in restoring the creek, which historically had been a source of food and a spiritual resource.

Today, water is shed much more quickly than in the past and the decline in water quality and the extremes of water levels (high in the winter and low in the summer) is in part due to changes in water movement across the land and through the ground. These changes are related to urbanization and the increase in impervious surfaces (pavement), straightening of the creek (e.g., Figure 2.2), loss of forest cover throughout the watershed and along the stream banks, loss of wetlands and recharge areas, and the loss of natural stream conditions.

The creek system within the watershed has been affected by human activity even more broadly. There are small clusters of suburban development interspersed with the farmers' fields. Storm drains and

**Fig. 2.2** View of "Stinky Ditch," a typical channelized stream, which has no more cover in the area behind from the camera. In the summer, there is hardly any water, and the levels of chemical contamination are high.

ditches channel rainwater—along with the pollutants of suburbia, such as lawn chemicals and car leakage—into Henderson Creek and its tributaries and away from these newly developed areas. The municipality of Oceanside introduced an industrial park to the watershed. Despite being carefully contained within a four-block boundary, drains of the machine shops and biotechnology labs in the park empty into a ditch, affectionately called "stinky ditch" (Figure 2.2), which, in turn, empties into Henderson Creek. To increase its potential to carry away water rapidly, the creek itself has been deepened and straightened, and much of the covering vegetation has been removed, thereby increasing erosion and pollution from the surrounding farmers' fields.

These physical changes have led to increased erosion and silt load in the wet winter months, and are responsible for low water levels and high water temperatures during the dry summer months when (legal and illegal) pumping for irrigation purposes taxes the creek.

We found out about the events in the municipality by following individuals involved in two major activity systems: environmental activists of the Henderson Creek Project, and children and teachers from Oceanside Middle School, who not only researched the creek but also published their results during open houses organized annually by the Henderson Creek Project. In the process, we came to interview and videotape many other individuals interested in Henderson Creek and its watershed.

The Henderson Creek Project arose from the concerns about water quality of three watershed residents. A farmer, a professor of environmental policy, and a research oceanographer obtained funding from a federal agency concerned with stream restoration to create the Henderson Creek Project. A coordinator and a steering committee of five to seven members head the Project. Its members enlist the support of many other people (e.g., hired high school and university students doing summer jobs) and institutions within the region. The activists initially believed that they were working in and against an adverse political climate. The interests of farmers, industry, and other landowners are often opposed to those that motivate the activists. Since most of the land in the municipality is private, the activists build and maintain good relationships with local residents. More recently the Henderson Creek Project has become an obligatory passage point: community and government agencies now request that individuals and groups coming to them with plans that have potential impact on the watershed discuss them first with the steering committee of the Henderson Creek Project.

## SCIENCE AND SCIENTIFIC LITERACY IN DIVERSE PLACES

Our extensive ethnographic research took us to a variety of places within Oceanside. As we researched events involving different members of the community, we came to understand that science is but one fiber in the thread of social life in the community. Even when scientists participated in an event, their contributions interacted with those made from different epistemological positions, and therefore were but an aspect of the work through which groups and the community as a whole entered into conflicts over different problems. We also noticed that Henderson Creek shows up in different societal activities including farming, cattle raising, horse riding, community activism, and producing industrial goods.

To be able to compare situated knowing and learning across these diverse activities, we take a systems view, which addresses the continuous, self-reproducing, systemic, and longitudinal-historical aspects of human functioning.[2] To understand activities (always motivated at the level of society) from a system perspective, we look for its *subjects* (individuals or groups), *objects* (artifacts or motives), *means of production* (tools, instruments), *rules*, *community*, and *division of labor*.

The object defines the activity. For example, farmers in Oceanside work their fields (the object of their actions), and produce crops, which secure their income. Relations between entities such as subject and object are never direct; there is never just farmer-working-his-field. Rather, relations of two entities are always mediated. Thus, farming requires tractors, plows, fertilizers, and pumps; these are the tools that mediate the farmers' productive activity. However, the farmer-tool relation is not arbitrary, as the way of using tractors and fertilizers, for example, is specific to farming and passed on within the farming community. That is, the community mediates the relation between subject and tool. Similar analyses can be conducted with all pairs of entities, each mediated by the remaining entities. It should also be noted that the basic entities (subject, object, tools, etc.) continuously undergo changes so that an activity system can only be understood when all its basic terms are viewed in their historical context. Such changes are often brought about by the contradictions that exist within and between activity systems; contradictions can therefore be thought of as growth points.

Each activity system involves different individuals or groups and tools; thus the representations of science, which are the results of the activities, are quite different. Depending on the particular instances of mediating entities, different discursive and inscribed representations were produced and subsequently contributed to a variety of interactional forums.[3] Furthermore, the same individuals could participate in different activity systems or take different roles in the respective division of labor. Our research shows that some of the instruments, such as the dissolved-oxygen meter and colorimeter, are used in different activity systems perhaps aspiring to the same standard uses, but for different intentions. In the following parts of this section, we describe five different situations where we found scientific literacy, not as a characteristic of individuals but rather as a property of collectives and their context. We foreground the emergent and interactive nature of each "literate moment" and thereby build a portrait of what citizen science looks like as it plays out in the community.

### Walking the Creek in Search of Suitable Trout Habitat

One of the central interests of the environmental activists is upgrading Henderson Creek to make it suitable as a trout habitat. A suitable trout habitat has all the characteristics of a healthy stream in the Pacific Northwest—meandering channel, plenty of large woody debris and boulders, overhanging vegetation, cool temperatures and high oxygen levels. Thus, restoring a creek to trout-bearing capacity is also a move to restore many of its other aspects to a healthy state. Before beginning this project, the steering committee of the Henderson Creek Project invited a consultant, Tom, to walk the stream with them and suggest rehabilitation strategies. Tom was a member of a group that restored another, nearby stream from a sorry state where there was no water, no habitat, and no fish, to one that now has its own yearly salmon run.

Despite his experience, Tom did not attempt to dominate the conversation as the group walked several hundred meters along different parts of Henderson Creek. Tom pointed out that he was not a biologist, but someone with more than fifteen years of experience working on another, nearby stream to restore it as a viable salmon habitat. During the conversation, Tom never claimed to be the all-knowing expert to enact power-knowledge dynamics. Indeed, he answered some questions by suggesting the group consult other sources for their information.

> Meagan: What is their life cycle, Tom?
> Tom: I don't know, you'll have to look it up. But certainly, there are two age classes of fish in here [pool], probably a bit more. There are probably a few big ones in here, too.

During the walk of the creek in search of suitable trout habitat, expertise and scientific literacy was distributed across the group. Bob, one of the environmentalists present to learn from Tom, has a Ph.D. in ecology and used to lecture at the local university. Meagan, has a Bachelors of Science degree in environmental studies, is an experienced environmental activist and campaigner, and is the (paid) coordinator of the Henderson Creek Project. Sally works on the steering committee of the Henderson Creek Project and took notes throughout the trip for constructing a report. Karen is also an activist in addition to her job as a trained water technician at Oceanside Farms. Geoffrey, as a local farmer, knows about farming practices and particularly about the impact cattle can have when they graze close to the creek.

Together, the group walked areas that could potentially be modified to allow the spawning of trout, and they looked at other spots where they were able to detect the presence of fry of different age classes. As they moved along, participants in the walk picked up bottles and plastic bags that floated by or hung in the brush. Tom pointed out particulars of each setting and explained what types of additions would change the existing stream into an ideal habitat for trout ("This is the right kind of stuff for them," "This is all good stuff for them").

Meagan: [The water] is so clear today. Normally, it is so brown.

Bob: When there is a bit of fall of rain.

Tom: The reason is because it is a bit of a steady, like that. But I don't think it is all that bad.

Michael: Do you think that there is enough oxygen for trout?

Tom: Well, it has got water in and water out. But that would be something interesting to do.

Meagan: We've been monitoring the $O_2$ levels in through here.

Bob: And it's not bad?

Meagan: Well, up in through there, just after it comes through Oceanside Farms' dam it was, you did it the last time, about ten [parts per million]?

Karen: Yeah.

Meagan: But it gets down to about five [parts per million] when we come down toward that dam.

Tom: So if there was any fish in there, it would be more toward this [upper] end?

Meagan: Yeah.

Tom: The temperature probably goes up down here, too.

Bob: Despite the overgrowth?

Meagan: Yeah.

Tom: I think this has more value just as it is.

Meagan: So you think that they could use this as habitat, but they couldn't spawn down here?

Tom: Oh, no, they wouldn't spawn down in here. There is not enough water supply, there is no gravel, and there is no water coming up through the gravel. But if there is larger fish, they could actually stay in this pool. You have cover over there, and there is lots of riparious stuff in there. I would just leave it.

In this conversation, the value of the stretch of creek emerges from the interaction of all utterances rather than from the analysis and assessment of a single (expert) individual. Bits of information emerge from the question-answer and comment-comment turns. For example, the creek is not only "normally brown" (a comment invoking historical knowledge of the creek), but also it exhibits this characteristic particularly when there is "a bit of rainfall." Oxygen levels have not only been monitored, but in the exchange involving Meagan, Bob, and Karen, specific levels between five and ten parts per million (ppm) became available to the group as a whole. Meagan and Karen had measured these levels during the previous year using a dissolved-oxygen meter, an instrument that was also used by summer work-study and middle school students in the same creek. Finally, the temperature of the creek in this reach does not just increase, but does so "despite the overgrowth" that shaded the spot where the group currently stood. In the final exchange between Tom and Meagan, the entire conversation concerned with the stretch was summarized in the assessment: this is a suitable trout habitat but not suitable spawning ground.

In this situation, scientific literacy and expertise with respect to the assessment of the suitability of the reach as habitat and spawning ground was distributed across the individuals and situation. Different individuals contributed to the emerging conversation as fibers contribute to a thread. Although the thread does not exist independently of the fibers, the properties of the former differ from those of the latter. Power-knowledge was distributed, with nobody trying to outsmart others and claim a position of superiority. Rather, power-knowledge itself was collective and democratic, with the desired outcome being to get most from this meeting for the watershed. Furthermore, scientific literacy that emerges as a thread of the conversation could not be predicted from the scientific literacy of the individual participants; scientific literacy in conversational interaction is an irreducibly social phenomenon. This becomes even clearer in the following episode. The division of labor associated with participation in conversation, which also includes a different set of rules, changes the nature of the activity and therefore the nature of knowing and learning that analysts infer from the situation.

### Scientific Representations in the Community: Sites of Struggle and Decentered Control

During our research, we witnessed presentations that one "expert" or another was asked to make. For example, Meagan and Karen frequently talked to a variety of audiences about their work in the environmental activist group or on the farm. However, expertise attributable to an individual was rarely visible. Usually, when someone in the respective audiences asked a question, the control over salient issues changed; the thread of the topic then emerged from the interaction between the participants, speaker and audience. Scientific literacy was again a social phenomenon irreducible to individual characteristics. We observed this change of control over scientific representation in different contexts, including the open house organized by the Henderson Creek Project. (See the section Public Meeting below and Chapter 7.) Although the various scientists (and, in the present example, the water technician Karen) "owned" the slides or some visual aid, what these inscriptions were about was no longer under the owner's control. What was relevant at the moment was how the information from the graph or photo related to the world more broadly, which emerged from the interaction between presenter and audience. Even more pertinent, the level of expertise that emerged from the interaction went beyond that which could have been attributed to any individual participant. Take the following example from our database.

The episode had been recorded near the open-house exhibit that Karen used to introduce members of the community to the variations in the Henderson Creek water quantity in the course of the year. For this purpose, she had joined several rolls of graph paper from a water-monitoring station and mounted them on the walls around the room. She guided visitors along the graph, explaining its features, and relating specific events (rainfall, opening of a dam) to the particular shape of the curve. In the following part of her conversation with a resident named Walter, Karen had begun to point to a step-like change in the curve, explaining that on this day the people on her farm began to irrigate the field. Again, collective knowledge is associated with collective power.

Karen: These very, you know, ninety degree angles in the lines, that's definitely straight, straight drops. That's definitely irrigation activity, people are all stopping at the same time, starting at the same time. Depending on the conditions, it's dry for a while here. (*Points to the rainfall chart.*)

Walter: Yeah, a lot of hay, people are into the hay and stuff.

Karen: Yeah, a lot of people cut it at the same time.

Walter: Further, you go toward the Fox's farm, down Henderson Creek. Because once you get past Fox's, it stops. There is corn. But of course, nowadays, there is late corn, too.

Karen: Yeah, they grow different varieties.

Walter: I think they grow mostly early corn (*gestures toward earlier parts of the graph*) on the fields that are around Henderson Creek.

Karen: Corn definitely has a lot, requires lots of water, doesn't it? Compared to hay.

Walter: Well, say, I guess, as you know, the structure of the material of the soil material in the valley is—So, like they say, it is the best place in the world to have septic fields. From the point of view of a person putting one in, not necessarily for the rest, if all they wanted was go down the first number of feet, they don't necessarily think what else I have to have in.

Karen: Yeah, they don't think beyond that.

Walter: That's right, but it's sort of a lot of sand, and coarse soil so it's—
Karen: A lot of clay in the valley.
Walter: It drains well. So, that's probably why they have to pump so much water here compared to over on Gordon Creek where Marie Flats are. I don't think that they have to pull that much....

Our recordings over the two days of the open house show that Karen wanted to move people through the exhibit rather quickly, explaining the parts of the entire chart that were salient (to her) and move on to the next person. In this interaction, Walter's questions (like those of other people present) codetermined what was interesting and being talked about. Walter was interested in more than simple propositions about step-like changes in the curve that are produced when different farmers simultaneously begin to irrigate. Walter had lived in the community for seventeen years. He was familiar not only with farming practices in general, but with the particular crops that specific farms along Henderson Creek are and had been growing. That is, Walter was much more familiar with the historical changes that the watershed has undergone than Karen, who had only recently arrived in the area when she took her job as water technician at one of the farms. We do not want to suggest that knowledge is necessarily attributable to either individual but highlight the fact that, through their interaction, considerable detail about the context that led to the current water crisis in the community was brought to the light of day. The science in the community that comes to be exhibited is not the output from the mind of an individual person, but rather emerges from the complex interactions with others and is, in its public nature, made available to other bystanders in the situation.

If knowledge is directly related to power, and if collective knowledge is more than the sum of (different) individual knowledge, then the collective power for dealing with environmental issues by far outstrips the sum of the power of individuals and individual fields of expertise. At the same time, when conversations over issues are analyzed as irreducible phenomena in their own right, scientific literacy becomes a property of the situation. The environmentalist's open house, and Karen's exhibition of the water-level graph, occasioned the possibility for conversations about the water problem in Henderson Creek and the watershed it drains. Here, then, water levels were mediated not only by farmers who all begin irrigating at the same time, but also by the differences in water needs of different crops. Characteristics of the soil, ideal for septic fields, allow the area to drain well and for farmers to pump more water than in other parts of the watershed (Marie Flats). This excerpt also exemplifies our more general observation that when scientific discourse and inscriptions (i.e., the representational tools) enter public forums, they are no longer in the control of scientists and their restrictive ways of talking, which are more appropriate to scientific laboratories than to situations in the community. Rather, we can think of discourse and representations as being taken into a more heterogeneous discourse, including many different concerns (ethics, politics, or economics), characteristic of the discourses that emerge over contentious issues and are characteristic for (political) struggle. At the level of the conversation as a whole, or discourse as a heterogeneous phenomenon, the scientific repertoire turns out to be no more than one fiber among many fibers in a thread—no more and no less than other fibers that contribute to the strength of the thread. Here, we understand that the strength of the thread comes from the integration of many different fibers.

### Student Summer Projects

In the community, scientific literacy is not isolated to adults. Rather, middle and high school and university students participate in various ways in the activity system and produce ecological knowledge about Henderson Creek and the watershed. This knowledge is exchanged and consumed within the community, where it will be distributed unevenly across individual members. In the process, these students not only contribute to the production of knowledge consumed in and by an environmentally conscious community but they also contribute to their own production as members of the community. In the context of the existing activity system of environmental activism, with its object-motive, tools, community, and division of labor, students are themselves subjects that contribute to the levels of scientific literacy that we observed.

In the summer, the Henderson Creek Project employs high school and college-level students to survey the Henderson Creek watershed and collect data for future stream restoration work. One summer, this involved five students. Their work started at Henderson Bight and included profile surveys of the creek bed, cross-sections of the creek, habitat assessments, water quality testing, and landowner research. The students spent the summer collecting data, and then entering it into a database at the Henderson Creek Project headquarters. For the in-stream work, Henderson Creek and its two contributing arms were divided into sections called "reaches." Abrupt changes in landscape, such as a transition from a field to a forested area, or at significant landmarks such as culverts, are used to demarcate a reach. The length of the reaches varied from 70 to 110 meters. In each reach, a series of tests were conducted. The ultimate goal was to assess the entire creek system.

Before they could begin their work, the students had to obtain permission from landowners to survey the creek. They located landowners, determined mailing addresses, and sent out letters requesting permission. They did not survey a reach unless the particular landowner had provided full consent.

The objective of conducting profile surveys was to develop an elevation survey of the entire creek, reach by reach, starting at sea level and ending at the headwaters. Students conducted the profile surveys drawing on a variety of tools such as a surveyor's level and rod. They took measurements every few meters in the deepest part of the creek, usually going from the bottom of the reach to the top. The number of cross-sections in a reach varied depending on the length of the reach. Usually, there was one cross-sectional survey every fifty meters. Looking at all the cross-sections in order allows the activists attempt to see trends in the creek bed (Figure 2.3). Lynne, a university student, commented:

> We tried to do flow rate and discharge measurement. But this didn't turn out too well because our flow meter was in the fritz. . . . The bankfull you have to kind of guess how high the water gets, because we are not here in

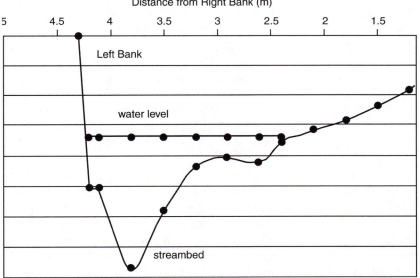

**Fig. 2.3** This cross section was constructed by Lynne, a university student working on a summer project, from measurements that she and other students took in Henderson Creek.

the winter. And this is very difficult, because I don't know how high the water gets.

Habitat assessments were done once in every reach. They included information on the percentage of gravel and silt in the creek, the size of the riparian zone, the types of vegetation in the riparian zone, the number of pieces of large woody debris, the number of rooted cutbanks and bank stabilization, and the percentage of channel covered by overhanging branches. Taking all these factors into account, one can come up with a habitat rating for each reach. Habitat assessment requires many situated decisions, which the students learned to arrive at by working collectively. Students used a variety of forms as tools that allowed them to enter their estimates for the different dimensions that contributed to an assessment. In the same way, attempting to assess water quality could have been an insurmountable task had it not been for the variety of tools available for this activity. Students used pinpoint meters, dissolved-oxygen meters, and colorimeters in conjunction with different forms that required entry of instrument readings and asked for particular calculations. Thus, the quality of the water in each reach was determined by testing temperature, dissolved oxygen, turbidity, and pH. As with habitat assessment, a water quality rating for each reach was obtained by using a form, the water quality assessment form, to combine different readings, conduct calculations, and compare the outcome to an established calculation-outcome to quality conversion. Lynne recalled the tools she used:

> Our main ones are oxygen meters, which measure dissolved oxygen and temperature. And you stick them into the water and wave them a little bit around and it gives you the results. And the pinpoint meters you just stick in and they give you the results. And the colorimeters are the big squinky things where you actually take a sample and you stick it in and it does, I think spectroscopy . . . it does a spectral analysis of the different components. But the colorimeter usually involves a lot of in-lab analysis; you can't just stick your colorimeter into the water.

The results from the students' work were not simply ends in themselves, stored in the Henderson Creek Project office. Rather, they were used as informational sources to guide their creek restoration work, to talk about the creek to different community members and landowners, and to persuade funding agencies to financially support additional projects in the creek specifically and the watershed more generally. For example, Figure 2.4 shows an excerpt from a proposal written to the municipal council, requesting access to the creek where it passes through a local park, drawing on the type of data collected and produced by the summer students. That is, producing knowledge about

Water quality tests were taken. Results are recorded in Table 2. The results indicate water quality in Reach 1 to be the poorest of the Centennial Park reaches (temperature and turbidity levels the highest and DO was the lowest). This is likely the influence of the open, chanellized reach upstream.

**Table 1: Channel Characteristics, Reach 1**

| length (m) | slope (%) | mean bankfull width (m) | mean bankfull depth (m) | width/depth ratio | mean paving material size (cm) |
|---|---|---|---|---|---|
| 290 | 0.35 | 3.26 | 0.66 | 4.93 | 2 |

**Table 2: Water Quality Conditions Reach 1**

| Dissolved Oxygen | Temperature | Turbidity |
|---|---|---|
| 6.34 mg/l (65.6% saturation) | 16.5 °C | 22 FTU |

**Limiting Factors for Reach 1**

1. *Reduced overall habitat complexity due to channelization.*
   The process of deepening and straightening the channel through this reach has removed habitat features such as deep pools, riffles, meanders, and off-channel habitat.
2. *Reduced juvenile and adult habitat due to removal of large woody debris and streambank vegetation.*
   Loss of these features results in an overall reduction in the amount and quality of habitat available to juvenile and adult cutthroat.
3. *Increased sediment transport and decreased water quality due to bank instability and erosion.*
   The vertical banks, lack of rooted vegetation, and loose soils throughout this reach have resulted in severe erosion. Sediments from these banks are deposited in pools and spawning gravel through the reach and downstream, reducing the quality of spawning, rearing, and adult habitat.

**Prescription for Reach 1**

1. *Increase pool and spawning habitat*
   Deepen pools by placing three 'Newbury' riffle structures where reformation of small riffles is occurring. These features mark the natural deposition and behavior patterns of the stream, indicating the logical locations for enhancement structures. Add spawning gravel at downstream end of pools.
2. *Increase habitat complexity via the addition of large woody debris and boulder clusters*
   Place woody debris and boulders at appropriate locations within new and augmented pools.
3. *Stabilize banks and increase habitat complexity*
   Limit the access to streambanks and channel. Plant the streambank paths with appropriate native vegetation. Provide interpretive signs to explain the restoration objectives, gain public support, and request cooperation from park users in keeping back from the stream channel.

**Fig. 2.4** Results of the stream survey and recommendations made to the community for improving the specific reach.

the creek was not an end in itself. Rather, students learned and enacted scientific literacy in the process of pursuing a worthy goal, representing the creek.

In this example, scientific literacy can be associated with the fact that the representations produced by the students were successfully employed to garner further funding for the Henderson Creek Project. However, this scientific literacy cannot be attributed only to the students. Rather, scientific literacy is a contingent product of the activity system and, in this case, emerged from the interaction of students in labor with each other and with the members of the Henderson Creek Project and the tools available for doing representation work. The activity system was not constituted by the students and the tools that they used; rather, students participated in an ongoing activity system whose motive is the preservation and recovery of the watershed. The students, guided by the environmentalists, used these (sometimes unfamiliar) tools in a fashion consistent with accepted practices; that is, tool use was mediated by the community in and for which the data were generated. Because the community mediated tool use (i.e., the tool-subject relation), the outcome was more than simply shaped by some individual's mind; rather, community was an integral part of the product or outcome of the students' actions. Here again, scientific literacy was a property of the activity system rather than of the students or the activists on their own. Scientific literacy emerged as a thread including subject, tools, division of labor, rules, object, and community, and all the mediated relations between pairs of these entities.

### Public Meeting

Public meetings, because they have the potential to add balance and depth to information collected by other means (such as surveys) are an important and widely used mechanism in democratic countries. Over the past decades, it has become increasingly evident that in risk management related to genetically modified organisms, those involved make value judgments at all stages of the risk management process. There exists therefore an "increasing contention that public participation in policy making in science and technology is necessary to reflect and acknowledge democratic ideals and enhance the trust in regulators and transparency in regulatory systems."[4]

One of the many forums documented in our research was a public meeting concerning the water in one part of Oceanside—Salina Point—which is not connected to the water main. During some summers, the groundwater levels are very low increasing the concentration of biological and chemical contamination in wells to such an extent that the residents have to get their drinking water at the nearest gas station, five kilometers away. After six different reports had been issued on the topic, the town council decided that there should be a public meeting where the sometimes conflicting discourses about cost, municipal intent, historical relations, and scientific details could be clarified in a situation where many of those concerned could be present.

According to some residents, the town council was heavily influenced by the majority report of the Water Advisory Task Force, which, in turn, had based its report on a report by an independent consultant, Dan Lowell. The scientists generally attempted to restrict themselves to a decontextualized kind of discourse that did not account for the particulars of the situation; especially, this discourse was unconcerned with human suffering.[5] For example, what the scientist called "unachieved aesthetical objectives" were experienced by the residents as corroding waterlines, washers and dryers that had to be replaced every other year, flowers that died off when irrigated with well water, scales on their skin after taking a shower, and so on. That is, real, objective concerns in the everyday lives of the people affected by the unusable water became mere "aesthetic objectives" in the discourse of science. Like all dialogic forms of interactions, public meetings involve a variety of people, who bring their own, quite different concerns and ways of understanding. As an interactional forum, therefore, a public meeting allows the emergence of rich forms of discourse, including but not limited to that of science. Scientific literacy emerges as a collective achievement and as something heterogeneous, taking into account various perspectives, interests, and needs that by far expand the limited notion of objectivity that is used by laboratory scientists. In fact, if anything, this heterogeneous discourse is more objective because it takes into account many more ways of seeing and perceiving the life world than is seen if only laboratory science discourse is brought to bear on a problem. To illustrate this, we pick one controversial issue, the problem of high chromium levels in the drinking water.

The chief environmental health officer of the regional health board, whose report had recommended connecting Salina Point to the water main, suggested that when he and his team had taken measurements in the well, there were unacceptably high levels of chromium:

> We had a problem and a high level with our chromium levels. Chromium can be a problem when it combines with chlorine and goes to the trivalent state. This is when a carcinogen is formed. Chromium as it generally occurs in the water system is fine. It is a nutrient. But when we have to chlorinate a water system, that's where we have the potential for some problems.

Dan Lowell, the consultant hired by the Water Advisory Task Force, reported that he had not found excesses of chromium levels and recommended that any metal contamination, which he called "aesthetic concerns," "be treated with in-home treatment systems." When the public came to ask questions and make comments, Lowell's report came under close scrutiny. In the first four utterances of the following exchange, which involved Lowell and a resident (Naught), a claim to scientific expertise was constructed.

> Naught: Let's turn to treatment of downstream water. Is that your area of familiarity and expertise?
>
> Lowell: I've worked with groundwater and water treatment for over twenty-five years.
>
> Naught: So, so you, so you would consider yourself an expert in that area?
>
> Lowell: Not in all aspects. An environmental engineer who's an expert in water treatment would know more about it than I do.
>
> Naught: Do you know, for example, whether chromium can be treated?
>
> Lowell: Yes, I do. It can, with ion exchange filtrate, a filter. I phoned the manufacturers of certain systems and they assured me that that can be done.
>
> Naught: And that's good enough for you?
>
> Lowell: Well, I read it in publications as well.
>
> Naught: Oh, there's a publication that we have here that says there is no commercial treatment for chromium.
>
> Bisgrove: Well, again Mr. Naught—
>
> Lowell: Again there wasn't any concern for chromium identified. So I'm not sure what point you're making.
>
> Naught: Well, it seems to me that Mr. Magee's [Water Advisory Task Force majority leader] report is relying very heavily on your information, which would suggest that it doesn't matter what the problem is with water, it can be treated. I would beg to differ on that because I think that when you do something to the water, you affect it regardless of what the treatment and where the treatment. And that it affects the water in another fashion. And so therefore this business of treating water is only a marginal thing with respect to water qualities.

The subsequent exchanges construct the possibility that chromium contamination can be successfully treated. Lowell claimed to have called manufacturers and read publications, whereas Naught pointed to one publication that suggested the contrary. Lowell's response—that there was no chromium contamination—attempted to shift the issue but in his response, Naught pointed out that the non-negligible effect of Lowell's report on the decision-making process warranted greater attention to the nature of the recommended treatments. Chromium had been found in the first sampling episode done by the scientists from the regional health authority. The claims that there were no problems with chromium levels not only contrasted those of the report by the regional health authority, but were further mediated by information subsequently entered into the meeting by other residents. For example, one resident said that the water samples taken from her home were "beyond the one that was done by Mr. Lowell, have always tested very high in the negative areas, the one in particular is chromium." She elaborated to have learned,

> about chromium after reading the [regional health board's] report that said it could possibly be carcinogenic. Part of the poisoning was through skin absorption, which was exactly what happens with the chromium in its carcinogenic state. The high pH encourages scale formation and decreases the efficiency of chlorine in disinfecting the water, which we can't use anyway because of the high chromium content.

Similar to the contributions made by other residents, some of whom had hired their own consulting firms, this resident's comments contributed to the construction of problems relating to chromium. When the public meeting is considered as an irreducibly social phenomenon (rather than consisting of the sum-total of individual contribution), we can understand high chromium levels as a contested issue. There are both pros and cons to the presence of high chromium levels. Not only the levels of chromium were contested, but also the claims that chromium could be treated. Finally, even the very status of scientific expertise was contested in contradictory claims about what the scientific literature says about the possibility of treating high chromium levels in drinking water.

Where is scientific literacy in this public meeting? Is it restricted to the scientists present (with or without master's degrees in a field)? Is scientific literacy an attribute of residents such as Naught and others who interrogated Lowell in ways that another presenter called a "cross-examination"? Naught is not a scientist, nor does he have scientific training. But during his exchange with Lowell, Lowell was presented as much less the expert than he had been pronounced to be; as a result of their interactions, the legitimacy of Lowell's declared levels of expertise came under question, appropriately acknowledged by an applauding audience. Here, we take a different route to scientific literacy. We suggest that scientific literacy thoroughly permeates the public meeting and the other situations that we described. Every person in the episodes is in some way related to scientific literacy as it emerges from the situation; and yet this scientific literacy enacted in and as everyday praxis, cannot be reduced to any single individual. Every participant is a part of the choreography that produces moments of the public appearance of scientific literacy. As we have shown with our excerpts from the meeting, scientific literacy, rather than being confined to an individual person or to several persons, arises from the dialectic relations that exist within the activity system. Thus, we suggest looking for scientific literacy not in the mind of the scientific expert consultant Lowell or in the heads of Naught and other participants in the public meeting, but in the thread of the conversation that dialectically (and irreducibly socially) relates all participants (fibers). Such an approach also has policy implications that are fundamentally democratic in the sense that as a society, we no longer just look for one type of expert to inform, but aim to bring together groups of diverse individuals (including those affected) to deliberate the contentious issues at hand. Solutions will (unpredictably) emerge from the weaving together of the individual fibers into a coherent but heterogeneous and variegated thread.

### An Aboriginal, Cultural, and Historical Perspective: On Henderson Creek and the Watershed It Drains

In our deliberation of scientific literacy as an emergent form we do not want to omit deliberation of individuals and groups that are or find themselves, for one reason or another, at the margins of ongoing debates and concerns. In Oceanside, the local First Nations band constitutes one such group. Different forms of scientific literacy emerge when we consider the aboriginal community that lives in the watershed and whose reservation borders Henderson Creek on the final kilometer before it sheds into the ocean. The W̲SÁNEC' people (also "the saltwater people") have lived there for centuries. Henderson Creek, the ocean shores where it drains, and the surrounding ocean have been central to their way of life. Their expertise reflects this long history. Yet in the local media, the W̲SÁNEC' and their elders seldom feature as the principal agents of activism. All efforts to restore the Henderson Creek watershed appear to be initiated and driven by non-natives; at best, aboriginal elders are featured in supportive roles of projects and meetings organized by others. Nowadays, as the environmental activists have found out, the W̲SÁNEC' are difficult to enroll in their efforts to restore the creek to the habitat it was decades ago. The reluctance of the W̲SÁNEC' to become involved can be understood as the outcome of historical processes that valued Western approaches to dealing with the environment at the detriment of their own ways of knowing.

One day, we were standing with Dan Daniels, an elder from the local First Nations people, looking over the watershed to the hillside where the reservation reaches down to Henderson Creek. (Our view was similar to that represented in Figure 2.1.) Dan talked about the different ways in which the W̱SÁNEC′ people related to Henderson Creek, the watershed, and the ocean into which the creek flows. Dan emphasized that their knowing is based on the oral tradition. Within the context of the oral tradition of his Nation, place names are irrevocably related to their narratives, which are teaching stories and historical accounts at the same time. Furthermore, each name that is evoked in a narrative stands for an idea that is more general than the account told by the storyteller. The meaning of words and stories, however, do not reside in the story or the intent of the storyteller. Rather, the meanings are thought to be stored in the listener, the only source of the wisdom. Because family histories expressed through oral tradition are often intertwined, each family maintaining its unique perspective of a shared event, the history of a people exists only in and as of the collective. A typical oral narrative of the W̱SÁNEC′ people is as follows:

> Once, long ago, the ocean's power was shown to an unsuspecting people. The tides began rising higher and higher than even the oldest people could remember. It became clear to these people that there was something very different and very dangerous about this tide. [ . . . ]
>
> The seawaters continued to rise for several days. Eventually the people needed their canoes. They tied all of their rope together and then to themselves. One end of the rope was tied to an arbutus tree on top of the mountain and when the water stopped rising, the people were left floating in their canoes above the mountain.
>
> It was the raven who appeared to tell them that the flood would soon be over. When the flood waters were going down, a small child noticed the raven circling in the child began to jump around and cry out in excitement, "NI QENNET T̵E W̱SÁNEC′" "Look what is emerging!" Below where the raven had been circling, a piece of land had begun to emerge. The old man pointed down to that place and said, "That is our new home, W̱SÁNEC′, and from now on we will be known as the W̱SÁNEC′ people." The old man also declared, on that day, that the mountain which had offered them protection would be treated with great care and respect, the same respect given to their greatest elders and it was to be known as ȽÁU,WEL,NEW—"The place of refuge." Also, arbutus trees would no longer be used for firewood.[6]

The W̱SÁNEC′ have a deep respect for the Henderson Creek watershed and all the plants and creatures inhabiting it, including themselves. That is, the culture and land of the W̱SÁNEC′ are inextricably bound together. The rich resources of the Inlet have fed the W̱SÁNEC′ for hundreds if not thousands of years. The environmental activists recognize that the knowledge of the W̱SÁNEC′ with respect to seasonal cycles, tides, and water movement was essential for their survival and have set the incorporation of this knowledge in the restoration of Henderson Creek to be an important goal of their own future planning.

In the past, the W̱SÁNEC' depended on Henderson Creek and the wetlands in its watershed for their food, everything from ducks to sources of medicinal plants and weaving materials. It is therefore not surprising that the W̱SÁNEC' were considerably affected by the draining of the wetlands and other changes to the watershed over the past 140 years. One elder recalled his mother's comment about Henderson Creek watershed, "This place will be no more good to us."[7] A local newspaper, the Peninsula News Review, ran an article about environmental changes (Dec. 13, 2000, p. 12):

> The availability of seafood, a traditional food source for West Coast First Nations, has slowly dwindled over the last couple of decades. Contaminated shellfish beds and fish-bearing streams have become all too common. Although many traditional shellfish closures result from the naturally occurring contamination of certain marine organisms, or biotoxins, other contaminants such as sewage, oil, antifreeze, detergents, paints and solvents are all finding their way into the marine environment and causing a different kind of contamination.

To the W̱SÁNEC', Henderson Creek was not only a place for food but also a place of cleansing, and therefore an integral part not only of their physical environment but of the very definition of themselves as people (Figure 2.5). The cleansing ritual was related to *skwinengut* (basic spirit). A person without the basic spirit was considered to be an "empty shell." Because the seeker of *skwinengut* had to be clean, sexually and physically, the individual would bathe in the saltwater at the mouth of Henderson Creek before retreating to the nearby mountain. Bathing in the creek was also an important part of the rite of passage from childhood to adolescence.

For the W̱SÁNEC', Henderson Creek is deeply integrated in their ways of living and knowing. Historically at least, the creek is deeply integrated in their activity system. Their local (traditional ecological) knowledge still preserves their ancient ties to the land. The W̱SÁNEC' are aware that their knowledge arises from their collective relation to the watershed. They know that their activity system includes all human and non-human (physical, spiritual) aspects as agents, by far expanding human forms of life.

The W̱SÁNEC' know that Henderson Creek is no longer the same place. Major changes have occurred during the past fifty years (e.g., Figure 2.2). These changes include pollution of the water bodies and lands around the inlet that bears their name, human encroachment in

**Fig. 2.5** Henderson Creek as it looks only in small sections. Before the settlers arrived in the mid-1800s, much of the creek looked like this and carried large cutthroat trout that provided food to the local First Nations people.

the form of development, resource extraction, and general invasion of privacy at sacred places and in other traditional-use areas, and lack of employment due to loss of subsistence activities within the inlet and other activities such as a viable commercial fishery. The brook trout, which had fed them as long as they their collective histories reach back, have gone. So have the humpback, gray whales, and orcas that had given rise to the aboriginal name K'ENNES for the mouth of Henderson Creek. The rich marine environment fed by freshwater from Henderson Creek, among others, has been killed off by rising levels of chemical contamination (fertilizers from the farms and heavy metals from industry) and by silting from the quickly draining straightened creeks. No longer does the actual state of the creek inspire cleansing rituals as it used to. The W̲SÁNEC′ do not need scientifically measured coliform counts, which are more than ten times the level appropriate for swimming, to know that the creek is unable to provide and sustain them as it has in the past. In fact, for the W̲SÁNEC′ science may have ended with the coming of schools. The coming of schools brought a separation of education from schooling. Thus, one elder writes:

> In our homes and in the privacy of our longhouses we continue to observe the wisdom of the past. The more we learn about the old ways the more we realize that science, mathematics and social studies did not begin with schools. For some of us it ended.[8]

In their ways, the W̲SÁNEC′ feel that they have much to offer for an ecological approach to living on the Peninsula: "If we bring back a deep respect for nature we can be an example to everyone and prevent our beautiful land from being destroyed."[9] But the W̲SÁNEC′ do not necessarily consider the environmentalists' activities as appropriate. Simply returning the creek to its state of 100 years ago does not address a more fundamental issue concerning the relationship between people and their life world. An aboriginal friend of ours, who has lived in and is familiar with the situation in the Henderson Creek watershed, made this point very clear:

> The activists are doing the same thing that the farmers did when they first cleared the forests, drained the swamps, and channelled the stream. They perpetuate the dynamics of colonialization. They haven't taken the time to educate themselves through dialogue with the Coast Salish people who've lived there for hundreds of years and who probably have stories about the birth of the creek. They've spent a summer measuring it with their meters and yardsticks and now they've got their machines in there, changing it. They haven't taken time to build relationships with the people who first inhabited the land. I do not understand how this can be called a democratic process.

The elder and our friend are right. If science and environmental activism simply impose themselves on collective processes, without seeking to involve communities as a whole and as equal partners, they are not keeping with democratic theory and practice. Such science and environmental activism patronize those with different epistemological commitments and values and, worse, perpetuate colonialism.

From our system perspective, we view knowing and learning as aspects of culturally and historically situated activity. Learning is discernable by noticing our own and others' changing participation in changing social practices. Because interaction and participation cannot be understood as the sum total of an individual acting toward a stable environment, scientific literacy cannot be understood in terms of what comes from and happens to individuals. The analogy of thread and fibers provides an appropriate framework for thinking about scientific literacy as it emerges from the complex interactions in the varying settings that we described. Here we focus on two salient issues emerging from our research. First, we propose to view scientific literacy as indeterminate outcome of conversational activity. Second, we propose to view participation in such scientific literacy as a lifelong curriculum.

## SCIENCE AS INDETERMINATE OUTCOME OF CONVERSATIONS

Conversations, which always involve at least two individuals drawing on language as a culturally mediated resource, are activity systems. The individuals participating in a conversation (e.g., those who walk the creek, speak up during the public meeting, or discuss the meaning of a hydrograph) constitute the central subjects focusing on some topic, the object of the activity. In the process, the conversationalists draw on (the same or different) discursive repertoires, diagrams, drawings, and graphs. Division of labor refers to the different roles of listener and speaker, which the individuals repeatedly exchange in the course of the conversation. Their interactions are mediated by the rules that mediate turn-taking or the rules of respect for one another.

In the conversational activity system, scientific literacy is neither a property of the individual participants nor something a priori available in the activity system as a resource. Rather, scientific literacy is the contingently achieved outcome that emerges from the local organization of the different conversations. In the same way, scientific literacy is produced in conversations that take place in other situations in the community, and where individual participants bring different resources based on a variety of socio-, ethico-, and politico-scientific practices. Each contribution to the conversation is not merely outcome but becomes itself a part of the context of the activity; that is, each outcome is reintegrated into the activity system where it can become a resource available to the community as a whole. Each contribution not only produces the conversation but also contributes to the production and reproduction of the individual *qua* member of the community; in addition, each contribution is also an aspect of the division of labor taken on by the co-participants in various ways. Because each contribution shapes the context of the conversation in ways that other participants cannot foresee, the unfolding of the topical thread is in principle unpredictable and indeterminate. The settlement of controversial issues, as scientific literacy, is therefore an outcome of the dialectic and dynamic conversational processes to which the different elements in an activity system contribute in non-deterministic ways.

Scientific literacy can be thought in terms of the right use of specialists, black boxes, simple models, interdisciplinary models, metaphors, standardized knowledge, and translations and transfer of knowledge.[10] Right use does not imply that decisions have to be made by individuals; right use can be accomplished within collectives that work in their specific ways on the resolution of the problems at hand. That is, right use of the above entities can be made to be a characteristic of situations, such as public meetings or other democratic forums that shape policy-setting and decision-making processes in public arenas. Such a view implies that our task as (school and adult) educators is to enable situations characterized by a collective scientific literacy rather than to think about the individual appropriation or construction of knowledge. In the same way, if educators were to think of science as but one fiber next to many other fibers in the thread of life, we might focus more on learning as participating in solving everyday (and societally relevant) problems. In our approach, we do not break individuals out of the societal contexts and material settings in which they normally conduct their activities. We do not sever the mediating relations of tools, community, division of labor, and situated rules, so forms of activity are observed that are not possible in currently normal circumstances.

Our approach puts the individual back into the system where it belongs and from which an increasingly individualistic culture has taken it. Historically, humans have transcended environmental conditions because, by banding together and dividing labor, they have increasingly taken control of and shaped their environment. Individual human beings no longer had to be able to hunt or gather food to survive; by contributing to the collective activities that sustain society, each individual also guaranteed his or her own survival. The claim that every human being needs to know science is not much different from saying that every human being needs to know to hunt, gather, or garden. Accordingly, as long as each individual contributes to a society that also supports science and contributes to an emerging conversation in which science figures as prominently as religion, ethics, philosophy, and so on, scientific literacy as a collective ability has been sustained.

## SCIENCE LITERACY AS LIVED AND LIFELONG CURRICULUM

Current efforts in rethinking scientific literacy have many shortcomings that impede the achievement of their goals of broad participation (e.g., the slogan "Science for all Americans"). Ways of enacting the reform agenda also fail to sufficiently address the wide gap between school and everyday knowledge, and therefore fail to set up a continuity of lifelong learning. The reform documents pay insufficient heed to the fact that students constitute a heterogeneous clientele; furthermore, it makes little sense to treat citizens as though they were a homogeneous group. In this chapter, we have depicted adults engaged in activities of their interest, drawing on those tools that best responded to their (intellectual, motivational) needs, and produced a variety of representations of stream and watershed health. Community members, activists, aboriginal elders, scientists, university students, and schoolchildren were an integral part of the community (thread) that also contains science. Various adults, including parents, high school and graduate students, activists, and aboriginal elders, assisted younger children in investigating the creek or painting signs next to culverts; the children, in turn, contributed with their actions and results of investigations to the community at large (see especially Chapters 6 and 7). Members from the environmental activist group contributed to the community by giving presentations, assisting in teaching kids how to use particular tools and how to do research in the creek, and by working with the citizens in the attempt to improve the environmental health of the watershed.

In this situation, each individual not only contributes to the ongoing conversation in the respective settings but also, as we showed earlier, to the context that the setting provides for others independent of age or levels of claimed expertise. Because of the emergent feature of these conversations, participating in producing and reproducing the changing conditions is equivalent to learning. Of particular interest to us as educators is the fact that the walls surrounding formal learning no longer separate school activities and community activities. We want to see involvement of community members in school and school members in the community, therefore integrating a variety of activity systems under the larger umbrella of achieving good for the community. That is, the various activities are motivated by the same concerns that drive the activities of other community members. In terms of our model, there is therefore legitimate peripheral participation because the motivations that drive the activity system share many elements. It is from this overlap that learning opportunities emerged for both children and adults.

Redefining scientific literacy in such ways that community members begin to participate in the community may come with considerable political consequences. Thus, when members of the community not only construct facts about environmental pollution but also begin naming and publishing the names of individuals, groups, and companies that perpetrate the pollution, communities will begin to change. We advocate direct participation in community affairs because it allows continuous trajectories of learning that neither stop nor are determined by the walls of institutional learning.

Our way of approaching scientific literacy directly acknowledges the limitations of (laboratory) science. Acknowledging the heterogeneous and collective nature of scientific literacy in the community opens doors to richer understandings of science as a "profoundly creative and imaginative activity tempered by a scrupulous honesty in the face of experimental evidence."[11] Such an approach permits groups and communities to enact different relations between traditional scientific and other forms of knowledge, including various forms of situated knowing (e.g., local, traditional ecological, relational). Rather than privileging disciplinary science, we ought to foster situations that allow conversations to emerge in which different forms of knowledge (geared to particular [controversial] problems as these arise in the daily life of a community) are negotiated. By creating conversational spaces where any form of knowledge may be entered and where learning trajectories are not marked by currently prevailing discontinuities when school boundaries are crossed, we allow new forms of literacy to emerge in non-deterministic ways that also include science as an integral component. Rather than science as a fiber involved in the hegemonic struggle to make all other fibers in its image, we accept a more democratic society in which science is but one of the many fibers, each of which contributes its part (as a practical form of the division of labor) to the survival of collective life.

# 3

## SCIENTIFIC LITERACY, HEGEMONY, AND STRUGGLE

What scientific literacy is depends very much on the conception of knowing and learning that one associates with it. Despite differences in the definition of scientific literacy, the current reform rhetoric describes the individual informed citizen as one who participates in public discourses and uses rather than produces science. Many citizens are said to have blanks in their background knowledge left by formal education and therefore need to be given information to fill those gaps; some even suggest more strongly that most people are not only ignorant but also incapable of scientific literacy. Like the makers of the film *A Private Universe*, many science educators mocked the answers that Harvard graduates gave to the question, "Why is it hotter in summer than in winter?" Thus, Bruce Matson, the flight director of the Challenger Center at Framingham State College, part of the Christa Corrigan McAuliffe Center for Education and Teaching Excellence, said, the Harvard graduates gave "bizarre and contrived explanations" to the most basic astronomy questions.[1] Matson, like many science educators, defined scientific literacy in terms of the answers that individuals give to questions in interviews or on questionnaires. Because every citizen should have some level of scientific literacy, so the general argument goes, the implications of such individualist takes on scientific literacy are finding ways in which the individual comes to know more of the facts (and sometimes processes) of science.

To rethink scientific literacy in radically different ways, we take our cues for thinking, knowing, and learning from everyday community-based activities in which science, scientific facts, and scientific methods are contested. We challenge reigning assumptions about knowing

**49**

and learning that depend "implicitly on a homogeneity of community, culture, participants, their motives, and the meaning of events."[2] But if we are not homogeneous, everyone knowing differently and different things, struggle will be inevitable whenever decisions are being made that affect people. We say struggle is inevitable because different versions of the issues at hand and how to resolve them compete for wider acceptance. With struggle come issues of knowledge and power, but we will analyze those issues more closely in Chapter 4.

## SCIENCE, SOCIETY, AND HEGEMONY

In the past, science and society have been thought of as two entities, two categories that are opposed like the citadel (of science) and the polis (the untutored public). Recent work in the anthropology of science suggests that the citadel is porous. Science and society cannot be separate, but, as categories, are produced inside a more general, heterogeneous matrix of culture. Culture itself, "meaning fundamental understandings and practices involving such terms as the person, action, time, space, work, value, agency, and so on, is produced by a far wider range of processes than those deployed by experts producing science."[3] Scientists claim that science is pure and that truth will come out whenever there is an instance of a rarely occurring mitigating social influence. Frequently, through their extensive and laborious boundary work, scientists attempt to encapsulate themselves and maintain the image of the citadel standing in opposition to the sullied polis, with its economic, ethico-moral, and political dimensions. But, in fact, science and scientists are just part of the discontinuous, fractured, and non-linear network of relationships from which science and the rest of society are made to emerge as constructs. When science and its role in society are studied as everyday activity, their collective nature begins to appear; using a systems perspective, we come to see science, knowing, and learning in and as of collective phenomena.

When we articulate human activity in non-reductionist terms of multiple interacting systems, we account for the many different ways in which the relationship between individuals and objects of their activities are mediated by means of (knowledge and artifact) production, community, rules, and division of labor available in the situation. Differences in the social location of individuals are inherent in societal structures and arise from specific practices that both produce and reproduce these differences. Differences in interest, motives, power, and action possibilities abound. From such a perspective, we see how much science really is tied up in the thread of life as a fiber among fibers. Individuals participate in and are part of the collective life as the fibers that make the thread (of life), each making it possible for human society to continue, which in turn makes it possible for each fiber to survive, even if it is not concerned with the production of basic necessities such as food. Thinking of the relationship between individual and collective life in terms of fiber and thread allows us a new approach to theorizing scientific literacy. It is no longer a property of a single fiber or a small number of fibers (scientific community), but a property that becomes recognizable and analyzable at the level of the thread. Thinking of science as a fiber among fibers helps us to understand it as an entity and as the context in a more general endeavor (thread). From the perspective of the thread, science plays a role as do all the other forms of knowledge and practices; any attempt to privilege it abstracts the fact that it itself exists only because of all the other threads. Science education would then be the endeavor to make scientific literacy possible as a collective rather than individual characteristic. It would amount to creating opportunities for individuals (fibers) to participate, each in their own ways, to contribute to the emergence of the phenomenon at a collective level. This means that not all individuals have to know a basic stock of scientific facts or concepts—much as most of us drive without knowing anything about car mechanics and most of us eat bread without knowing how to bake it.

When decisions are made, different fibers that make society often bring competing perspectives. For example, whereas AIDS researchers wanted to use double-blind experimental methodology for testing new drugs, those afflicted with the disease who were potential research participants refused to be part of the control group. AIDS patients wanted to be given experimental drugs rather than the placebos, even though it was not known whether the drugs really could help in alleviating the suffering. In the resulting struggle, scientists attempted to articulate their leadership across that terrain of social, cultural, and political life concerned with the testing of new drugs. Such struggle for the superiority of one perspective, one discourse, over all other perspectives and discourses with the consent of those who hold them has come to be known as hegemony. In the process, consent comes to be structured through a matrix of relations that define an ongoing political struggle—between dominant and subordinated groups—over competing perspectives and ways of understanding the world.

In this chapter, we tell the story of one such struggle. In the last chapter, we featured an excerpt from a public meeting in which various reports concerning the water in the wells of the residents of Salina Drive were discussed. The residents wanted to be connected to the water main that supplies the remainder of the community. However, the mayor and town council opposed the connection because they feared that it would increase the values of the properties at Salina Drive, which might lead to further development and urbanization of the area. The mayor and town council established the Water Advisory Task Force, made up of members of the Oceanside municipality, only some of whom lived on Salina Drive. Various scientist consultants, including Lowell Consulting, were brought in to test the water. Although their findings that there were no water problems were contradicted by the results of other studies and by the lived experience of the residents, the town officials used those findings to decline a petition for a connection to the water main. To a great part, the public meeting became a struggle over the legitimacy of the consultant report and the legitimacy of the methodology that had been used. We argue that a new form of scientific literacy emerges in this struggle between hegemonic (science, town officials) and counter-hegemonic (residents) views of the water issue at Salina Drive. It is a new form, because its discourse is no longer solely that of laboratory science, but is heterogeneous, appropriate for a heterogeneous community, culture, participants, their motives, and the meaning of events. More broadly, then, scientific literacy is the contingent outcome of the encounter of hegemony and counter-hegemony over contentious issues.

## ORDINARY KNOWLEDGEABILITY AS STRUGGLE

The currently dominant, folk-psychological view takes knowledge to be a collection of entities (representations, concepts, or structures) in the heads of people and of learning as a process of internalizing or constructing them. In this view, learning is problematic because (school, adult) educators are concerned with the ways in which the external environment has to be configured to allow, depending on the theoretical commitments, knowledge appropriation, transfer, or (internal) construction to occur. A minority view takes knowing and learning to be engagement in changing processes of human activity. In this approach, knowledge as we have come to know it changes, becoming itself a complex and problematic category. What constitutes knowledge at a given moment or across a range of situations is a matter of analysis, which has to take account of the motives, interests, relations of power, goals, and contingencies that shape the activity. It may therefore be more appropriate to rethink knowing and learning as production of knowledgeability, a flexible process from which individuals and their life worlds emerge. Knowledgeability is a concept that suits our purpose of redefining scientific literacy, because it implies struggle over competing definitions of situations (hegemony) and contradictions in complex systems, all of which are potential drivers of change and development. Thus, knowledgeability:

> is routinely in a state of change rather than stasis, in the medium of so-cially, culturally, and historically ongoing systems of activity, involving people who are related in multiple and heterogeneous ways, whose social locations, interests, reasons, and subjective possibilities are different, and who improvise struggles in situated ways with each other over the value of particular definitions of the situation, in both immediate and compre-hensive terms, and for whom the production of failure is as much a part of routine collective activity as the production of average, ordinary knowledgeability.[4]

When we think about scientific literacy as the outcome of contingent struggles over the value of competing situation definitions, it is no longer something that is owned by (or characterizes) individuals. It is no longer stuff that is exhibited by individuals on international tests of basic science knowledge. Rather, scientific literacy is continuously pro-duced, routinely changing and therefore an emergent phenomenon. Thought of in this way, scientific literacy is a form of knowledgeability. Thus, everyone (speakers, listeners, moderator) and everything (re-ports, spatial arrangements, historical context) in the public meeting that we analyze below was part of the production of scientific literacy.

Reconfiguring scientific literacy in this way requires us to rethink the notion of "context" of human activity, and the relation between in-dividual and context. Thus, the context of human activity is not a con-tainer filled with people nor is context, situationally and individually created experiential space. Rather, context is an activity system, het-erogeneous and historically constituted entities composed of many, often dissimilar and contradictory, elements, lives, experiences, and voices and discontinuous, fractured and non-linear relationships be-tween these elements, lives, experiences, and voices. Context is not so much something into which someone is put, but an order of behavior of which the individual is a constitutive part. Context, therefore, gives rise to interactional possibilities, which are the source of individuals, scientific literacy, and so forth.

## STRUGGLE OVER TROUBLED WATER: THE CONTEXT

Oceanside is a rural community that spreads over a considerable area, with two neighborhoods of higher concentration. Salina Drive, the part of town involved in the controversy, lies in a wooded area on the ocean, about five kilometers away from each of the two high-concentration areas. The residents have individual wells that draw on several local aquifers. For years, the local and regional newspapers reported that in the summer months, the water in the Salina Drive area was biologically and chemically contaminated. In some years and for some periods, the residents had been advised by the regional health board not to use their water at all or to boil it considerably; many residents have opted to get their water from nearby gas stations. For the past thirty years, the residents of Salina Drive demanded to be connected to the water main that supplies other residents of Oceanside. The residents brought the issues forward to the local Water Commission, which decided that the issue was a municipal concern. However, the Oceanside town council and mayor blocked all demands, attempting to keep the water main away from Salina Drive to prevent the area from being developed.

At issue is not just the water for Salina Drive: the residents of Cross Road, which connects Salina Drive to one of the higher density areas, currently draw their water from wells and would benefit from a water main. Furthermore, a water main would also come with fire hydrants and decreased fire insurance costs for the currently unprotected homes. However, the appropriate capacity for fire protection by far outstrips the water use by the existing homes, so that laying a water main opens up the possibility for further development of the area—though it is currently protected from development by its Agricultural Land Reserve status.

In the past, individual families (through consultants they hired) and the regional health board had tested the water. Invariably, a variety of problems were noted including chemical and biological contaminants. However, the Water Advisory Task Force decided that previous studies and testimonial evidence was insufficient or flawed, so it hired a consultant firm, Lowell Consulting, that regularly works for various municipalities in the region and is said to have a special expertise in groundwater and in the impact of effluents and sewage on water quality. The consulting firm is used to controversy, as there have been cases where their studies have been contradicted by the results of other studies. This has led litigants in such cases to play on the contested nature of Lowell's reports.

Because the Water Advisory Task Force could not come to a unanimous recommendation, two reports were filed with the town council, the majority report and the minority report. The majority report largely based its recommendations on the data provided by Lowell Consulting. The minority report grounded its assessment on two major pieces of information: the degree of the problem on Salina Drive as apparent from testimonial evidence of residents and the lower-than-recommended water quantity available to nearly two-thirds of the families on Salina Drive.

The senior engineering technologist for Oceanside, Don Bisgrove, prepared a report for the Council that summarizes the results of all other reports and proposes a series of policies and options. A large part of the report focuses on the Official Community Plan (OCP) and the Land Use Bylaws. (This report had been reviewed and endorsed by the town's director of financial services and the director of planning and building services. Furthermore, the municipal engineer and clerk administrator had signed to concur with the recommendations.) In particular, the report notes that these existing documents do not allow the subdivision of existing rural and agricultural properties for the development of new housing units.

> The direct implications of having a water main extension are difficult to quantify. The availability of water could encourage some property owners to either develop under the existing zoning, or to apply for rezoning.
>
> With the current Provincial support for the ALR and given the policies of the OCP, however, it would be difficult to support any rezoning of or development of the lands zoned Agriculture.
>
> For the lands designated Rural, the OCP and the Land Use Bylaw should continue as constraints on development. Another constraint on development would be the suitability of the soil for sewage disposal. (Memorandum, p. 7)

At issue, therefore, was not merely whether and how to get sufficient and suitable water to the residents of Salina Drive but also whether any changes would allow further development of the area. Following the meeting in which the report was accepted, the Council decided to provide the public with a forum in which reports and issues could be discussed. It organized an one-and-a-half-hour open house, where the different reports and graphics prepared by the technical presenters were available. This event was immediately followed by the public meeting in which technical and advisory bodies made presentations (45 minutes), the public could ask questions about the technical presentations (15 minutes), and members of the public made comments.

## HETEROGENEITY OF SCIENCE: BEYOND THE RIGID BODY LANGUAGE

Our research in the Oceanside community (and particularly in public meetings) shows that ordinary citizens often feel disenfranchised by scientists who talk in decontextualized ways about the issues at hand, which deeply affect residents' lives (presence of a high-power radio emitter, access to the water main). Scientists exhibit a very limited (laboratory science) discourse and a rigid body language, which they consider to be value-free. They attempt to impose this discourse and body language wherever they are involved and to co-opt others into accepting their ways of talking about and representing the issues at hand. In this community, as elsewhere, scientists are involved in a struggle for hegemony. They hope to emerge victoriously by bludgeoning the general public with what they call "scientific" facts, mostly ignoring the culturally embedded understandings that the general public brings to the forum. That is, scientists practice a rigid body language that frequently alienates and disillusions their lay audiences.[5]

The first part of the public meeting constructed the scientists and engineers present as the "experts." Each expert was provided with the opportunity to elaborate key issues in the reports they had produced, and took the amount of time they deemed necessary. There was no attempt to shorten or curtail any of the presenters. The experts were constructed as such also by their and the moderator's description of the positions, titles, or degrees they held. Thus, individuals were variously introduced as "professional engineer and a professional geologist," "public health engineer serving the regional district," "environmental health officer for the Oceanside area . . . [with] a Masters of Science degree, and has significant experience with water quality issues and he has been involved extensively in both reports in the sampling episodes" or "chief environmental health officer for our health region."

All of these presenters had considerable time to make their presentations—something that is significant when held against the attempt by the moderator to limit questions and contributions of other participants. The independent consultant Dan Lowell, an engineer and hydro-geologist, provided a report in which there was no uncertainty left about his methods of data collection and the facts that resulted from them. Lowell stated:

> The sampling methodology was, "sample as close to the well as possible and at an outside tap or right at the wellhead." We tried to avoid house plumbing and cisterns as much as possible. So we pumped the wells for as little as fifteen minutes and as much as one hour to get a fresh water supply coming straight from the aquifer and not coming from storage. The results of our testing showed that according to the Guidelines for Canadian Drinking Water Quality, there are no concerns related to health. None were identified in the parameters that we tested. Some aesthetic objectives from the Guidelines for Canadian Drinking Water Quality were exceeded for some of the wells. . . . For all of the bacteriological testing done, no wells were found to be unacceptable. All of the bacterial, bacteriological results were acceptable.

Mike Magee, university professor, chairperson of the Water Advisory Task Force, and the representative of its majority, presented a report that was very much built on the facticity of Lowell's report. Repeatedly, Magee emphasized that Lowell's report was the "first systematic" and "unbiased" study of the water problems at Salina Drive. Magee and the report he presented articulated Lowell's science as definitive and all other forms of data as "mere opinion." It was a rhetoric effort to discredit other, competing reports and data that supported different versions of the situation. By describing the report as "systematic" and "unbiased" and Lowell as an "independent consultant," Magee draws on the negative connotations that everyone in the audience and the Salina Drive residents understand as the polar opposites of these terms. Magee made a clear move in the struggle for hegemony of science and the ruling town council:

> Our suggestion, our conclusions in the final report and recommendations to Council were as follows. Number one, a systematic problem of groundwater supply in the Salina Drive area has not been identified. Instead, solutions to problems of both quantity and quality can be provided on an individual basis. In this light Council may wish to provide individual homeowners with technical design advice as to the nature of each individually designed solution. Second, it is anticipated this approach will solve the Salina Drive water issue in possibly every case. However at the end of a case-by-case household assessment where we actually look at solutions and Council facilitate people to do their own, as Mr. Lowell has said, to solve problems individually.

The presentations by Lowell and Magee did not pass by uncontested. Another scientist, the representative of the regional health district, presented those present with a very different set of facts. Unlike Lowell, he emphasized the seasonal variations in the concentrations of various contaminants. He also talked about the differences between the concentration measures taken in the field (where Lowell had taken them) and those measured in the lab (where his engineers had analyzed the water). Accordingly, Robert Radford, a public health engineer, had come to the conclusion that there were substantial problems both with biological and physico-chemical pollutants (e.g., chromium), at least during particular times of the year:

> There is a very pronounced effect on the aquifer relative to rainwater as evidenced by the pH tested. A pH of 6.8 to 7.2 is similar to the pH of rainwater and if you look at the data you'll see a lot of the pH values in that range. The well data for a log at 617 Salina Drive demonstrates that groundwater-level fluctuation and that information is from 1996, October, to June of 1999. So we do have a couple of years of data in there that shows us what that water table is doing. The total dissolved solids, or TDS, show the significance of dilution and if you look at the aquifer, you'll find that as the aquifer is drawn down, the chemical constituents

increase so there is a fairly significant influence by dilution of the rainwater. . . . We had a problem and a high level with our chromium levels.
Chromium can be a problem when it combines with chlorine and goes to
the trivalent state. This is when a carcinogen is formed. Chromium as it
generally occurs in the water system if fine. It is a nutrient. But when we
have to chlorinate a water system that's where we have the potential for
some problems.

The minority report from the Water Advisory Task Force, here presented by a citizen named Rees, emphasized the problematic nature of
a variety of measures and of several technical solutions proposed in
the majority report.

The report says itself that the analysis is done from the well logs of the
area. Well logs, as you probably know, are what the well-drillers report
when they hit water. And assumption in the report is made that those
water volumes are accurate, they assume that they, that the well will run at
that capacity all year long and that they will run at that capacity for eter-
nity. Well, all of those assumptions are false. So if you're basing your
analysis on false data I think that puts to great speculation the analysis itself. They say that there's no quantity problem and they're quoting, for
example, simple math. If, say, you have 0.2 gallons per minute in a
twenty-four-hour period, you'll generate enough water for a household.
Well, 0.2 gallons per minute is a very, very small amount, and there are
neighbors around us that have ten times that flow according to their well
logs and they still have shortages throughout the year.

In sum, there was no agreement between the scientists and within
the Water Advisory Task Force as to the problem and its solutions.
Lowell, Magee, and the community engineer used a very limited (scientific) discourse; they represented the traditional assumption that
there is something like science unfettered from social influences. But
the present data show that science itself is heterogeneous; science
arises as a thread from the interaction of its heterogeneous practitioners and practices. Despite this heterogeneity, the town council took the
stand (largely as the consequence of the majority report of the task
force presented by Magee) that the residents of the Salina Drive could
not have a water main. Here, the question was not whether every citizen in a community of an industrialized nation has the right to sufficient and safe drinking water but whether those supplied with the
water had to pay for the cost of putting in solutions even if the solutions excluded the water main.

Contradictory reports from scientists working for different sides on
controversial issues have led to decreased credibility of scientists, of
the infallibility of their knowledge, and of their supposedly neutral
role in policy. Fortunately, public meetings provide opportunities for

ordinary citizens to participate irrespective of their level of scientific training; or rather, scientific literacy emerges only if public meetings provide spaces for people to talk and be heard. New forms of scientific literacy emerge from the struggle between hegemonic and counter-hegemonic efforts to articulate what the real problems and solutions are. The thread of public meetings, then, includes citizens and different types of expertise as fibers. Although the initial part of the hearing could be read as a claim to the scientists' and engineers' authority over the water problem at Salina Drive, the participation of the citizens turned up problems in scientific facts and methodology. What the appropriate facts and appropriate methodology in the public forum and the political process were could not be determined a priori—attributing them to the scientists and engineers—but had to await the outcome of the process.

## SCIENCE, ACCESS, AND THE POLITICS OF VOICE

An important point that is seldom addressed in the context of scientific literacy pertains to access. If access to ongoing conversations is not enabled, particular citizens cannot become part of the choreography of scientific literacy. In the following situation, a citizen named Fowler wanted to elaborate on an issue raised by the previous speaker, Ted, a member of the Water Advisory Task Force. However, the moderator of the session, Bisgrove, wanted to prevent Fowler from making a comment, stating that "everyone has a bias or concern about" the issues raised. (The square brackets in consecutive lines indicate where the speakers overlapped.)

> Fowler: I too would like to make a comment about the previous speaker's comments. I believe we all [have a—]
> Bisgrove: [Frank?!]
> Fowler: Frank Fowler.
> Bisgrove: Yeah, I know but everybody has a bias or a concern about it.
> Fowler: No, [I could—]
> Bisgrove: [I don't know,] if Ted said anything in particular. All he was doing was presenting his [side—]
> Fowler: [This is,] this is just a [comment—]
> Bisgrove: [his side of] the Water Advisory Task Force. Well, okay. Let's try [and—]
> Fowler: [It's very] brief.
> Bisgrove: Well, let's try not to bash each other, please.

The overlapping turns show how both Fowler and Bisgrove tried to access the floor. Fowler attempted to get the floor in order to make the desired comment, whereas Bisgrove wanted to prevent Fowler, or anyone else, from engaging in a critique that might lead to a confrontation ("let's try not to bash each other"). That is, the choreography of hegemony and counter-hegemony from which scientific literacy emerges has to include not only what is said but also the ways in which it is said and the struggles to say something in the first place.

This episode shows that scientific literacy is not just about knowing science in a traditional sense, or participating in a public meeting from which scientific literacy can emerge as a recognizable feature. Rather, scientific literacy also means participating in the choreography of the public meeting, enacting access to participation and thereby contributing in different and changing ways as the event unfolds. Preventing access to the speaking floor is also part of the choreography of the public meeting, and an integral part of scientific literacy that can be observed. During the second part of the hearing, Bisgrove repeatedly asked "Are there any other questions of a technical nature?" That is, this second part itself was distinguishable from the first because of the type of questions that Bisgrove, a gatekeeper and obligatory point of passage, attempted to allow. It is not that other types of questions could not arise. As we have seen, Fowler was able to make a contribution where Bisgrove did not foresee one. Rather, "second part" characterized by "technical questions only" are descriptors whose usefulness in this context can be established only after the fact. Negotiating access and preventing it, involving different people with different social positions, is part of the choreography of hegemony and counter-hegemony that gives rise to scientific literacy.

In schools, science is (generally) taught as if it and its results were value-free and independent of opportunities of access. This, as much research in the sociology of science has shown, is not the case. Students or citizens cannot be part of scientific literacy if they are prevented from access to the floor of ongoing conversations. In reconsidering scientific literacy as an emergent feature of the practical struggle between hegemony and counter-hegemony, the question of access and legitimate peripheral participation become crucial. The citizens in this community in general and in this public meeting more specifically realized that due process should allow their voices to be heard. As recurrent newspaper features showed, the people in this community did not feel that their voices were heard or that their knowledge, which has emerged and evolved over thirty years of experience, was not valued. This is evident in the following episode, which began with a statement by a citizen named Naught about the ripple effect that Lowell's report had. It first influenced heavily the majority report by the Water Advisory Task Force, here represented by Magee, which itself—as other speakers also pointed out—heavily influenced the decision by the town council.

Naught: Well, it seems to me that the report is relying— Mr. Magee's report is relying on very heavily on your information, which would suggest that it doesn't matter what the problem is with water, it can be treated. And I would beg to differ on that because I think that when you do something to the water, you affect it, regardless of what the treatment is and where the treatment occurs. And that it affects the water in another fashion. So therefore this business of treating water is only a marginal thing with respect to water qualities.

Bisgrove: We are straying sort of into the area of public opinion and your comments—

Naught: He's an expert, he just told us.

Magee: Well, I'd like to make one comment on this—

Naught: I'm addressing, I'm addressing—

Magee: You're looking for technical— This is supposed to be a technical discussion and I think—

Naught: No, I'm talking to Mr. Lowell. I'm not talking to you. I don't think—

Several: (*Clapping.*) Yeah, we wanna hear.

Bisgrove: Mr. Naught, I'm sorry but you're really not. If we can keep to a specific question, you are certainly able to ask questions if we're going somewhere with it, but I don't want to get in to a detailed bit-by-bit tearing something apart.

Naught: Why? I mean, I'm asking—

Bisgrove: Because, because—

Naught: This is our only chance to talk to this man who has made a report that influences our lives.

Bisgrove: Yeah, but it doesn't directly influence your life to the extent that everything is going to hinge on his report. It's merely one bit of information and we've got lots of information back and forth. Other people are presenting as well—

Naught: Well, I disagree with you.

Bisgrove: Can I ask— Sorry, can I ask you if there is a specific question that you wish to ask of Dan [Lowell] specifically?

Naught: Well, I'll ask him another question.

In this episode, Naught attempted to generalize the earlier issue of downstream treatment by claiming that any water treatment constituted a change, probably undesirable. This comment was never elaborated because Bisgrove intervened, followed by an exchange that also included Magee, who had spoken in favor of local treatment solutions. Magee attempted to enter the exchange, insinuating that Naught's comment was inappropriate for this part of the hearing devoted to "technical discussions" ("This is supposed to be a technical discussion"). However, Naught reclaimed the floor by suggesting that he was talking to Lowell rather than to Magee, thereby contesting Magee's claim to the floor. Importantly, several individuals clapped and loudly voiced the desire to hear more from Naught. The choreography of the hearing then involved Naught and Bisgrove, the former wanting to continue and the latter attempting to limit Naught's questioning. Most importantly, Bisgrove, who had earlier asked Naught not to ask specific questions, now reminded him to ask more specific questions. That is, the nature of the specificity of permissible questions is also open for contention. The point here is that scientific literacy is enacted as praxis, involving listeners and applauding audiences as much as speakers and the public demonstration that the expertise of an individual present is more limited than it first appeared. A key point in the struggle, one relevant to our theorizing of scientific literacy and science education was made by Naught. *This* meeting was their chance of directly interacting with the person whose report appeared to have most influenced the decision by the community not to pay for the water main extension. This decision affected the lives of the people living at Salina Drive—their participation in the choreography of hegemony and counter-hegemony that made the public meeting was motivated by concerns for the quality of their everyday lives. In this case, Naught and other members of the community were able to gain the floor, making it possible for scientific literacy to emerge as collective praxis in a variety of ways.

## SCIENCE AS FIBER IN THE THREAD OF THE CONTROVERSY

In this public meeting, the choreography changed when citizens were provided with the opportunity to question the experts and to make statements on their own behalf. Here, a more general type of scientific literacy emerged, exhibiting local expertise, historical knowledge of the problems, their emergence, and a variety of (abandoned) solutions. Whereas one might be tempted to attribute scientific literacy to the individual scientists—based on their talks when they did not have to interact—such attributions make no longer sense when one analyses conversations, which are irreducibly social in nature. In the present situation, detailed understandings of the trajectories of individual wells became apparent, including a variety of consultant reports, often contradicting the one-time assessments outlined by those present. A different kind of expertise became evident, one that was very pertinent to the greatly varying water problems in the Salina Drive area. Although in this meeting, as in other situations reported by sociologists of science, the scientists were discursively marked and set apart by introducing them with their titles and positions, the previous section showed that the (impromptu) choreography did not relegate citizens to mere listeners. The citizens who attended contributed their part for scientific literacy to emerge in the various forms that we will describe here. They contributed to raising questions such as "What are scientific data representative of?" "What are the limits of scientific expertise?" and "What links fire, water-treatment systems, and other conflicting things?"

### What Do Scientific Data Represent?

One of the citizens who struggled for and got a longer turn at talk was Tom Naught. We pick up the public meeting after Tom Naught had already been able to raise doubts about the claim by Lowell, the hydrogeologist, that his measures of biological contamination and dissolved substances represent average values. The following excerpt starts when Naught suggested that the tremendous increase in rain probably led to an increase in the water in the aquifer and therefore to much lower-than-average concentration of the contaminants.

Naught: Well, well, it's, okay this is true but the thing is, is that what we've experienced is, rainfall in the order of 522 percent on average, as far as monthly averages are concerned increase over the summer months. In other words what we've got through the winter period, through the five months previously preceding your test results. If you took that and compared that to an average summer month, a month through that period, it is, there were 522 percent more. Now, it would seem to me that we're probably not dealing on an average result with your tests. We are probably dealing with the hydrostatic head feeding that aquifer up in the higher, very much higher ends, so that the readings that you are getting are very much diluted.

Lowell: The hydrograph that we have shows that the water levels are average in late April early May, and I put the average water level on the hydrograph here and the—

Naught: Could it be an error? Could you be in error here?

Lowell: Well, I don't take the water level readings but I take the Ministry of Environment—

Naught: Well, you mean to say that on these particular aquifers out at Salina Drive that they are taking the readings? And, and—

Lowell: The Ministry of Environment produced these readings.

Naught: And could there be an error? Could they be, for example, relevant for some. . . ?

Bisgrove: I'm not, I'm really, I really don't want to get into— I hate to cut you off but what I would like to do— Dan [Lowell]'s report deals with a specific time that he took the samples. We recognize already through Mr. Radford's comments on their original testing that there are differences in the quality of the water throughout the time. I don't think that you're going to find a smoking gun one way or the other. You may be able to pick [it] apart on specific instances but in general, I don't want to, as I say, get into a slugfest over particular pieces of the report. Dan is not here to defend every little bit of it. I don't, I really would like to move on with it and carry on with the meeting.

Lowell responded that he relied on the hydrograph readings, which were halfway between the minimum and maximum water levels. He clearly made the attempt to construct "halfway between minimum and maximum" as "average level." A detailed consideration of the issue suggests that even if the water was at an average level this would still be consistent with the water supply to be contaminated for a major part of the year. Lowell defended his claim by suggesting that he based his claim on the readings from the hydrograph. Naught questioned whether there could be an error (it is unclear what type error this might be). Lowell drew on the readings taken by the Ministry of Environment, presumably an authoritative and accurate source of environmental data. (Authoritative repertoire [register] is one of the discursive resources available when issues of science and scientific knowledge are contested.) The subsequent question relativized the recourse to the authoritative repertoire by raising doubt about whether the Ministry of Environment technicians had actually sampled the particular aquifers at Salina Drive, that is, the only aquifer relevant to the people living there.

Although it is crucial for the evaluation of the case to know whether the engineer's data represent the normal, mid-level, or average situation in terms of contaminant concentration, Bisgrove made an attempt to stop the line of questioning. He did, however, point out that the other scientist had established seasonal variation in contaminant concentration. It was also important to know whether the water levels brought into the discussion actually represented those at Salina Drive or whether they were taken elsewhere and therefore not representative. There is, then, a double methodological issue: What is the extent to which the available data are representative of the specific case that is for discussion? Naught relativized claims that the concentrations represent an average by questioning the representativeness of water levels and the representativeness of extant readings for the particular location. Here, the legitimacy of the questions is at issue. This part of the evening had been designated as the opportunity for technical questions. Although Naught did ask technical questions, Bisgrove attempted to limit the detail with which technical questions could be asked. Being able to maintain the floor and thereby contribute to the choreography of the public meeting under such mediating circumstances is as much part of scientific literacy as knowing the effect of chromium on the human body.

### What Are the Limits of Scientific Expertise?

In the analogy of thread and fiber, it is less important to know a scientific fact than to know how to find and use expertise; an important aspect of scientific literacy is therefore the appropriate use of a specialist. However, even if a scientist involved in a socio-scientific controversy is recognized and used as *a* specialist, there still remains the question whether he or she is *the* appropriate specialist for the case at hand. Appropriate use of specialists therefore means not only drawing on scientists but also delimiting the extent and level of the expertise and evaluating them in the context of the specific problem. Here, we return to the episode when the geologist is led to admit that his expertise is limited relative to a specific aspect of the water problem. That is, this move directly questioned the legitimacy of the scientist whose claim to hegemony requires others to buy into the superiority of science and scientists when it comes to scientific method. He also emerged as someone who is, at a minimum, not informed about the current state of the field, and at worse, gullible in the face of manufacturers' assurances.

> Naught: Treatment of downstream water, is that your area of familiarity and expertise?
>
> Lowell: I've worked with groundwater and water treatment for over twenty-five years.
>
> Naught: So, you would consider yourself an expert in that area?
>
> Lowell: Not in all aspects. An environmental engineer who's an expert in water treatment would know more about it than I do.
>
> Naught: Do you know, for example, whether chromium can be treated successfully?
>
> Lowell: Yes, I do. It can, with ion exchange filtrate, a filter. I phoned the manufacturers of certain systems and they assured me that that can be done.
>
> Naught: And that's good enough for you?
>
> Lowell: Well, I read it in publications as well.
>
> Naught: Oh, there's a publication that we have here that says there is no commercial treatment for chromium.
>
> Bisgrove: Well, again Mr. Naught—
>
> Lowell: Again, there wasn't any concern for chromium identified. So I'm not sure what point you're making.

At issue in this exchange is Lowell's claim that individualized local solutions better address the problems experienced by the citizens living on Salina Drive than a water main. Not only a particular solution is being questioned but the very expertise Lowell brought to the study ("Is that your familiarity and expertise?"). Naught questioned Lowell whether he considered himself a specialist on downstream-treatment of water. After Lowell admitted that an environmental engineer "would know more about it," Naught asked a specific question about the treatment of water for chromium. Lowell suggested that an ion exchanger would deal with the problem and that he had the assurance of several manufacturers that this could be done. Naught questioned whether such assurance was sufficient and, after Lowell indicated use of publications, Naught noted the availability of a publication that suggested the impossibility of chromium removal by means of ion exchange mechanisms. The episode ended with the statement that there was no "concern for chromium identified" in the study conducted by the engineer and geologist. Although Bisgrove's intervention and the shortage of time prevented further elaboration of the chromium issue, other speakers did contest this statement. For example, in his introductory remarks, Radford (from the regional health authority) had already identified chromium as a significant contaminant in some wells. Furthermore, among the reports commissioned by the citizens themselves, chromium was identified as a significant pollutant. Thus, one citizen said, "Our water samples, beyond the one that was done by Mr. Lowell, have always tested very high in the negative areas, one in particular is chromium."

Some readers might automatically assume that scientists and engineers are de facto scientifically literate. If the efficient use of black boxes is a criterion of scientific literacy, one could construct Lowell as not being scientifically literate. Here, "ion exchanger" together with "manufacturer assurance" constituted an unopened black box. This black box is one of those that scientists have to trust, rightly or wrongly, in their everyday work. It is only when things go wrong or when knowledge and facts become contested that the problems in this system of trust become evident. However, we prefer to look at the entire situation; here, scientific literacy emerges from the struggle between hegemony and counter-hegemony in the form of an argument over the use of a black box. Scientific literacy is embodied in the argument rather than attributable to Lowell (on de facto grounds) or Naught (as the one who detected the error).

Scientific literacy is also recognizable when the understanding of technology is contrasted with the understanding of its scientific principle. In the present case, the scientific principle is the exchange of ions. Water softeners working on this principle exchange calcium ions, which are responsible for hard water, with sodium ions. From the technological perspective, the problem of hard water has been alleviated or eliminated by the water softener. However, from a scientific perspective, what happens is an exchange. That is, the ions removed have been replaced by other ions. The most common ion used is sodium. That is, in the process of softening the water, sodium ions, one half of sodium chloride, are introduced into the water supply. Whereas these ions are not necessarily dangerous, it is well known that they contribute to health risks—they constitute hidden sodium for those individuals on strict sodium-reduced diets. Contrasting the understanding of technology with understanding of its underlying scientific principles was also played out in the following episode.

Naught continued his questioning of the recommended methods for treating the water and thereby contributed to the emergence of other aspects of scientific literacy. Scientific literacy arose here from the back and forth between his questions and the engineer's responses. Naught constructed the case that the use of cisterns would make water treatments work on an intermittent basis, which, according to the information available to him, was not as effective as a continuously operating treatment. At first, Lowell suggested that water treatment was in fact continuous and that he did not understand Lowell's point. Then, he admitted again that he had simply recommended extant systems rather than comparing them. At this point, Magee finally succeeded in taking the speaking floor.

> Naught: Is it a good policy to treat water on an intermittent method? In other words, downstream treating of water after a cistern-Okay, where you are pumping only on occasion, isn't it true that water treatment in that fact is less effective than if you are going to treat something that is moving on a continuous basis at a constant flow?
>
> Lowell: When the water is being treated and moving through the treatment system, it is coming through at a constant flow. Yeah, I don't know what point you're making.
>
> Naught: Well, it isn't really, well, it's puzzling.
>
> Lowell: Most systems are, you know, with a certain flow through them.
>
> Naught: Yeah, but they start and they stop, they start and they stop. And that kind of a treatment is less effective than on a treatment system that is working on a constant basis.
>
> Lowell: Yeah, I didn't compare treatment systems. All I know is that the treatment system, any treatment system that I recommended, has been tried and proven effective over many years.
>
> Magee: I would like to make a comment on that, on his discussion because I think that as Mr. Lowell is being questioned, cross-examined as it were, it should be pointed out that Mr. Lowell's report is the first systematic assessment of the aquifer. And up

until the time at which that was requested, the [town] council was being barraged with demands to make high levels of public expenditure based upon information from the taps. And the Health Region's testing methodology, which we supplied— we made an assessment of it. If we want to talk about a testing methodology, the testing methodology up until the time that Mr. Lowell came in was wholly inadequate. And Mr. Lowell's is the first systematic attempt.

Naught: But his results are greatly affected by the time of year.

In this "technical question" period, the credibility of Lowell had been undermined not only by Naught but also by the speakers before him, as well as by others yet to come. Given that there was a public perception that Lowell's report had greatly influenced the reports filed by the Water Advisory Task Force and the technical staff of the community, it comes as no surprise that the questioning had focused on Lowell. Magee described the questioning as a "cross-examination" and defended the report as the "first systematic assessment" contrasting the "wholly inadequate" testing methodology by the officers from the Health Region. Naught reiterated that seasonal variations influenced and biased Lowell's assessment. Which version of the events will ultimately be adopted? The answer depends on the contingent achievement of the divergent claims of hegemonic and counter-hegemonic forces in the community. It is important to note that this is not a political struggle between an imposing dominant culture of the community and a weak subordinated group; the next municipal elections can change the composition of town council and with it the political positions taken by the group as a whole. Because every hegemonic relation is also an educational relation, the dominant group can garner the consent of the (temporarily) subordinate group only by taking seriously and articulating the values and interests of the latter. Here, both hegemonic and counter-hegemonic forces, if they aspire to win over the other, require mutual consent of a common ground. But this achievement of a common ground is the site of struggle; here science has become the battleground.

### Fire, Water-Treatment Systems, and Other Conflicting Things

One of the received assumptions is the notion of science or technology as entities that exist independent of other ways of knowing, interests, and human pursuits. Accordingly, science and technology are, in the dominant educational discourses, thought of outside their everyday real-world involvement with economy, politics, aesthetics, and so forth. Science and technology are thought of as pure pursuits happening in science laboratories that are sullied once they hit the street. Scientists and engineers often appear to be sociologically naive. They promote the facticity of their abstract laboratory-dependent knowledge as wholly unproblematic only to realize that laboratory knowledge cannot be imposed on the world outside the laboratory but has to engage with all the other forms of knowledge and ways of conceptualizing the world. That scientists and engineers might be thinking in this way would not surprise anyone who followed their career paths from middle school to the end of formal schooling. Their domains are always presented in pure form.

In everyday life (at least outside the laboratory and outside of school classrooms), science is but a fiber in a more complex thread. The properties of the thread cannot be deduced from the properties of each (much shorter) fiber; and conversely, the properties of each fiber are difficult to discern from the continuity of the thread. This is the image we get of science when we look at the activities in our community where "science" can be identified. In the following excerpt, Clay Bolton—an Oceanside resident who would be affected by the placement of a water main—wanted to find out about the criteria for the size of water main to be considered.

> Bolton: Clay Bolton, 1082 Mount Nemo Crossroad. The report mentions the six- or an eight-inch pipeline to Salina Drive and then a six-inch pipeline. What capacity are you looking at in terms of population levels that can be met? And obviously agriculture is an issue there too. So what are you dealing with? Why that size as opposed to a two-inch or four-inch? I'd just like to know what the difference is.
>
> Bisgrove: That's a good question. The line was sized to provide residential flows and a bare minimum fire flow. Between 500 and 800 gallons a minute sustain flow for a fire anywhere along that line. This would be the bare minimum that we would recommend to be installed under good engineering practice. If you were to try and provide water for agriculture, you would have to increase the size of the new line. And you would also have to increase the size of the line that runs along Mount Nemo Crossroad from Wendy Drive all the way down past the school where it exists now. It's only an eight-inch line as well. So the line that is proposed at the moment is simply an extension of that system for residential and fire flow purposes. So, if that water main were to be approved, we as staff would take it forward as a recommendation to Council to at least consider upgrading that for agricultural purposes and to pay the increased cost for it. But yet again that would be a secondary step well after a lot of other things had taken place. Have I answered your question?

Bolton: No you haven't. My question was, what population would serve—

Bisgrove: I'm sorry, population. The existing population could be served quite readily. Residential flow is really quite small by comparison to fire flow so my concern would be the fire flows. But I can't give you off the top of my head what would be a residential number, but at least probably twice the amount of people that are there now could easily be supported by that from the residential point and still have a fire flow capability. Fire flow capability is always the governing thing in a water main system design.

In the consideration of a solution to the water-quality problem, water quantity also becomes an issue. At the present time, the residents do not have sufficient water for regular fire protection. There are no fire hydrants in their area of town, leading to insurance policies that cost much more than those of residents in other parts of town. From the perspective of the town council (here represented by the engineering staff member Bisgrove), considerations of improving water quality by means of bringing the water main to Salina Drive are irremediably tied to considerations of water quantity. But water quantity is related to the possibility for the expansion of new housing, the realization of which is imputed by some to the developers who own property in the area that would be served by a new water main. The size of the water main also depends on whether the water it carries would be used for agriculture—which at the current price would not be viable in any case from the perspective of the local farmers.

Not building the water main, in effect, supports current policies for limited expansion of the community. Adding a water main means opening up the possibility for further expansion of residential housing into this agricultural community, because residential flow has a small impact compared to required fire flow capacities. Any solution to be considered does not exist on its own but in a context of other possible solutions, each constituting a fiber of its own in the thread of the community and the water problems. In the public meeting, alternative solutions were also presented and discussed. Each of these solutions was itself tied to other issues such as cost, flow rate, ease of access, and so forth. For example, some residents had already had their water trucked in until the delivery company had to stop operations "on sanitary grounds," as ordered by the regional health authority. Furthermore, within a few years, the cost for the water shipped in this way increased threefold, thereby making trucking prohibitive as a long-term solution. Another solution proposed was that of recycling wastewater. Recycling could be tailored to the individual needs of each property. But, as the following excerpt shows, presented by a citizen named Rees, the person who promoted this solution had stakes in the only local company that would deliver such services.

> Rees: The last thing that I wanted to say was, I wanted to ask a question directly to Mr. Magee. In your report, you make some references to recycled wastewater and you say that there is a local company that has the technology to recycle wastewater. This company, we know, is called HydroSystems, and as I said they're out by the airport. This is a local company. This is great news. But at the end of one of the Water Advisory Task Force meetings, those of us that were there heard Mr. Magee say that he has an investment interest in this company. He owns stock, a block of shares, however he described it. It seems to me that that might just possibly buy us his assessment of the area and perhaps even put himself into a conflict of interest, so I would be interested to know if that is still the case.

## TOWARD PERVASIVE SCIENTIFIC LITERATE PRAXIS

In this chapter, we present a case study of everyday people involved in the struggle over access to potable drinking water. In the public meeting, they question those scientists whose reports have provided the grounds for the town council and mayor to make a decision against extending a water main that would provide them with water of a consistent quality and quantity. The meeting was characterized by the struggle between the currently ruling group in the community (mayor, council, part of the Water Advisory Task Force), which drew on the help of one consultant, and the residents of Salina Drive, the area in need of the water main. Whereas the ruling group represented through the scientist consultant attempted to persuade the remaining community to buy into a purely scientific perspective, the residents invoked their historical knowledge of the water issue, personal suffering, ethics, and so on to convince members of the community and its political representatives to connect Salina Drive to the water main. In this struggle between hegemony and counter-hegemony, a new form of scientific literacy emerges. No longer is it modeled on the purist discourse characteristic of laboratories isolated and elevated as the citadel separated from and standing above the polis. No longer is it a decontextualized and decontextualizing science that can only exist in the isolation of the citadel, but it is a science that actually lives and can survive in everyday ordinary society. It is involved in ongoing political struggles as other forms of knowledge over competing conceptions and views of the problems at hand; it is this struggle (as process and product) that constitutes a new form of scientific literacy. This literacy is not something that we might find in individual minds but in situations where people draw on various resources to get different views of contested issues accepted and taken on as the majority approach. Scientific literacy, in this approach, is a massive form of collective everyday praxis.

To date, the controversy over the water supply is not closed; the residents of Salina Drive still pursue their struggle to get access to community water by means of an extension to the water main. This open nature of the controversy helps us resist the temptation to put closure to this issue or to provide a master narrative in favor of the ultimate outcome of the debate. We cannot attribute the outcome to more or less scientific knowledge held by one or the other party in the controversy. We do not know how the various fibers contribute to the unfolding events, and which fibers will be constructed as the dominant themes after the fact. However, not arriving at a solution is also a form of action, which contributes to further debates, costs, and impact on the environment, that is, the very shape the controversy will take over its course. As some speakers suggested, the projected costs for a water main already doubled over the four or five years during which the community and the residents have not come to a solution of the issue, and during which six different and sometimes contradictory reports have been produced.

In this public meeting, science was but one of various forms of knowledge that was brought to bear on the decision-making process over the water main or any of its alternatives. Science was but one of different fibers in a thread of knowledge available in general. Our research in Oceanside showed that in the daily life of the community, science was always but one of the many forms of knowledge, always but one fiber that contributed to the framing of problems and solutions. When twisted together with all the other fibers, it was not science that became continuous but the thread. We think of the thread as a continuous entity that forces us to think of scientific literacy as something that emerges from the collectivity. It is only when we unravel the thread that we find a fiber. We cannot understand the continuity of thread by imaging all fibers going the entire length; we do not understand each fiber by thinking of it from the continuity of the thread. The science (water quality) is connected in deep ways with technological, economic, political, and aesthetic issues. There are different water treatment solutions, each with its own interconnected range of scientific and technological possibilities and constraints, there are costs to the community and individuals, and there are a variety of potential economic benefits.

We should not think of the fibers as living side-by-side happily forever. In collectivities, struggle is an inherent element, for different perspectives frequently come with contradictions. Democracy does not mean eradicating contradictions but working out solutions that serve general rather than particular, special interests. The form that such struggle will take is likely a function of the way power and knowledge come to be played out in the service of one another (see the next chapter).

The analogy of fiber and thread for the relationship between science and other forms of knowledge in controversies about different problems forces us to rethink what knowledge means in the curriculum. Does everyone have to know the same things? Does every student have to be competent on the same issues? We contend that there is simply too much specific knowledge currently available for any individual to know the relevant facts even in more constrained contexts. We do not have to master all areas of knowledge to live successfully in our society, and awareness of this fact may free us to explore more creatively how to deal with questions of scientific literacy. Educators may be tempted to teach science so that all students exhibit knowledgeability at the level that arose from the interaction of Naught, the scientists, and many others in this public meeting. But then, we would spend much more time in school even if knowledge transfer from school to workplace and everyday life was less problematic than it already is. If we think of scientific literacy in different terms, as choreography that teaches us to participate from the beginning, we take radically different approaches to teaching science in schools. Our children would already participate in doing things that benefit the community, and participate in the ongoing discourses and concerns that are relevant to their parents and the community at large. The children and students would already participate in truly authentic activity, that is, in activities driven by the motives that are also relevant in the lives of other community members. The notion of "zone of proximal development" can further help us think through these issues.

In the education literature the "zone of proximal development" has been used to describe the distance between individual, unaided performance, and performance under guidance. Learners are thought to appropriate higher levels of performance into their own repertoires. Here we want to pursue a different avenue for thinking and theorizing the notion, an avenue that focuses on collective activity. The zone of proximal development can be thought of as the distance between the everyday actions of individuals and the historically new form of the societal activity that can be collectively generated. That is, the zone of proximal development arises from the dialectic relation between social and individual development. In this way, the public meeting is a zone of proximal development, a new form of collectively generated societal activity (in this community).

Collectively, the public meeting has provided an opportunity for scientific literacy to become a recognizable and analyzable phenomenon. A new form of collectively generated societal activity was made possible in the organization of the public meeting and in the provision of the questioning and comment periods. Scientific literacy also emerged because the citizens were involved in an issue where there was something at stake. As practical activity in the face of problems arising from everyday life, scientific literacy is constituted by a number of competencies. These include how to use specialists; how to use black boxes efficiently; how to invent interdisciplinary rationality islands; how to use metaphors; how to use standardized knowledge; how to translate, negotiate, and transfer knowledge; how to use (different types of) knowledge in everyday life to make ethical and political decisions; and how to contrast the understanding of technology with the understanding of its scientific principle. Here, these aspects of scientific literacy emerge as aspects of the public meeting, which is an irreducibly collective praxis of the struggle between hegemony and counter-hegemony.

When, how, and where do we allow young people to be scientifically literate in these terms? The classical approach is to expose children and older students to the images of scientists' science. This science is a pure subject, often taught in special physically separated rooms, unsullied by common sense, aesthetics, economics, politics, or other characteristics of everyday life. It is also a subject in which each individual, so goes the idealist rhetoric, must appropriate and exhibit certain "basic skills." Whether students have gained this knowledge and these skills is usually assessed by isolating them from any resource normally available in everyday situations. Conceptualizing scientific literacy as a feature of collective praxis changes the situation. Educators now have to think about how to set up situations so that contexts (rather than individuals) exhibit scientific literacy. How can we (teachers) possibly do this? Such a view of scientific literacy provides new opportunities for conceiving of science curriculum (see Chapter 7). Rather than preparing students for life in a technological world, we propose to create opportunities for participating in this world and to learn science in the process of contributing to the everyday life in their community. Sample contexts are environmental activism, salmon enhancement programs, farming, or traditional food gathering ceremonies among aboriginal peoples. Early participation in community-relevant practices provides for continuous (legitimate peripheral) participation and a greater relevance of schooling to the everyday life of its main constituents.

Rethinking knowing and learning, science and scientific literacy, and collective public meetings and individual contributions from the perspective of fibers and thread, leads us to radically different conclusions about what and how curriculum should be designed and enacted. When learning is no longer identified with gray matter between the ears but with the relations between people, our views of teaching will change. When learning no longer "belong[s] to individual persons, but to the various conversations of which they are part,"[6] we need to rethink what science curriculum ought to look like. Scientific literacy is then no longer something that is acquired by the child and carried into other settings within and outside of schools. Rather, scientific literacy is something that emerges as a recognizable and analyzable feature of (collective) human struggle in which the child is but one part.

In many ways, schools and society treat children and youths as marginal until they are recognized as full members in society. Even more marginal are those who are homeless and live in shelters. What does scientific literacy as collective praxis mean in the context of homeless children and youths? More specifically, what may participation in scientific literacy and knowledgeability mean for them? In the subsequent two chapters, we follow several children and youths through their after-school activities. These chapters show that science and scientific literacy are bound up with politics, power, and marginality (the state of finding oneself somewhere between margin and center).

# 4

## POLITICS, POWER, AND SCIENCE IN INNER-CITY COMMUNITIES

### INTRODUCTION: POWER, KNOWLEDGE, AND SCIENCE

The stories of Henderson Creek and Salina Drive in the previous two chapters demonstrate just how complex and socially mediated the construction of scientific literacies can be. Scientific literacy in the case of Henderson Creek involved the creek (the subject itself) and the different ways in which the constituents interacted with and understood that creek. The needs of the farmers, including the quality and quantity of the water that reached their fields, was just as much a part of the story about understanding the health and sustenance of the creek as were the needs and practices of the suburban developers, the community activists and residents, the First Nations tribes, or the consulting engineers, all of whom understood the creek in relation to their needs quite differently.

Overlaying this public and collective construction of scientific literacies are relationships between individuals, organizations, and subjects of study that ultimately frame what kind of work or talk gets done. As pointed out in previous chapters, how the residents of Salina Drive vied for speaking time and space shaped the science that emerged just as did the scientists' attempt to control what knowledge was displayed, when, and how. Knowing that this interplay happens is important in understanding the public construction of science. This alone, however, is not enough. Knowing how power relationships and the ways in which power is commanded within such relationships frame such interplay is also important.

Addressing the nature of power in the collective construction of scientific literacy goes beyond assumed understandings of who has power at a particular moment (i.e., elected officials, highly funded programs) to also consider how power is distributed within networks and contingent upon knowledge, position, and historical context. Again, in the case of Henderson Creek, power was negotiated and reconstructed among the various constituents as they interacted at community meetings, through face-to-face and written communication between environmentalists and community officials, or during encounters of environmentalists and landowners over environmentally friendly cattle-grazing practices.

We develop two claims in this chapter along the lines of power that we believe add depth to our understandings around scientific literacy as collective praxis. First, extending discourse networks and the accessible forms of discourse among inner-city youth provides them with opportunities to engage in new forms of knowledge and power. Second, the political power associated with scientific literacy as a collective praxis changes power relations because it not only changes the science that gets done and who has a voice in that process, it changes the very nature of the relationship between science and society. We develop these claims in some detail by exploring the construction of science and scientific literacies among homeless youth and their efforts to convert an abandoned lot into a community garden.

## KNOWLEDGE AS POWER

David Dickson, the former news editor of the scientific journal *Nature*, has publicly taken up the challenge to engage the scientific community in a discussion about the relationship between science and the public.[1] He acknowledges that communication between the scientific community and the public over such issues as bovine spongiform encephalopathy (BSE), or mad cow disease, genetically modified (GM) foods, or the history and origins of HIV/AIDS, even as it has been moderated through governmental and media channels, has rocked the faith that the public has in science. This lack of trust, Dickson argues, is not so much a lack of trust in the science itself but in how that science has been applied without public consultation—consumers want to know that they are getting potentially tainted beef or of modified soya. He traces how this currently tenuous position of science in the public space is rooted in the "complexities of the links between modern science and corporate power."[2]

An important lesson to be learned from the case of the public trust in science is about how the lack of involvement of the public in the development and application of science yields certain messages about what kinds of knowledge count in science and in the decision-making process around the application of science. In the case of genetically modified foods, Dickson reports that the public distrusts science because of the "exclusion of consumers from decisions about the use of genetically modified soya in staple foods, or of Third World farmers from the chance to choose whether to preserve seed from one season to the next, indeed often what seed to plant."[3] For example, in the case of genetically modified foods, there are few questions about whether Monsanto's science is sound. The debate stems more from the research questions Monsanto chose to pursue. The company has not asked tough questions around the safety of GM foods in human consumption (and has found little evidence suggesting that such foods are harmful to human health in the short term). However, without sustained conversation and debate with those who use GM seed (farmers), those who study its impact on global sustainability (ecologists), or even those who eat its product (consumers), then questions investigated by the Monsanto community—the financially influential community—had not taken into account the needs, concerns, or livelihoods of all those affected by their science.[4]

Thus, it seems, the public has been looked upon as a passive consumer of science. Their input is not important in the scope or focus of science and bears little relevance to how that science might or ought to be applied. Indeed, the public has had little power in influencing the fate of GM foods. This scenario is important because it demonstrates not so much that the science itself was problematic, but that its direction and application were problematic.

There are other cases similar to the GM foods controversy that demonstrate how the public has gained, or failed to gain, entrée into science-corporate power discourse. A telling account of "how not to construct a radioactive waste incinerator" shows how an educated public stood up to academic and corporate science to dismantle plans for a radioactive waste incinerator.[5] In this particular case, Lawrence Livermore National Laboratory (LLNL) had developed plans to build a decontamination and waste-treatment facility to handle their radioactive waste. Political and ecological concerns prevented the laboratory from shipping their radioactive waste to sites in Nevada and Utah. LLNL was unsuccessful in their bid for a number of reasons, including lessening cold war tensions and problems at nuclear facilities in the United States. However, LLNL was unprepared to handle their most devastating challenge: protestation by members of the local community. Thus, "the political economy of Livermore itself had produced a population of young professionals and working families who were not beholden to LLNL for their livelihood and had brought to office a mayor and a council more oriented to the local development than to LLNL."[6]

These individuals had the collective means to generate an effective campaign against the incinerator, which focused on health and the environment. They attended LLNL-sponsored meetings and challenged the ritual of assent common at such events. They hired their own experts to present data and findings on their behalf. A process that was meant to go smoothly and public meetings that were meant to inform rather than invite input gave way to a very different kind of multiperspective process. Stepping back from this study, one wonders what the outcome might have been if the community had been involved in the conversation from its inception. Probably we will never know. What we do know is that community members who were perceived by LLNL as without power created the space and the knowledge to change the progress of the incinerator. Most powerfully, the community members knew their needs—the safety and well-being of the families who lived in Livermore—and capitalized upon those needs to change the direction of science at that moment.

This story shows that the application of science can be altered when those who live and work outside the power boundaries of science find ways to engage the "science elite" on their terms. As this story shows, scientific discourse is an important mediating factor between power, knowledge, and position. If we return to the case of Henderson Creek, we can see the same sort of shift in power dynamics when the scientific assessments of the quality and quantity of the well water were challenged at the community meeting.

What does it mean to engage the discourse? How does engagement in science discourse change power relationships in settings where individuals have been marginalized in participation in the sciences? Unlike the participants in the LLNL case study, who were, for the most part, professional and financially privileged themselves, how do youth from an inner-city setting go about repositioning themselves in relation to science and society? How do they extend the discourse around science to get their ideas heard? How do they bring about a practice of scientific literacy, which is more complex, publicly shared, and collective?

## COLLECTIVE PRAXIS: THE BUILDING OF A COMMUNITY GARDEN IN AN INNER-CITY COMMUNITY
### Teaching and Learning at Southside Shelter

I have been teaching and researching with homeless youth in urban settings for the past several years. During the 1998–99 school year my research team[7] and I worked with teens at Southside Shelter, a shelter in an impoverished New York City neighborhood, on community-based science. For the purpose of this project, we defined community-based science as the science we did together that was with and for those who lived in the local neighborhood.

To understand the development of after-school science and the youths' building of a practice of science, we employed critical ethnography.[8] We planned activities with the youth by listening to their concerns and ideas, but also by bringing in our own experiences and expertise. We prepared field notes based on our participant observations, conducted both individual and group interviews, kept copies or photographs of the work they produced, and generally just hung out with the youth during out-of-school hours.

Given my own deep involvement in this work, it is hard to tell a story about my work at Southside without more actively positioning myself into this text. I am an academic science education researcher and activist. In short, I was a visitor at Southside, required to wear the visitor badge in plain sight at all times. I began my work with homeless families as a result of my own experiences as a homeless individual.[9] In 1995 I spent three summer months homeless with my partner and our dog. Like many homeless families, we spent the initial weeks bouncing around from family to friends. We then "graduated" to living in our car. The experience left me reeling as I struggled to balance preparing to teach in the fall with finding adequate privacy, places to clean, and places to sleep.

Despite the difficulties we faced while being homeless, we recognized it could have been worse. Our cultural capital as educated white people offered us luxuries that made the daily struggle of living possible. We could enter fast-food establishments, go directly to the bathrooms to wash up, and rarely be harassed for using the bathrooms for these purposes. We also could hang out in the public library for hours on end during the hot summer months (there was an extreme heat wave that summer) without appearing suspicious. And, as a test of society's norms, we even dared ourselves to go to a local university gym, enter without IDs and take showers. Sadly, the evidence mounted that our homeless lives were, indeed, privileged. Our experience unearthed a deep-seated and pervasive enactment of cultural practices built on racist and classist intentions that in our society and schools are treated as normal and natural. This set of experiences, specifically, led me to focus my own educational efforts in science education on the experiences of urban homeless youth and their families.

Southside Shelter was one of three shelters in New York City where I spent time teaching and researching since 1995. I began working with Southside in the spring of 1998 because they invited me to work with their staff on providing science-related resources and activities to the families who resided there. They were also interested in "research" to better document the role and importance of the kinds of compensatory programs they offered to families. There are two events, in particular, which marked my own participation at the shelter that I believe are important to present here. First, after my second week at the shelter, I stopped wearing my identification badge after making my way past the security entrance. I did this as an act of resistance, as if my own whiteness didn't already set me apart from the shelter residents. After all, of the 212 families who lived at Southside, two were white. Yet, even without the badge, I was often approached by adults at the shelter for information about WIC and other aid programs. Clearly my outsider status did not need to be identified with a badge.

Second, about two-thirds of the way through my first school year at Southside I learned that many of the youth with whom I met weekly believed me to be Latina. This issue arose one day when I was working on a paper coauthored with one of the youth there.[10] He was typing the title page and listed the authorship as Angela Martinez and Darkside. When I informed Darkside that my name was not Martinez, that it was, in fact, Calabrese Barton he seemed astounded. He got up and started informing the teens about my "real identity." As it turns out, the youth were surprised because they said I "did not act or talk white." While statements like "acting or talking white" were surprising on the one hand; they seemed appropriate on the other hand. The youth were reacting to what their lived experiences allowed them to distinguish—for instance, that there is a "white" way of acting and talking. Because I did not fit their understanding, they allowed me into their community to share and learn with them.

### Living at Southside Shelter in New York City

Although family homelessness has been a part of the New York cityscape since the city was founded, it was not recognized as a public issue until the 1980s.[11] Since the city began to seriously document these statistics, the demographics of homeless families have been strikingly similar. In 1992, females headed 97 percent of all homeless families, with 56 percent being under the age of twenty-five, and with black and Latino/a families disproportionately represented in these statistics.[12] Children from homeless families constitute two-thirds of all homeless individuals and disproportionately suffer from educational deprivation, social stigma, weak social circles, and a lack of adequate health care. They also develop chronic respiratory infections, gastrointestinal diseases, ear disorders, and dermatological problems at a rate double to "homed"[13] poor urban children.[14] Furthermore, one in five homeless families have one or more children in foster care. This is a rate much higher than homed families, for whom the emphasis is more likely to be on working closely with the families to help them address underlying problems that put their children at risk rather than on punishing the family, as is the case with homelessness.

Conservative public and social policies[15] have not met the needs of homeless families and in fact have contributed to the increase in the number of homeless families in New York City and nationwide almost tenfold. Cuts in federal and state assistance to the poor have destabilized families such that the historical one-time housing emergencies (fires, hazardous living conditions, personal calamities) no longer constitute the primary cause of family homelessness. According to Ralph de Costa Nunez systematic reductions in programs that serve the urban poor led to the "notching down" of an entire generation into a chronic and debilitating poverty that claims homelessness as one of its most defining characteristics.[16]

Southside Shelter, built in 1997, is a relatively new family homeless shelter in the Top Hill neighborhood of New York City. Top Hill, in the South Bronx, is home mainly to black and Latino/a populations, many of whom are recent immigrants to the United States (documented and undocumented) from places like the Dominican Republic, the West Indies, Mexico, and Africa. There is also a significant Puerto Rican population, as well as a multigenerational black population.

Top Hill has gone through many changes. Since the late 1800's Top Hill has been home to many different immigrant populations: Irish, Jewish, Italian, Russian, African, and Caribbean. As each ethnic group made its way into U.S. culture, they moved from Top Hill to more affluent suburbs on Long Island and in New Jersey and the northern Bronx. However, in the 1970s these dynamics changed. Many of the Black families chose to stay in the neighborhood, in part because they were not as welcome in the more traditional stepping-stone communities as other white ethnic groups were, in part because their economic successes had not mirrored that of the previous (white) ethnic groups to inhabit Top Hill. Consequently, many turf wars now take place in Top Hill between recent immigrants (mainly Latino/a) and the black community. There are even turf wars among the highly diverse Latino/a populations, with Puerto Rican and Dominican Republic families often claiming dominance over those from their poorer Central American neighbors such as El Salvador, Guatemala, and Nicaragua.

As these turf wars suggest, Top Hill is a tough place to live. After having experienced economic decline in the 1970s and 1980s, Top Hill is just beginning to recover. Several bodegas, check-cashing stores, and fast food restaurants line the streets. However, the recovery has been hampered by the most recent economic downturn. The neighborhood is mainly home to towering residential apartments, boarded up buildings, abandoned lots, and a large comprehensive high school. A walk around the neighborhood reveals that although the streets teem with adolescent life, they also tend to be littered with garbage and dog feces. The kinds of city-sponsored clean-up efforts seen on Manhattan's Upper East Side are not a part of Top Hill's reality.

Additionally, Top Hill also has a long history of gang- and drug-related activity. Not many weeks pass where one does not hear about gang-related violence that has ended in the death of or severe injury to a young person. In fact, the reputation of this neighborhood has been depicted in a negative manner by the local and national media, and the residents of the other parts of this city often refer to this neighborhood as undesirable and dangerous.

Southside Shelter is one of the largest family shelters in the city. It is sandwiched between one of the larger high schools, which has had the reputation of ranking below the city and state average in standardized test scores, and a city park known for its violence. Southside is different from many other shelters in the city because it serves all kinds of families, whereas many of the family shelters in the city are strictly earmarked for domestic abuse, drug-related homelessness, or people living with HIV. Southside is run by a private organization that receives private and public funding to sustain its operations in order to serve people displaced from their permanent residences. The founders of Southside pride themselves on their commitment to "living for today and building for tomorrow." They believe their multifaceted approach to homeless families (education and job training, housing, and counseling) will help their families assimilate more easily and more quickly into a "self-sufficient society."

The shelter itself is well kept and simultaneously resembles a motor lodge that one might see on an interstate freeway and a prison (depending on perspective). It is a two-winged, four-story complex painted in a burnt orange hue and has a playground for young children. The whole complex is separated from the rest of the neighborhood by a metal fence on all four sides. The buildings that house the residents are constructed of cinder block. Some residents have complained that the buildings are cold in the winter and do not have acoustic privacy. Each unit has a kitchenette, bathroom, living room, and bedroom; however, there are no formal dividing partitions for these areas. The main entrance has a check-in desk and waiting area.

This shelter also serves as a working facility with administrative offices, recreation rooms, a computer room, a conference room, maintenance department, day care, and preschool programs for children between the ages of two and a half to five. There are on-site social workers, counselors, GED programs, school-age children's programs, and city administrators.

The shelter is also highly regulated. Where one enters the shelter through the front gate (the only entrance) there are two security guards and a check-in desk. All visitors for any nature of business must sign in and out at the front desk and show picture identification before being allowed onto the premises. Adult residents may not stay out past ten P.M., teenage children may not hang out around the building, and young children cannot run around except in the playground supervised by adults or preschool workers. Residents may not have guests, even if these guests are family members. Infractions of these rules along with violations of drug use, domestic violence, child abuse, or any other criminal activity result in immediate eviction or discharge from the facility. Personal adornments to the individual units are also discouraged. Shelter directors want the residents to remember that this place is not home.

Many of the youth who live at Southside feel that the shelter rules, along with its physical construction, make the shelter feel like a prison or cage. They also described the worst aspects of living at Southside as curfews, having to deal with security guards on a daily basis, and having no privacy. Indeed, many of the teens wished that, at the very least, the shelter would add doors and some private spaces within the family unit. Finally, many of the youth were embarrassed if friends found out they lived at Southside Shelter. As one boy, Kobe, explained in the spring of 1999:

> I don't like [my high school] because, you know, it's too close to home. And the friends I might make there might live around the way, which they sure enough do, they might laugh at where I live. But see, and another reason I wouldn't wanna go there is because, if they call home, my mom could just walk right in. I like being in far distant schools, where my mother doesn't know the way, or doesn't know how to get there, or probably even the name. So, that's why I don't like my high school, because I live right across the street from it.

Locating and keeping space at Southside, as at all other city shelters, is riddled with bureaucracy and games of chance. One youth described to me how his family was denied shelter housing three times because his parents, who had lived together for fifteen years, were not officially married. They were finally granted shelter housing once the parents scraped together enough money to formalize their living arrangements in a civil ceremony. The process of securing and maintaining homeless housing is dehumanizing and makes attendance at school or work nearly impossible. Youth are moved around the city in a process that takes up to two weeks, if the family is lucky enough to be deemed eligible on their first try. Youth and their families must follow strict regulations regarding behavior and curfew not required of the more affluent segments of society. Yet, many of the youths recognized the double bind of this situation: they were indeed grateful for the space. They also recognized that people who worked at the shelters were trapped into following the same rules and regulations that made their own lives difficult and different. Thus, these kind of bureaucratic decisions led to subtractive social experiences for youth in shelters.

### *Building a Community Garden in an Abandoned Lot across the Street*

In the fall of 1998, we (adults from Teachers College) began a science program with youth in collaboration with an after-school program operating out of a temporary housing shelter for homeless families called Teen Services, for youth ages twelve to eighteen. However, we did not discourage younger children from participating, and when they did we worked to allow heterogeneous learning environments to form. While some younger children sporadically participated, others became core members of the project.

The program was cotaught by Dana, a postdoctoral fellow on my research team, and Courtney, a doctoral student of mine, while I served as the project leader and researcher. The goal of the program was to create a community-based and action-oriented science project. Even though we initiated the project and encouraged the youth to think about projects that connected to their communities and their lives, the actual goals and purposes of the project were wholly up to the youth. The project began with Dana and Courtney talking with the youth about their concerns as a community and how to productively address those concerns. For example, during the first week with the teenagers, Dana, the main teacher, began by engaging the youth in group conversations around questions such as: What are the concerns of young people today? The youth described teen pregnancy, being shot or making it to the next day, AIDS, unprotected sex, gangs, alcohol use, and adults' perceptions of youth, described as negative especially if you're black.

At first, when asked about how they might use the space of after-school science to address these issues that concern them, the youth were focused on raising money and giving to charity as a way to bring about positive change. However, as Dana talked with them about why charities were important to them, one of the youths clearly stated his opinion that, as homeless kids, "we are charity." This statement, although harsh enough to cause the group to become silent for some time, also helped to make apparent how they were thinking about themselves in relation to their community. The consensus that they were charity made more urgent the notion that if they wanted to make changes in their community, they might have to begin to do so themselves.

Dana helped the teens focus on those concerns they cared most about and believed they could do something about. She had them design murals, write raps, and role-play their concerns. One concern that emerged was that of an abandoned lot across the street from the shelter. Mainly, the youth were concerned that the lot was the site of drug deals and was generally an unsafe place to be. Furthermore, the lot was an eyesore. It was abandoned and full of litter, including ripped open garbage bags, feces, broken bottles, and crack vials. A metal link fence surrounding the lot had sharp fragments protruding in several places from a car crash. In talking about the lot, the youth realized that though they might not be able to do something about the drugs or drug paraphernalia that got passed through the lot, and though they might not be able to protect themselves from the gangs who threw bottles into the lot, they could at least try to improve the lot so that eventually it might not be the kind of place that drug users or gangs wanted to exploit.

The youth decided that one thing they could do was to clean up the lot and turn it into a useable community space. A community space would be clean and inviting and would deter criminal activity because the space would no longer be abandoned. Dana led the students through brainstorming possibilities for the empty lot. Ideas included a basketball court, swimming pool, arcade, playground, sandbox, garden, stage, set for cyber games or laser challenge, and a penny store. She had them conduct a site assessment to determine the feasibility of their ideas. Was the space large enough to house all of these suggestions? What existed in the lot currently and what was its history? Was the soil viable for planting?

To evaluate the lot, the youth formed four teams. They measured the space, recorded its contents (living and nonliving things), took photographs, and drew diagrams of the present condition of the space. Each team, although pursuing the collective motive of documenting the lot qualities, also had their own motive that framed their work. Some teams were more interested in the possibility of building a stage and painting a mural, while other teams were more interested in a playground. Some members of some teams did not really know (or yet care) what should happen to the lot. Dana had all the teams report their findings back to the larger group. Student reports and drawings ranged from one-page pencil sketches of possible designs to elaborate presentations of the kind of litter found in the lot and the feasibility of preparing the lot for future use. Each group answered questions and defended the feasibility of their ideas with information gathered in the lot assessment. The sharing process helped to refine the youths' ideas. It also resulted in some ideas being dropped altogether because they were not realistic or somehow did not fit the space and its qualities properly (i.e., cyber games, laser challenge, and basketball were rejected based on the findings of the site measurement). This process enabled the youth to narrow this list of ideas to seven realistic possibilities: playground, garden, clubhouse, penny store, jungle gym, sandbox, and stage.

Eventually, through ongoing research, presentation, and debate, the youths' ideas were ultimately funneled into one larger idea: a multipurpose community garden. The garden would contain fruit and vegetable plants that would be tended, harvested, and sold by the teens. It would also house a stage for community performances and a mural depicting the work and worlds of the youth who built the garden.

The youth then revised a conceptual drawing and design complete with garden, stage, and mural. Once a final design was agreed upon, a three-dimensional model was built. The teens worked on various structures, planning the layout of the design and the materials they would need (a process modeled by a landscape designer who had been recruited for the project). They used pictures from magazines as guides. Tiny rocks and twigs were used as the boundaries of the path. One youth sculpted a pond and a birdbath from clay, while another built flowerbeds from model wood. The process continued for several sessions, each time people adding or revising from where others left off. Even youth who rarely participated found a way to contribute (e.g., going to the store for supplies or taking pictures of the model in progress). The number of structures included in the design plan increased steadily from the initial drawings in October to the conceptual drawings in January to the model in March. One youth's initial drawing, for instance, included a laser park and an arcade. In the later designs there were trees, a pond, a stage, flowerbeds, garbage cans, and more. The plans also showed how ideas continued to emerge. Through conversations with professionals, visits to local gardens, and pictures of other community gardens, structures, such as a trellis, unknown and unimaginable beforehand, were added to the overall design. Further, because the design products were visual and public, participants (and others) could continuously add to the funds of knowledge that were circulating.

This model was then shared and revised at a public community meeting. At this meeting the youth presented their model, distributed flyers, and answered questions. Prior to the meeting, some of the youth were nervous sharing their ideas with the community. As one youth put it, "Who wants to listen to shelter kids?" The meeting was lightly attended, but the youth felt confident after sharing their ideas. The group decided that the community needed to be more involved and developed what they called "Community Day." The Community Days were all-day events on Saturdays when the larger community was invited to help the kids with their lot clean-up and gardening plans. A Community Day both culminated months of research and initiated putting the design plan into action. The teens publicized the event, distributing flyers to families, staff, local storeowners, and neighbors. The days were mainly planned by Dana and the youth, but were tailored by the expertise of those present each Saturday. About fifty parents, staff, volunteers, neighbors and children attended the first Community Day. The youth displayed their three-dimensional design model to passersby and family members. Youths had various roles and responsibilities for the day, such as welcoming guests, managing the overall production, organizing the refreshments, and video-interviewing participants. Extra help proved crucial in picking up the litter and debris in the lot, replacing the fence, and planting trees.

The youths' transformation of the lot was captured in at least four ways. First, it was captured in the design of the mural, which included pictures of the youth working on the garden and slogans that represented their thinking about the garden. Second, it was captured in the name the youths selected for themselves: REAL, for Restoring Environments and Landscapes. Third, it was captured by the youth in what became known as *The Book*, a three-ring binder that held the history of the group and project. Fourth, it was captured by a smaller group of the participants who produced and directed a sixty-minute video entitled "The Urban Atmosphere," which focused on life and science and the building of a garden in the inner-city by teens for teens.

## EXTENDING THE DISCOURSE

The development of REAL in some ways is a nice, neat story. Inner-city youth joined together to improve their neighborhood. They learned about gardening, what kinds of plants survive in a northeast urban climate, and how plants grow. They learned about soil and water quality, measurement, and scale. They learned how to gather evidence and use it in support of their own developing ideas in private and public settings. Stacked up against the national science standards for their grade levels, they learned a lot of science (see Table 4.1).

The scientific ideas the youths learned were important. Not only did understanding scientific ideas play a role in the success of their gardening practices, but also these ideas were part of the standards to which the youths were held accountable for learning in schools (in order to receive state-certified high school diplomas). Yet, this simple listing of scientific ideas is only a small fraction of the science that transpired and what the youth learned in the process of participating in the lot transformation. Indeed, more important in the youths' participation in REAL than their learning of these key concepts is that the youths learned to engage in a practice of science that was framed around an extended set of discursive practices. They learned to share ideas, listen, challenge, and respond around and through REAL in a variety of ways (talking, writing, art, music, etc.) among themselves and with members of their neighborhood and outside experts and government officials. These extended discourse practices, whether they be constitutive of talk about science with their peers, new ways of interacting and communicating with their neighbors through community meetings and announcements, or exchanging ideas and concerns with gardening, architecture, and science experts from outside their community, became their shared knowledge of science and positioned them with power in science. Indeed, we can look at REAL as one way in which youth came to understand "knowledge as power."

### Knowledge and Extended Discourses: Living Dangerously in the Margins

At a certain level, "knowledge as power" seems trite, especially in an inner-city context. How much scientific knowledge will help bring about change in the youths' lives or in their neighborhoods? Realistically, it is important to acknowledge how social structures in U.S. society have positioned youth in the inner-city without power or voice in processes of schooling or society. As described earlier, the youths' lives are regulated by shelter rules that leave them with little independence or freedom. They attend schools that are looked upon by the intellectual elite as inferior. And, they are afforded few opportunities in these schools to gain the experiences and the résumé for upward mobility. (We use the word *résumé*, because it represents not so much what students learn in their school-based experiences but what they can report

**Table 4.1** National Science Standard 1 Grades 9–12 (Understanding Scientific Inquiry) and the Youths' Work

| Standard | Youths' Accomplishments |
|---|---|
| Identify questions and concepts that guide scientific inquiry | Youth generated issues and research questions about how to make life better for themselves and their peers. They refined questions, making them manageable for exploration on a teenage level with minimal resources. They settled on transforming the lot into a garden with flowers and vegetables, benches, a stage, and a mural. |
| Design and conduct scientific investigations | Students evaluated the state of the lot (kinds, quantities, and location of trash, living plants and animals, fence, soil, surrounding buildings). They used evaluation to determine clean-up activities. They researched the resources necessary for such clean-up activities and determined what kinds of plants they wanted and that the garden could support. They researched what it would take to fix the fence and to paint a sign for their lot. They generated a work plan to accomplish these tasks. |
| Use technology and mathematics to improve investigations and communications | Youth measured lot dimensions and the kinds of things contained in and around the lot (fence, building wall for mural, etc.), including such properties as perimeter and area, and used these calculations to determine what they would need for clean-up and transformation efforts. |
| Formulate and revise scientific explanations and models using logic and evidence, and recognize and analyze alternative explanations and models | In the process of generating plans for the lot, the youth researched multiple ideas. They developed multiple plans (based on their ideas), debated and defended these plans among themselves, and built two- and three-dimensional models of the most agreed-upon plans. |
| Communicate and defend a scientific argument | The youth presented their favorite plans to the larger community. They advertised their presentation through fliers, signs, and word of mouth. Through the presentations the youth elicited feedback from the community. |
| Understand scientific inquiry | Youth learned through experiences how all of the processes listed above were critical to the development of their lot-transformation project. |

they have experienced and learned, i.e., advanced placement or honors classes, science- and technology-based extracurricular activities.) If they transfer to elite schools they are often tracked into lower-level courses or looked upon suspiciously because of their skin color and socioeconomic background. And, so we must wonder why it might be important to view knowledge as power.

If we view extended discourses as knowledge, then we can begin to see how youth learn to play the knowledge and power card in science and in their communities in nontraditional ways. They may still attend high-poverty schools with few opportunities for college-preparatory science courses and strangers who know no better may still look upon them suspiciously (although these things still need to change). However, participation in these extended discourses provide the youths with opportunities to gain a deepened sense of the ways in which their lives and science are wound up together in collective daily life. They generate a network of resources, including people, organizations, and places that will listen to them make sense of their connectedness to science for good and for bad, provide input, and potentially change themselves, in response to the youths.

In the beginning of the after-school program, before REAL or the gardening project were envisioned by the teens, it was interesting to note that when Dana engaged the youth in conversation about their needs, their talk focused around survival and around dangerous activities: Gangs, AIDS, or racism. It was also interesting to note that even though the youths had ideas about how and why their lives were affected by such dangerous experiences, their critical discursive practices were by and large internal to their own grouping. Many of the teens certainly asked tough questions in the program and in their daily lives about racism and classism and about how their community received little attention or help—a dynamic quite different from the white, rich communities of Manhattan. As one youth noted, "We don't get the same [garbage removal] services as Manhattan." Yet, their critical talk remained within their own circle of friends and peers as a matter of self-preservation and as matter of marginalization. Either the youths did not know who to complain to or what to say (outside of complaining to the mayor) or they resisted opportunities to do so. When they did offer public critique, for example, as some did by raising concerns with their teachers or counselors, many of the youth, with few exceptions, believed their complaints were rendered invisible at best and deviant at worst by those in power. One youth told me that students who complained at school about being treated unfairly were marked as troublemakers. Ultimately, he had decided that school was about control; too much learning or too much student independence in what or how they learn was not tolerated because it took away from the teacher's control. Many teens also told stories about how it was not worth complaining or trying to fix the system because the "system never works for minorities." It is not surprising that the youths held these beliefs. When they first attempted to get the city to replace the torn fence around the lot, they were denied over and over again. They called and wrote letters to various individuals in city government, but regardless of the tactic employed, they were never successful. Such recurring denials left some teens wanting to make their critique of society visible through acts of defiance or resistance with little sincerity (on either side of the issue—youth or the government) to actually work to make things right.

For many of the youth involved in REAL, extending their discourse practices and networks around doing science with and in the community was much more complex then learning a list of science concepts. Extending their discourse practices and networks involved learning how to negotiate and renegotiate power structures and one's place within those structures. A good example of how difficult this process of learning how to renegotiate their place in larger societal power relations was for youth, psychologically and intellectually, can be found in their talk about charity. When Dana challenged the youths to begin to think about what kinds of activities they could engage in to respond to their concerns, the youths' initial ideas focused on giving to charity, or raising money for the community. However, when one of the teens stated that they were the subjects of charity, the teens were forced to confront difficult notions of what it might mean for them to respond to their concerns. The teen's statement was met with silence, but in the end opened a whole new way of thinking about their involvement in improving the local community—that activities and actions did not always have to involve money, or at least money did not have to be the final or most important dimension to their actions.

### Community Sharing: A Two-Way Dialog

At many different stages in the development of the community garden, the youth shared their work formally and informally with those in their neighborhood through events such as community meetings and community days. These events were formally arranged opportunities for youth to come together with the people who lived and worked near them to share their ideas, exchange concerns, and to gather input. The kinds of exchanges youths had with their neighbors at community meetings provided opportunities for greater public participation in their project. Community input is crucial because it allowed "those affected by a decision to have an input into that decision."[17] The teens reported on their work. The attendees offered support, suggestions, and challenges. The youths responded to those concerns at the meeting and again in their later efforts.

The exchanges were much more open-ended and contextually situated at Community Day. There was also wider participation. Whereas the community meetings required interested individuals to attend a meeting at Southside Shelter, Community Days were held in the lot being transformed, and participation was just as much about having fun as it was about debating ideas. For example, during the first Community Day, a neighbor who was also a DJ set up his equipment so people could work to music. Adults, children and youth from the shelter worked and played side by side with those from the surrounding neighborhood, a relationship with much historical tension. The refreshments team barbecued hamburgers and chicken and the media team video-interviewed people about the benefits of the garden to the community. This kind of open-ended participation allowed the project to develop as extensions of the expertise present at the lot that day. For example, the teens had planned to erect a new fence around the lot, but had not planned in detail what that process might involve. They knew they needed new fencing materials, some concrete, and tools. However, with the assistance of a professional carpenter, they dug holes for fence posts and cut the wood to the proper size to create sturdy structures for a new fence. Seeds and seedlings were planted with the assistance of one of the residents of the shelter who was an expert gardener from Trinidad.

Another interesting extension of the lot transformation project was the "courtyard chats." Courtyard chats were impromptu conversations held in the shelter courtyard among the teens and between the teens and other individuals who lived or worked at the shelter about the development of the garden project. Most notable about the courtyard chats were the ways in which they involved members of the community who were not members of REAL, yet these conversations had a significant impact on the development of the project.

For example, Tanda, a nineteen-year-old mother of two children, was not a member of REAL because she was older than eighteen and not enrolled in school. Tanda loved to talk and she could often be found in the courtyard chatting away with some of the older teens, both girls and boys. Over time she became quite interested in the garden project because she wanted her children to have a safe place to play. As time went on, Tanda talked with the other teens about the development of the garden project. Tanda's talk with the teens most often seemed to focus on the need to make the lot a safe place for young children, such as her own. She challenged the teens in these chats to describe how their garden plans would be safe for kids. But, the courtyard chats did more than provide a channel for Tanda's ideas to be heard by project participants. They also gave her information and insight into the project. Eventually Tanda participated in the Community Days. She also coproduced "The Urban Atmosphere." Her personal goal in participating in the video project was to help to educate others that the South Bronx can be beautiful but that it is up to the members of the community to make it so:

> We need to be doing these projects, using science, to make this a better place. I want to get out of this hellhole. It shouldn't be that way. We should work together. Make this place better, safer, make it a fun place for the children and all of us. We ain't gonna wait for no government to help, because they ain't ever gonna do it.

### Engaging with Experts

Periodically throughout the development of the garden, Dana invited urban environmental designers, architects, and gardeners to share their expertise with the youth and to help the youth refine their plans for the community garden. These meetings were interactive (intentionally so) and took place in a variety of locations, but mainly at the shelter. Meetings with the experts were not rituals of assent or instruction for how to build the garden, but rather working meetings where the youth had opportunities to receive, question, and play around with information and ideas from outside resources. During a gardener's slide-show presentation of outdoor spaces, the youth saw elements that had not been considered, such as, storage space, a path large enough for wheelchair access, and signs. After watching the slide show, one boy wrote that having storage was important because "we need a place for our tools"; in the construction of the model (several months later), he designed a storage space underneath the steps to the stage. To another participant, signs were important, "to tell people not to litter." In the model, she made a sign that read "Help keep the R.E.A.L. garden clean!" The gardener's slide show also led the youth to discuss new design considerations, such as a design that required low maintenance, structures that could be built with simple materials (hammers, nails, wood, etc.), and structures that supported social activity for all community members. Design features that were not previously considered—a trellis, birdhouse, tool shed, pond, and signs—became added possibilities.

Dana's role in the negotiation of ideas and expert space between the youths and the outsiders was crucial. In working with the teens to explore the experts' ideas she neither privileged nor valued the expert opinion over the youths. She simply kept those ideas on the table as ideas worthy of exploration and interrogation by the teens. She also used those interactions to frame the authenticity of the youths' efforts. She recalls:

> Aside from easily discernible steps (i.e., cleaning out the garbage, fixing the surrounding fence), at this point in the project conversations with colleagues, design professionals, and community members became critical to furthering our collective performance as urban landscape designers. With other adults eager to hear their plans and ideas, many of the participants began to realize that the project was not "fake." This sentiment was first voiced during a visit to the lot's owner/manager, an older Latina woman and longtime community activist. Two of the teens [one of whom spoke Spanish] and myself made the trip. In my field notes I wrote, "There was an intimate excitement about our walk to visit Mrs. D. [They] started saying that they didn't think we'd really be doing anything. [One boy] said, "I thought it was going to be a project, like in school, you know, like a fake project." [The other boy] chimed in saying, "Yeah, I didn't think we were actually going to do it until you started talking about picking up the garbage and stuff." The youth began to realize that they were not simply researching ideas [talking about science] but enacting them [doing science].

What is important here is not that the youths needed the outside expert validation to make their project real, but rather this kind of extended discourse practice situated their efforts in ways that both made their project real and gave the youths the perspective to know so.

### Creating a Public Record: Beginning to Define One's Work

How the teens came to name their lot transformation project reflected a changed stance in what they understood science to be in their lives through this project. Initially the group called themselves "Shelter Boys" even though several girls were participating in the project. Their primary identification with the project had been that they were working together on after-school science because they lived together at a shelter. However, as the project progressed the teens began to debate a new name for the project. When brainstorming a name for the group with Dana, the youth thought up words like: Designer, Activity, Community, Gardener, Service, Caring, Caring Squad, Agriculture, Helping Hands, and Environmental. From these words, they decided upon REAL, which originally stood for Realizing Environmental Architecture League. Dana reported that the word *league* was hotly debated:

> Ty did not like *league* and ran downstairs to get a dictionary. Meka and he began reading every word beginning with the letter L. When Ty came across the word leader, he became very excited and adamant that we change the name. Meka, conversely, wanted to keep league. To Meka, league represented the cooperative and holistic nature of REAL; it fit with her personal mission to change the lives of the children in the neighborhood. She wrote that participating in REAL "gives me a sense of responsibility and gives me a good feeling about helping people in the community." To Ty, perhaps leader represented his sense of his own participation as well as his vision for an entrepreneurial garden.

Eventually the word *league* was dropped and the youth changed the name to Restoring Environments and Landscapes. The name REAL signified so much in terms of how the youth thought about themselves, about science, and about how these two come together in their neighborhood. It reflected a vision for science education that is inclusive, meaningful, and relevant to the lives of young people. The boy who feared REAL was going to be "a fake project," unwittingly raised the question: Toward what end are students "doing" science in school? It also raised the question of just how much the youths' participation in their community could transform their community for the better.

Getting to this point of REAL was a process and did not happen at the same time for all participating teens and certainly did not happen at the same time for the community members looking in. Perhaps the biggest challenge faced by the teens was in how REAL affected members of their peer group at the shelter and in the neighborhood who had not actively participated in the project.

I am reminded of a conversation that occurred between Steve, who was highly active in REAL, and Kobe, who was not at all active in REAL. They had an exchange over the "realness" of REAL one afternoon when Steve was interviewing Kobe. I often interviewed and hung out with participating teens on Tuesday and Thursday afternoons (REAL formally met on Mondays and Wednesday). One of the places where I would hang out with the teens was in the computer room. It was a spacious room at the shelter (an asset in itself), was quiet and always closed at that time (so my presence there made it available for student use), and gave some of the teens, who had come to hang out, things to do when I engaged other teens in interviews. Not all interviews followed the conventional one-on-one interview style. Many were interviews of teens by teens, or informal conversations between the teens and me. These interviews were particularly important because the youth did not see me as their after-school science teacher—that was Dana and Courtney's job. During the time I spent with them we were often engaged in activities and conversations that diverged from the garden itself. Steve interviewed Kobe because Kobe began hanging out with us in the computer room and Steve wanted to know why Kobe never participated in REAL. This section of the conversation began when Steve was questioning Kobe about why he did not like science or participate in the lot-transformation project.[18]

> Kobe: Related to science, you know, I just don't like that lot that we have across the street because it's all garbage and I don't know why they try to fix it up. It's gonna stay an empty lot. All that's gonna be there is the same junk there is now.
>
> Steve: Kobe, how come you don't get hope again? (*Pause.*) Yeah.
>
> Kobe: Because, I mean, look at it. Who's really gonna be here? Who's really gonna spend their time over there working, and it's built on a sewer. I mean, not a sewer. (*Pause.*) What do you call it—a swamp. And all these rats. People have little children running around here, man. They could seriously get bit, or hurt. Excuse me.
>
> Steve: Okay, Kobe. Got kind of touchy there, but see, I don't agree with you because people might get hope in that lot. And they might build something good on there, so what's your thoughts?
>
> Kobe: But, you can't build, well, you can build, but you just can't build concrete, because, it will collapse, and then the sewage stuff. (*Pause.*) Stuff like that. So, all right, there you go.
>
> Steve: But we could do the garden or a playground or something.
>
> Kobe: Now see, to build a playground, you need concrete. All right, how do you expect the swings to stay on, to stay down into the dirt?
>
> Steve: On the spongy mats.
>
> Kobe: Well, one day I might, you know. It's like a bad neigh— you know, kids drive by, throwing things out their car. Bottles. It might hit the building and cut a kid. All right?
>
> Steve: You do got a point, but we gonna build a fence around it. And we gonna have securities on it.
>
> Kobe: But, excuse me, like I said, they drive by and throw bottles and stuff like that out their window. How is a security guard gonna stop them from doing that while they're just standing there? In a car, they're in a car. How are they gonna stop them? And what's that fence gonna do? The bottle could hit the building behind the fence, and the fence doesn't stop glass from going through the little holes in the fence really. It doesn't really help, you know.
>
> Steve: Again, you got a point.

After this last point, Steve paused in his line of questioning, seemingly out of ideas for how to debate Kobe, and moved on to ask him about his favorite basketball stars. Nevertheless, this conversation is important in many ways. In this exchange, Steve pushed Kobe to consider his critique of how successful the lot transformation project would be. Kobe, on the other hand, pushed Steve to consider different challenges to the success of the project that he had overlooked. However, this conversation, at another level, is about having "hope," or belief in a better future for the community, and the role that teens can or should play in that process. Kobe had not been involved in the lot project for a variety of complicated reasons, the least of which was that he had not been attending school regularly, a shelter requirement for participation in any after-school program. Yet, this conversation between Kobe and Steve marked a turning point of sorts for Kobe. Although skeptical about REAL, Kobe began to observe the development of the project with more interest and ultimately became one of three coproducers of "The Urban Atmosphere."

### Other Public Documents:
### Raising Questions about the Audience and Its Role in Science

On the one hand, it is extremely important to note that the actual transformation of the lot space had a major impact on how the youth or the community members thought about what was happening in this space. Indeed, after the youth began to clean up the lot, neighbors who lived in nearby apartment buildings, on their own initiative, helped with the daily upkeep of the lot. On the other hand, the ways in which the lot transformation story was officially recorded and retold also frames the practice of science engaged by the youth.

The youth created two public documents that recorded and described the development of REAL and its impact on the neighborhood: *The Book* and "The Urban Atmosphere." *The Book* started off as a photo album, but became a space for public documentation of the development of the garden as new items were added each week. *The Book* contained documents (letters, notes, flyers, drawings, etc.), visual representations (photographs), direct inquiries (obtained through surveys, written evaluations/reflections), an attendance log, and a weekly summary of activities (or "lesson plans"). Some entries were included for the explicit purpose of keeping track of the things the youths were learning and doing together, while other entries were actual products, such as diagrammatic models.

The documentary "The Urban Atmosphere" was the brainchild of Darkside, a participant in REAL. He had been participating in the

Tuesday and Thursday interviews and decided that he had a better way to document kids' ideas about REAL—by creating a video. He also believed the video would be important because they could give it to other teens to teach them how to create their own garden. He also felt they could give it to teachers to teach them about life and science in the inner-city. The video was coproduced and narrated by three teens (Darkside, Kobe, and Tanda). The final product consisted of interviews with fifteen teens about science, their lives' ambitions, life in the inner-city, and the garden project; interviews with adult members of the community on the same topics; and footage from activity and conversations in the garden, the neighborhood, and the shelter.

Both documents, *The Book* and "The Urban Atmosphere," were dynamic constructions of public records that, although meant to inform others of the project, were crafted by both those involved in REAL and those outside the REAL project. They were public stories that portrayed how the youth extended their science discourse practices and networks and how those extensions radically changed their position and power within the community. Both public documents show how their understandings and practices of science changed as well. In terms of *The Book*, several weeks into the process, the teens began adding personal summaries of daily activities about what they thought was important in the project. Later they also began adding materials that were not specifically related to the lot, but to their thinking about what to do with the lot, such as data sheets from urban gardeners and landscapers. After the first community meeting, the teens opened up *The Book* to the larger community in order to better include and learn from their ideas and reactions. Decisions to add new kinds of data to *The Book* influenced the emerging science, which then in turn impacted the kinds of things that were added. The "Urban Atmosphere" video was created by teens who were originally peripheral to the project, and it included aspects of REAL that might not be construed as science at all. Thus, in addition to filming the garden and teens' and adults' ideas on the garden, they interviewed the security guards at the shelter to get their perspective on the rules that govern the community—those same rules the youths feel so oppressed by. They interviewed a local grocery store manager to get his perspective on the neighborhood and the kinds of things that might happen to make people feel safe shopping at his store. They surveyed the family units to show the living conditions at the shelter. And, they followed youth in daily activities (buying bread at the store, buying food at a local fried-chicken place, babysitting children) to get their perspective on all the pieces that made up youths' lives. Most of the interviews were open-ended, leaving it up to the interviewee to contribute what she or he felt was important for such a documentary.

## CHANGING SCIENCE AND CHANGING SOCIETY

As the story of REAL suggests, the political power associated with scientific literacy as a collective praxis changes power relations because it not only changes the science that gets done and who has voice in that process, it changes the very nature of the relationship between science and society. Indeed, the very doing of science through collective praxis helps to change how those in power define that relationship.

We described earlier how David Dickson, the former news editor of *Nature*, challenges the relationship between science and, as he says, "its public." As part of this argument, he also makes the claim that it is important to understand that there is a tension between science and society, but that it is more important to understand "why governments and politicians feel it appropriate to address them and suggest solutions in the specific way that they currently do. . . ."[19] In other words, Dickson finds it more telling to make sense of how those in positions of power attempt to mediate a relationship between science and the public.

Sandra Harding makes a similar claim but more critically. Instead of wondering how those in positions of power attempt to mediate relationships, she suggests that those in political power use the traditional constructions of "objectivity" and "neutrality" in science to remove the possibility of political debate and controversy.[20] Although she first raises this point by exploring Nazi science, she pushes her argument into modern science in democratic communities as well.

Dickson and Harding provide us with a powerful line of thought. It is helpful to step back for a moment to examine how the relationship between science and society in the inner-city has been framed by those in power through science education. Indeed, the route taken by governmental officials and policymakers has been to increase the rigors of science standards without changing how that science gets framed as a tool for change. Current school reform efforts—and this includes (a) the writing and dissemination of national standards and the use of such standards in rewriting state and local science requirements; (b) the move toward high-stakes testing and accountability; and (c) the linking of test performance with school-based funding—are all based on a model of engagement in science that is ultimately unidirectional. Science gets framed as a set of ideas to be learned and reported back. The purpose of learning science is to meet a list of state objectives rather than a set of human needs. The power of science as a tool to change society, self, and ultimately to define and control inner-city communities is substituted for shake-and-bake experiments with little utility beyond grades and classrooms. One might argue that this system is in place in all schools, not just those in the inner-city. And at one level this is true. However, there are two key differences that allow this setup to further distance inner-city youth from science. The first is that such shake-and-bake approaches to teaching science are enacted in much more extreme measures in inner-city schools because of the triple threat of insufficient resources (lack of new books and lab equipment); understaffed science programs (majority of teachers are not deeply knowledgeable in science, i.e., are teaching without a certificate); and a desire to equate teacher-centered methods into tactics of behavior management and control. Second, good grades—indeed, even mediocre grades—in affluent and middle-class systems place youth in colleges and on science-based trajectories if they so choose. Even if these youths do not have opportunities in K–12 schooling to experience science as an empowering tool, they are ultimately granted the opportunities to gain the credentials necessary to engage in science at the professional level. However, youth who attend inner-city schools, even with the best of grades, still face several barriers that they must penetrate if they are to move easily into science-based trajectories.

Government policies meant to "empower" youth in science by demanding that they become scientifically literate have instead generated a setting where youth involvement in science is further reduced. Participation in science is reduced to knowing or not knowing concepts. Using concepts and participating in their enactment from multiple angles are discouraged because they take time away from the mandated curriculum. The involvement that does occur—coverage of state-mandated concepts and participation in high-stakes exams—further solidifies how youth ought to be positioned with and in science.

The Top Hill students' out-of-school participation in REAL raises questions and points toward opportunities for how thinking around the importance of scientific literacy as a collective praxis can help to change this unidirectional dynamic.

The purpose of REAL was to transform the physical and social landscape and to engage students in science and research as part of urban life and community. Revitalization of the natural world and understanding the interdependency of life (physical and social) offered a view of science as a means for improving human conditions, in addition to the contemporary school view that, in order to advance, society requires technological innovations based on rational models of science. The youth were producers of a science that meant something to them. Science was not an abstract body of knowledge to be learned but was "something to be proud of, to be remembered by, and to help beautify the community," as one youth put it.

The model and other artifacts of REAL were often produced toward a collective goal. To the extent that equity was created, it was because these products were public, and publicly enacted. That is, young people could add to or borrow from the pool of knowledge that existed. This pool was soon broadened to the larger community, including after-school staff, parents, neighbors, and friends, who also added their feedback. During Community Days, the teenagers publicized their design plan using assessment tools (*The Book*) and the model to represent REAL. In addition to advertising the design plan/model, the goals for those days were to clean the garbage, fix the fence, make signs, and create a fun and productive environment. Ty volunteered to be on the media team to videotape the day as well as interview people. Meka was on the welcoming committee that invited guests to sign a book and to have their questions about the project answered. In addition, Meka spent most of the day cleaning out garbage with a group of teenage girls.

The effect of extending the discourse from individual students to the larger group of teens, the community, urban landscape experts, and teens outside the community positioned youth as having valuable knowledge. They learned to believe that what they had to offer the community was worthwhile, although they had to struggle to find the appropriate physical and intellectual spaces to do so. Through the experience of shared conversation around what doing science in the community could mean, the youth created the opportunity to articulate what they knew about their community's and their community's needs. In planning for the mural, Meka, who wanted the community to care for the environment and for the children who lived and played there, wanted to include slogans such as "Environmental Is Fundamental," "Help Keep the Garden Clean," "Stay in School," and "Speak Up."

The youth were also able to think through how they are positioned "as charity" and how to go about changing that perception. Of course, the youth did not always agree on the best next steps or courses for action, as the debate been Kobe and Steve highlighted, but it was this very sort of debate that strengthened and refined their thinking about how they understand their own needs.

How they moved out from their small group is also important. Dana had brought in experts who were both insiders and outsiders to the teens' community. Some experts knew about urban gardening or urban architecture but not much about homeless teens. Some knew about high-poverty urban youth, but not much about science. The youth learned to engage these outside sources through their project. This balance was important because the youth always had a space in which to be experts even when the so-called experts shared their knowledge. Here the teens knew their abandoned lot in ways that the outside expert could not, but in ways that the outside expert needed to learn about in order to be helpful. The science of the moment needed both perspectives to move forward in ways that would be positively productive.

The youths' interactions with the larger community, similar to their interactions with the experts, reveal the levels of support community-based science requires. The youth were initially nervous to share their plans with the members of their community because they did not want others to object; they did not want their months of labor to be diminished. This black and white expectation on the part of the teens mirrors the right and wrong approach to youths' achievement in school science. What their interactions with the larger community began to unravel was that extending the discourse around the lot-transformation project meant figuring out how the garden might best serve the needs of the community and how the community might best participate and support the garden (and locating other forms of expertise to push the project along). They needed the support of the community but they also needed to support the community.

How they chose to communicate with the community also advanced their agency in shaping and extending their science activities. The youths who created "The Urban Atmosphere" began to see that in addition to offering the community a safe and clean garden instead of an abandoned lot, they could also offer their experiences and recommendations for how other teens might engage in a similar project. They assumed teaching positions, but those positions were framed by stories of their experiences rather than right or wrong ways to build a community garden. Community fliers also provided for more genuine involvement in science by the public. Instead of being a passive form of communication, these fliers informed the community of new ideas and developments and invited their participation and input.

## LOOKING AHEAD

Scientific literacy in the inner-city raises many issues around knowledge, power, and position. Youth in inner-city settings have been actively marginalized in schools and in science through tracking and school funding practices thereby minimizing their opportunities to engage in the discourse and practices of the power elite in our society. They are also demonized in the popular media, minimizes the importance of their own unique contributions to society. Even in some of the best-intentioned policies around inner-city youth's development, they have been positioned as other, or as recipients (rather than framers) of policies and programs that affect their daily lives.

Yet, as this chapter shows, scientific literacy exists within relationships between individuals, organizations, and subjects of study through multiple forms of discourse practices (the video, the book, the community meetings and Community Days, etc.) and the networks they represent. More importantly for youth in the inner-city, they also show how such relations are framed through power and knowledge. The example of the Community Days helps to make problematic the framing of power through individuals. How the youths were able to communicate their goals for the project and their visions for the future in both of these informal settings elevated the importance of REAL and their work in REAL within their neighborhood. The Community Days also show how the power of moment existed within relationships and, most importantly, is understood through the way it is distributed within networks and contingent upon knowledge, position, and historical context. The Community Days brought together shelter residents and their neighbors—a relationship marred by historical tension—to work together on making their lot transformation real. Individuals who rarely, if ever, talked to one another contributed their own skills and understandings to the group allowing the garden to be transformed in ways the youths had not anticipated or imagined. The very fence the youths had unsuccessfully tried for three months to get the city to replace was repaired in a day with help from the neighborhood. Courtyard chats and "The Urban Atmosphere" allowed the progress of the lot transformation project to be understood and developed within groups of teens who had not before participated in the project. These extended discourse networks and the accessible forms of discourse among inner-city youth provided them with opportunities to engage in new forms of knowledge and power.

Clearly, the youth involved in REAL learned a great deal about science, if one examines their participation through traditional lenses (again, see Table 4.1). However, the youth also learned to use the various resources to which they had access to renegotiate both what science looked like and their own power in their community. Understanding how science and power were created by youths in networks provided the youths with news ways of talking to and relating with their community. Considering that their lives represented were highly regulated through shelter rules and that the youths signified the historical tension generated by neighbors not wanting a shelter in their neighborhood, their abilities to use an extended range of discursive practices to create science *with* the community give witness to just how much power and knowledge can change and be changed. To us, this story about power and knowledge raises questions about youth participation in science, and how such participation must be understood, valued, evaluated, and legitimized with and in a broader social order to include the histories, cultures, and life worlds of those who do, use and in whatever way are affected by the science. And, participation must be evaluated by how it can transform both science and the community in which such science transpires. These are the questions that we take up in the next chapter.

# 5

## MARGIN AND CENTER

> *What the moon tells about science*
> *The moon is for night,*
> *it's a light for while you're sleeping.*
> *The moon is special,*
> *it's a light,*
> *a globe light,*
> *sometime it's a half.*
> *It's a thing that's in the sky night*
> *and day.*
> *The sun is for morning.*
> —Latisha[1]

During the time we worked with her, Latisha, the author of "What the moon tells us about science," was a fourth grader who lived with her mother, sister, and brother at a family homeless shelter in New York City. She is a year older than her school peers because she was held back in the first grade in an effort to promote her literacy levels. Three years later, Latisha is still angry about being held back, as she says it is "embarrassing" to be older and taller than her classmates. Latisha presents us with a dilemma. She is able to articulate her thoughts about the moon and about science in her poem; yet she is still not doing well in school. Her report shows a line of U's—unsatisfactories in all subject areas.

Latisha's story raises questions about power, knowledge, and what it means to be scientifically literate. Although Latisha's report card indicates below-average performance, we are moved by the clarity, insight, and science and literacy capabilities expressed in her poem. We are also challenged by her poem to raise difficult questions regarding conceptions of science and knowledge, and how these things intertwine in science classrooms that serve children in poverty.

In the last chapter, we described how knowledge and power intermingled in the lives of inner-city youth who worked together to transform an abandoned lot into a community garden. Their story demonstrated how knowing and doing science were dynamic forces that shaped how youth took up and transformed their social and political spaces in their urban neighborhood. In this chapter, we continue to explore how power and knowledge frame youth's collective praxis of science. However, in this chapter, we focus on how institutional and disciplinary settings with their inherent power hierarchies are co-opted by children while they learn science. Processes of co-opting power hierarchies are integral to enacting science and to learning to identify with and against science.

To make this argument, we first develop the metaphor of margin and center as ideological and material. We then link the margin and center with a scientific literacy that is defined as existing when the center and margin are understood as constructed dependently. This allows us to understand them in a reflexive relationship that challenges and collapses the other. In making this argument, we also describe how this relationship exists as a tension muddled up by social and political power structures for it is a lived relationship defined by those who experience it as well as those upon whom it is imposed. We then share three stories of youth doing science in ways that co-opt power hierarchies. It is this act of learning to use the margin and center dichotomy—or to transform institutionally and socially imposed power arrangements—that allows youth to enact a practice of science that is much more powerful than the science in books they learn in schools. They learn to understand and enact science as a practice that draws its strengths from collective knowledge and individual agency. We show why this stance is particularly important for youths whose lives— whose experiences, knowledge, and culture—are consistently marginalized by dominant culture.

## MARGIN AND CENTER

bell hooks describes the separation between margin and center as based on social and political power relationships:

> To be in the margin is to be part of the whole but outside the main body. As black Americans living in a small Kentucky town, the railroad tracks were a daily reminder of our marginality. Across those tracks were paved

streets, stores we could not look directly in the face. Across those tracks was a world we could work in as maids, as janitors, as prostitutes, as long as it was in a service capacity. We could enter that world but we could not live there. We had always to return to the margin, to cross the tracks to shacks and abandoned houses on the edge of town.[2]

In science education, we often talk about students as being either marginal or central to science through the lenses of the nature of science, participation in science, and inclusive classroom practice. Whose values, beliefs, and experiences are parts of science historically, and whose are not? What does it mean to understand margin and center in the lives of homeless youth or of youth living and learning in poverty?

Chicana feminists have written about how marginalized peoples often live within the margins of dominant culture or on the "borderland."[3] The borderland reflects the ideological strength of the margins; it suggests a kind of critical consciousness held by those in the margins about how power, culture, and experience intersect in social contexts. A critical consciousness of the margin and center dichotomy is a powerful, political place for those in the margins because it suggests survival on one's own terms as well as a cultural and political standpoint and place of solidarity from which to critically understand the assumptions and practices that guide dominant culture. In short, there is social and political power in knowing margin and center in multiple and shifting contexts, because these understandings provide numerous ways for challenging relationships of power and knowledge in science education.

Urban homeless youth live within multiplicities of identities and borderlands. Many of these youth are members of ethnic and racial minority culture, in particular black and Latino/a culture. As homeless individuals, they also are members of the underclass, silently tucked away at the bottom of the social and power hierarchy in U.S. society. Finally, they have been stripped of a sense of place, leaving their privacy (and all the privileges that come with that privacy such as private baths, quiet study areas, kitchens to prepare meals or sneak snacks, or storage spaces for personal belongings) behind for shelter life. They learn to experience schooling and science from multiple dimensions, including skin color, gender, language, class, and a sense of place. Indeed, homeless children are positioned within the margin and center dichotomy in particular ways. These include: (a) material resources, such as access to quiet space and materials for homework; (b) expectations embedded within material circumstances, such as a lack of parental concern about whether they complete their homework; (c) institutional structures framed around cultural and class conditions of children's lives, values, and needs, such as the tension between school-work and home life; and (d) ideologies of who and what counts.

The ways in which these structures, values, and circumstances influence margin and center are shifting, insidious, and dependent on time and place. Yet, because the margin and center metaphor is created and maintained through physical circumstances and institutionalized rules, structures and assumptions about children, knowledge, and schooling, we, as science educators, often talk about the margin and center metaphor as if it were fixed, making the margin and center seem natural rather than constructed.

The margin and center metaphor raises questions about the situated nature of power, knowledge, authority, and cultural production and has much to contribute to how we understand the practice of science education. Any sort of scientific literacy exists within critical reflections around margin and center, including such reflections as: How are margin and center constructed in classrooms, and how is their existence used to hinder or promote education for particular groups of people in particular contexts? What does it mean to be positioned in the margin or in the center, and what are the implications this has for ways of knowing, talking, and acting? What happens when the center or margin is used to understand, challenge, and collapse the other? The following three stories help us to contextualize the power of the margin and center metaphor: Latisha and the purse, Jason and the edible paper, and Claudia and the desk.

## LATISHA AND THE PURSE

Latisha, who wrote the poem that opens this chapter, was a quiet girl unless in the company of close friends. She appeared to have stronger relationships with adults than with the other children. Although she rarely volunteered information about herself or school to me (Angie), she often hung by my side or by the side of other adults who helped out at the shelter. Our more informal conversations revolved around the things she wanted, like to bake with me.[4] When we talked about school, it was almost always because I asked her about it. Her responses tended to focus on three things: spelling, because this was a frustrating topic for her; reading, because she loved stories and wanted to become a writer; and gun violence in the school and on the playground.

The story that follows is taken from the after-school science program in which Latisha participated. One particular day the children made homemade microscopes from orange juice containers, small hand-held lenses, paper clips, colored construction paper, glue, and

Magic Markers. In addition to these supplies, each child had his or her own notebook, and there was a common large container filled with materials for science, arts, and crafts (scissors, rulers, feathers, glitter, beads, books, copper wire, etc.).

Latisha finished her microscope early. Usually Latisha gave a great deal of attention to detail. She often ripped out and threw away paper from her after-school science journal because she misspelled one word, or did not like the way her handwriting looked. When she worked on projects, she took her time to color or decorate them thoroughly in such a way that they not only looked nice, but also expressed a certain thoroughness and style. I was drawn to Latisha's actions because she did not give her microscope that kind of attention. My gut reaction was that she did not care about microscopes, that something had happened at school, among her family members or peers, or perhaps that she was hungry or not feeling well.

After completing the microscope, Latisha ran up to me and asked if she could do something else. I was not sure what that something else was, but agreed to the plan. Latisha ran to grab an extra orange juice carton, and some glue and paper. She then pulled out beads, string, copper wire, and glitter, and moved to a corner of the room alone.

Latisha later showed me the "something else" she had made. She had covered the bottom half of a large rectangular orange juice container with construction paper glued into place. On the construction paper she had drawn designs in marker and glued gold glitter and a few colorful single beads. Strips of construction paper separated the inside of the container into three separate compartments. Across the opening of the container was what appeared to be a handle made of a short string of beads. Unlike the microscope Latisha made, this thing appeared to be carefully designed and crafted.

> Teacher: Latisha, that is a very beautiful thing you made. What is it?
> Latisha: It is a purse.
> Teacher: Oh, I see. The beads are the handle?
> Latisha: Um hmm. I invented it.
> Teacher: You invented it? What do you mean?
> Latisha: I made it myself. I didn't copy no one. I used them things on the table. And, now I got me a purse.

Latisha pointed to the table where the cartons, glue, and other materials were. There was a period of silence in the conversation as Latisha fiddled with the way the beads were connected to the carton.

> Teacher: Latisha, I think this is very interesting. Can you tell me how you got this idea and how you decided to make it?
> Latisha: I just saw the orange juice, um, what's it called?

Teacher: The container?

Latisha: Yeah, the container, and I thought, I am going to make me a purse. I am going to make me a purse to carry around. See, it's got colors and jewels.

Latisha seemed satisfied with that answer. When she finished talking, she looked away from me back to her purse, and again started fiddling with the beads. Earlier, while she had been working on this creation, she had become agitated that she did not have a string of beads long enough for her needs. Another young boy, Ray, had seen her making something else with the beads in the corner. He had gone to the supply box and taken the longest string of beads and used them to decorate his microscope, and later to make a purse resembling Latisha's. When Latisha saw Ray "copying" her, she became extremely upset. She tried to pull the beads away from him. It was not clear to me through her explanation whether this act was motivated by her desire to have a longer string of beads, to prevent Ray from finishing a purse similar to her own (although Ray referred to his purse as a basket), or for some other reason.

## LEARNING FROM LATISHA ABOUT MARGIN AND CENTER

Returning to the ways in which margin and center are manifested in science education helps me to answer my questions. First, the material separation is significant in Latisha's life. Although I might have known this intuitively as a teacher, and used this as one reason to make take-home microscopes, Latisha shows me the immediacy of this separation. Using nearly the very same materials, in a rather similar arrangement, Latisha created a purse. This is significant because it suggests a link between environmental conditions and what Latisha chose to make. Latisha quite often asked me for school supplies. Her most frequent requests were pencils, pens, and papers, although she sometimes asked for rulers, scissors, glue, and beads. Latisha developed her purse from the materials and activities at hand. She rushed through her microscope project, and upon completion gathered the same basic set of materials used to design the microscope along with other readily available materials to complete her purse. She worked quickly and efficiently to finish her purse before the after-school science program came to an end and the materials were stored away for another week. Equally significant, Latisha used the materials to construct something that would allow her to hold on to the resources she scavenged in a more systematized way.

Latisha's actions also challenged how margin and center are separated through institutional structures framed around cultural and class conditions of children's lives, values, and needs. For example, in an interview after the purse episode Latisha told me that she "likes after-school science because [she] gets to make things." When one of my graduate students asked her what her favorite things are in science, Latisha said:

> We planted flowers, and made glue and paper, that was fun. And I want to make pencils and pencil sharpeners. I'd like to make an oven, and make toys, and the sea, the sand, make sand. Science after-school is better than school because science is for making things. In school we only do lots of reading. I don't like my teacher. Only good people [should teach science]. People who know science very well and love to grow flowers. People who know how to make experiments, like you and Angie.

Latisha learned in school that doing well in school science meant "doing what the teacher said," reading the books and filling out assigned worksheets. She also learned that when she did not follow her teacher's rules she would get in trouble and she would get unsatisfactories on her report card. Spaces such as the after-school program, where children invent and experiment in deviation of the prescribed curriculum, challenge and blur the implications for following—or not following—prescribed school practices.

Finally, Latisha's invented purse challenged how disciplinary knowledge gets framed. Latisha created a fluid continuum between microscopes and invented purses. Although a cursory glance at the creation of a purse may not seem too radical on Latisha's part, I believe it is. She used the resources available to her to make what she needed in her life. Although simple, and not very durable, it was functional, and physically represented Latisha's agency to act on her environment.

As science teachers and science educators, we are drawn not only to the question why Latisha invented a purse from the microscope materials, but also to the question of what empowered her to push the regular activity to the side to invent at all? These questions raised by the story about Latisha are examined in the next story.

## JASON AND THE EDIBLE PAPER

This second story is about Jason, a thirteen year old who lived at the Carla Voster Inn in New York for six months with four siblings and his mother. Jason was a quiet boy compared to his siblings, but he exuded determination when his efforts were actively supported. He liked school for social reasons—he could see his friends (unlike at home), and his brother and sister went to the same school. Jason also believed that school was going to help him make something of his life; however, such positive generalized statements about school often contradicted his descriptions of his personal success in school. He often referred to his sisters as the smart ones in the family, unlike his brother and himself.

During the time Jason lived at Carla Voster, I (Angie) had the children in after-school science engaged in a long-term environmental study. As part of our explorations, I wanted to help the children make recycled paper. In addition to learning about the process of recycling, it was near the winter holidays, and I wanted the children to have their own paper to make cards and gifts to send to family and friends. Such holiday gifts were a topic of their informal conversations during this project. For example, the children talked about the kind of things they wanted to get and give for the holidays, most of which were "dream" items—such as a "car for my mom."

To make recycled paper, I had the children collect leaves, twigs, dirt, and other natural items from around the neighborhood. I brought with me a stack of old newspapers, string, fabric, and office paper, for the recycled paper, as well as popcorn, juice, and graham crackers for a snack. Although I planned for the children to invent their own recipes for recycled paper, I had also planned their inventions around the ingredients I thought the children might use and how they might go about using them. After all, I had made recycled paper successfully with several other children in the past. When the children began mixing their choice of ingredients for recycled paper, Jason and his two friends separated themselves from the rest of the group. In their bowl, instead of mixing the materials from outside with the newspapers, they were mixing popcorn and graham crackers that I had brought for snack along with some leftover flour used in an activity a few weeks earlier. They mixed their concoction to a thick paste, spread it into a thin sheet on a large rectangular pan where they were to have put their recycled paper to dry. They asked if they could bake it.

While their concoction was baking I asked them about what they were doing. I had waited until this point to question them on their activities because I did not want to interrupt their somewhat secretive and definitely intense efforts. The oldest of the three boys, Jason informed me that they had decided to make "edible paper." When they were done, they cut their product up into tree shapes, ate some of them, and made plans to give the rest of them out as edible cards.

## LEARNING FROM JASON ABOUT COLLAPSING MARGIN AND CENTER

From the perspective of science educators, the boys' choice to make edible paper is fascinating as are the kinds of questions the boys were asked by their peers, and the responses they gave when their peers learned about their covert actions. In this conversation, Jason, as the spokesperson for the boys, indicated that they examined and discussed the sample pieces of recycled paper I had brought for the children. The boys understood that there was a particular way to make recycled paper, and based on their analysis of the sample pieces, they described what that process was. The boys also described what it was they wanted to do differently from the prescribed activity.

For example, Jason when he was asked why he made the edible paper he responded that he "didn't want to make ordinary paper," that he "saw how you could do it" and had "different ideas for something [he] wanted to try." He also said that when they "took a close look at the paper" they knew it could be "done different ways," and that the purpose of recycled paper was to "make it from what you already got, using materials that already served a purpose." In making this point he picked up the sample paper I had made and pointed to the pine needles, then compared that to the popcorn kernels in his own paper. Finally, Jason also told how if he gave away "edible cards" that "people could eat," it would be "like a two-way present."

In some ways the very act of making recycled paper promoted the material separation of the haves and the have-nots: We were making recycled paper so that the children could have cards to give away as gifts. In fact, as the teacher, I, like the students, was conscious of this positioning through their stories about dream gifts. I wanted to recognize this reality, because it seemed particularly salient during the holiday season, and because I did not want to actively participate in how such material differences separate children through the have and have-not status. Besides recycled paper was fashionable, and making and giving recycled paper could be read as an environmentally friendly and even politically correct act, just as it could also have been read as an act of poverty.

When I first noticed Jason and his friends mixing food together, I chose to leave them alone rather than draw attention to their difference. She did not think of their actions as deviant. However, I also did not recognize the boys' actions as being related to the group activity of learning about and making recycled paper. In fact, I thought they were not interested in our project that day and were simply mucking about with food. As the teacher in this setting, I wanted to value what I perceived as the boys' needs at that moment, while simultaneously not drawing too much attention to them.

My decisions were based on my perceptions of the influence that the shelter's rules about food and eating have on the children. Residents were not allowed to bring food into the shelter because of potential rat and roach infestations. Any food eaten by residents is provided by the shelter and must be consumed within the dining room. Much of this food has been donated by area markets and restaurants, and is best described by a girl at the shelter: "This food is disgusting. They fed us pizza for supper that was burnt. . . . Nobody wanted it. It was hard. Gross." Given the fact that children are growing and frequently hungry, it is no wonder that such regulations regarding food are a constant source of stress and a reminder of their social and physical status as homeless.

Yet, Jason's actions push us to consider the whole analysis on another level. Jason's and his friends' activity was much more than simply mucking about with food, although this is important, and my choices were about much more than collapsing material separations between margin and center. Jason's actions have much to say about the margin and center dichotomy. Jason used the after-school science program to position himself as one with power who could act on his needs and environment. He addressed his desire to give a particular kind of present rather than a prescribed one. He used the available resources to meet his self-defined needs. He challenged rules about where food can be used and eaten at the shelter. Finally, he challenged the marginalization created by definitions of acceptable science through challenging the production, uses, and nature of science. Science no longer was something done by scientists far away in labs or by teachers who tell the students how to do the science through explicit directions or persuasion. Science became the active intersection between Jason and his social, political, cultural, and physical conditions and contexts. With these actions, Jason centralized the multiple ways in which margin and center were positioned and interconnected in his life together at that moment. He also articulated how he could use these momentary structures as political tools that could help sustain and aid those on the margin in what bell hooks calls the "struggle to transcend poverty and despair" and to strengthen "our sense of self and our solidarity."[5]

Jason's choices teach us about the complexities of margin and center in school science and, in particular, how margin and center come together (or at least are not thought of as a dichotomy). For example, Jason chose to center his desires and dreams in a way that simultaneously valued and challenged school-based and home-based experience and knowledge. This move on Jason's part positioned the boys within margin *and* center. He acknowledged how he had been positioned on the margin, but used this understanding to refuse marginalization. This is important. A traditional rendering of science or self as stable and objective could not have accommodated what Jason did because his actions required simultaneous positioning on margin and center.

Jason's actions promoted a critical reading of the science in his life and his life in science, thereby providing a safe space for a critique of margin and center. This critical reading of margin and center politicized and destabilized the boundaries between the two. Such politicized and destabilized boundaries reposition the traditional power-knowledge relationships, which, in turn, influence how students learn to label valued knowledge—knowledge about self, others, and science. Jason repositioned himself relative to science and society by valuing the need to eat and the idea of agency through food, the authority of what constitutes recycled paper, and how it gets made.

Yet Jason's story also leaves us with questions. How did he understand his authority? How was his authority, not solely based on him, as an individual, but rather situated within the collective authority of the margin? How can Jason's implicit challenge of "what counts as science" shed some light on how an understanding of margin and center is critical to a more empowering rendering of scientific literacy? We take up these questions in the next story.

## CLAUDIA AND THE DESK

Claudia stood with her hands on both hips, looking proudly at the desk in front of her.[6] Even a brief glance in her direction evoked the immediate response, "This desk is mine!" along with a determined look on her face that suggested she meant business. The desk was small but functional. It contained no drawers, but furnished a writing surface large enough for any young person, and stood sturdily upon the floor. The desk, or rather, "Claudia's desk," as it became affectionately known among the youth and teachers at Hope Shelter[7] where Claudia lived, in Well Springs, Texas, was crafted carefully from six pieces of wood, each piece 30 inches by 12 inches, and with many, many nails. In the end, the desk stood two and a half feet tall, two and half feet wide and two feet deep. However simple, the desk was a testament to Claudia's generative capacities. Indeed, during a single afternoon, Claudia, a lively fourth grader, conceptualized, designed, and built her desk with only limited adult help.

Claudia's desk building was not a part of the plan for after-school science at Hope Shelter that day. Rather, the plan had been to continue with the butterfly garden project by building aboveground planters. For the six weeks prior to this episode, the youth had been caring for caterpillars. We had begun this project for several reasons. The youth in the after-school program had expressed an ongoing interest in having pets, and they constantly used after-school science as a way—a legitimate space—to bring living creatures into the shelter community, where such things were normally prohibited. Caring for caterpillars captured this interest among the students. There were other reasons why I (Angie) selected this particular project: monarch butterflies are the state insect of Texas, and Texas is a primary resting point on their migration route between their more northern summer homes and their southern winter destinations of Mexico and South America. Further, butterflies are a rich part of Mexican and indigenous American culture. For example, among some tribes of Mexico, the butterfly is a symbol of the fertility of the earth, and in pre-Hispanic, Mexican Indian culture, the butterfly was one of the symbols of the god of rain. Finally, ecological interactions, migration, and life cycles are key concepts in science and would help us pull together our ongoing efforts to understand the local neighborhood scientifically.

Because Hope Shelter planned to construct new housing in the future, we were prevented from planting the butterfly garden in the ground near the portable building that housed the after-school program. Instead, we had to use aboveground planters so that we could move the garden to another location if necessary. The youth conducted research on butterflies and their habitats, then designed their gardens through blueprints, pictures, supply lists, and much debate over what was really needed. On the day we brought in the agreed-upon materials, the majority of the youth eagerly set about assembling their planters. Claudia, on the other hand, who appeared to be disinterested in the activity, asked me if she could use some of the wood to build a desk. I encouraged her creativity, and while the other students built planters, Claudia and one of the other teachers went inside the portable building to work on Claudia's desk.

In Claudia's hands, the six pieces of wood intended to form the sides and bottom of a planter became the sides and top of a desk, a piece of furniture that she wanted for her shelter apartment. She never told any of the adults explicitly that the planter-building activity did not meet her needs, but her actions clearly demonstrated that fact. Although I had thought that I was being student-centered in my teaching decisions about the caterpillars and butterfly garden, the story of Claudia's desk shows that we have to think more deeply about the youth's personal experiences or the kinds of science that might emerge from them. As one of the other teachers later noted, there was further evidence of this lack of insight: when Claudia's family moved out the shelter, Claudia took her desk with her. Two other youth about the same age as Claudia, who had built a planter the same afternoon that Claudia built her desk, moved out of Hope Shelter around the same time as Claudia's family, but did not take their planter with them.

Upon their departure, their beautifully decorated planter remained outside the door of their former shelter apartment.

## LEARNING FROM CLAUDIA: CREATING A NEW AUTHORITY FROM THE MARGIN

I first met Claudia when she was in fourth grade and lived at a long-term homeless shelter in Well Springs, Texas where I taught after-school science and conducted ethnographic research around science education and youth living in poverty. Through many informal conversations alongside a set of formal interviews with Claudia, we learned that she was born and lived the first three years of her life in one of the neighboring Mexican states. Claudia's family emigrated to Texas when she was three. When Claudia was six, she and her mother and two brothers moved to a local short-term homeless shelter to escape domestic violence. Claudia's mother attributed the violence to the stresses of living in a new land with few resources and to differing priorities for the distribution of what few resources they had, especially as they related to her children's opportunities. Claudia's mother was a strong woman who resisted traditional channels of authority to create opportunities for her children. Although Claudia's mother believed leaving her husband was the best decision for her children, she talked about feeling "ashamed" for leaving him and for moving to a shelter. When Claudia's family's time in a short-term shelter expired, they were granted space in a long-term shelter because they met three key criteria: the family income was below the poverty level, they did not have immediate family in the area, and the mother was actively seeking better-paying employment.

Claudia was bright and energetic. Not only was she fluent in English and Spanish, but she also moved easily back and forth between languages as situations dictated. In fact, her mother often kept her home from school to translate in official settings such as medical care and social services. Claudia was mentally and physically strong. On several occasions, she ended up as the brunt of boys' jokes. Many boys attempted to pick on her because her beautiful, large, round eyes reminded them of a frog. They called her *El Sapo*, bringing Claudia close to tears. These same boys pulled her clothes and threw paper at her as she walked home from the bus stop. Claudia did not take this harassment lightly. She always fought back. On several occasions Claudia instigated physical fights with some of the boys to prove her status and strength. Although she was small, she was strong, quick, and aggressive. Many other girls who lived at the shelter looked up to Claudia for these qualities. However, by the same token, she was also somewhat alienated from the cliques of more traditionally feminine girls.

Perhaps even more than her willful spirit in dealing with the boys, what really marked Claudia for me was how her willful spirit manifested itself in her relationship to schooling. Claudia received tremendous amounts of homework from her teachers. Quite often, Claudia could be found in the children's activity space copying all of her times tables, writing out lists of a hundred words that begin with the letter *a*, *b*, and so on, and completing multipage worksheets of basic skills mathematics problems. Even when other youth were building kites or playing tag, she often resisted the games to work on her assigned homework until the temptation became too great. What makes this so remarkable is that despite these grand and conscientious efforts to succeed in school, Claudia's report card indicated that she was barely making average grades. And, although Claudia expressed a desire to do well in school, she spoke passionately about how much she hated school and her teachers. In fact, Claudia admitted on more than one occasion that she did not talk very much in school and did not raise her hands in class in an attempt to send a message:

> I never like school, mostly because it's boring. It's boring because we have teachers and work, and we never play. I always have to be here, be there, do this, do that, and I am always getting in trouble. It's not even my fault, and I get in trouble. If schools did not have teachers, then it might be fun. . . . You know why I don't raise my hand in school? Because I want my teacher to know I'm bored!

Claudia understood the kinds of work she was asked to do in school as boring and stupid and she wished she had more opportunities to work on things that interested her. She even said that some subjects that she liked, such as math, are boring in school. As she said of science, "I don't like science. It is boring. All we do is read."

When the desk-building incident occurred, Claudia's intent was surprising, especially after she had appeared, over the weeks that preceded the building incident, to be very devoted to taking care of the caterpillars and researching and making decisions about how to best care for the soon-to-be butterflies. She had thoughtfully planned her butterfly garden and had carefully selected the pattern and colors for her flowers in order to best please her fledgling butterfly. When she asked if she could use her planter wood to make a desk, I agreed because Claudia seemed quite earnest and eager in her request and because it would pose an interesting scientific and technological challenge to Claudia to decide how best to design and build a desk with the selection of building materials to which she had access. I knew that another teacher would be helping her and felt confident that Claudia would at least have some degree of success. There was also extra wood, so she would not be, in the end, left without a planter. I also suspected at the time that Claudia's project might provide an interesting context to talk with the other youth about how scientific decisions get made in the "real world." The situation had the possibility (and indeed did) create a moment for the other youth, Claudia, and I to talk about how Claudia's needs as a student influenced her decision to use the resources available to build a desk instead of a planter, just as a scientist might change his or her mind about research directions based on new information and new contexts. However, Claudia's desk-making experience was much more political and consequential terms than simply how one's experiences, in a rather narrow sense (i.e. the need to have a place to do homework), drive the direction of scientific research, particularly among poor, urban youth.

Returning to the desk-building experience, it seems to me that Claudia's desk was about much more than demonstrating how context influences scientific decisions. Claudia's decision, and indeed her science, was situated much more deeply and profoundly than that. Claudia's desk was a testimony to her knowledge of life in the margins and her determination to merge the science of after-school with her personal experience as well as her ability to translate her mastery of scientific ideas (measurement, scale, and geometry) into a project of her own making. Claudia's desk combined her knowledge of design and construction with, of course, her need for a desk *and* with her familial and community memory. Through the experiences of her mother and grandmother she has learned, at an early age, stories of schooling, power, and resistance and has brought those to bear on science. Neither her mother nor her grandmother graduated from eighth grade. Her mother now works for minimum wage in the service industry while raising three children. They receive no financial or other support from the father. Claudia strongly desired to succeed academically but struggled in school. She desired to be independent and stand up for herself even while her life remained highly regulated at the shelter. Building a desk instead of a planter took on a profound significance.

Claudia's authority in the margins helped to reposition her in relation to science and to the rules that govern life in an urban homeless shelter. Claudia had been critical of how she was often positioned as the one without power or authority. She was angry with how her science class made her bored, how her teacher did not listen to her, and how the hours she spent on her homework never seemed to help her grades. She was also critical of how regulated her shelter life was and frustrated with how little those regulations failed to make her life better. The boys still picked on her, she did not have a quiet place to do homework, and she had few friends. One might argue that Claudia was not achieving in school because of differences in what was valued at school and what was valued at home, and that success for Claudia would only occur if she learned how to cross the school-home border. Yet, Claudia's desk-making experience suggests that doing science was much more complicated than simply crossing the border from home to school. Claudia had to understand and find ways to resist how schools and normative social practices play a role in reproducing race, ethnic, class, and gender inequalities. Claudia's desk allowed her to recreate science in ways that addressed her perceptions of the domains on either side of the home-school border including perceptions of self.

## SCIENTIFIC LITERACY IN THE MARGIN AND THE CENTER

Reading Latisha's, Jason's, and Claudia's actions through the margin and center metaphor from a variety of perspectives (material resources, expectations, cultural practices, and definitions of science) sheds some meanings on their actions. The most important lesson about scientific literacy we can learn from these three students is that scientific literacy depends more on how ideas, activities, and actions get framed by teachers and students doing science together than on what actual ideas, activities, and actions that teachers and students do or have, although these are also important.

For example, reflecting on how multiple articulations, understandings, and repositioning of the margin and center metaphor occurs led us to wonder about just how much scientific literacy exists only within the moment; always positioned by those who are doing—doing science and doing education. It is not certain that if we were to go back to the shelter and introduced edible recycled paper to the children it would result in the same set of events, or that Jason would enact the same kind of scientific authority to transform the activity at hand. This suggests that enacting scientific literacy hinges on much more than the content of the educational activities explored. It hinges on the expression of community from moment to moment. What would have happened if I had been more prescriptive in my directions for recycled paper or microscopes? Would the boys have continued on with their edible paper? Would Latisha have made her purse? Would the idea that they could have done something else ever been actualized? What would have happened if the boys or Latisha were questioned earlier in their activities? Would the rest of the children have engaged in a more explicit conversation of why they were doing what they were doing? Finally, what was it about the moment, and about those who acted in that moment, that demanded the neat and orderly progression of margin and center to be turned on its side?

Latisha's choice to make a purse, Jason's choice to make edible paper, and Claudia's choice to make a desk positioned each of these children within margin *and* center. All three children's actions spoke to their position on the margin—desiring a purse to store and organized personal things, desiring food and the ability to give food away as gifts, and desiring a desk for homework and personal space. Yet, all three children used their understandings of themselves, their situations, and science to refuse marginalization—they acted on their positions in productive and political ways. As I described earlier in the case of the edible paper, a traditional rendering of science or self as stable and objective could not have created a space where Claudia, Jason, or Latisha could make their creations because their actions required simultaneous positioning in both margin and center. For example, I could have been more like one of Latisha's schoolteachers and asked her to complete her microscope more carefully before moving on to another project, or before sitting or reading quietly in her seat. I could also have chosen to learn more about Latisha by finding out what she wanted to make, why she wanted to make it, and how she saw this as connecting to the science lesson that day (or not). But instead we know that doing experiments is central to Latisha in after-school science and it is important for her to do things *her* way. She consistently asked me to stay late so that she could experiment (and she needed the space of the recreation room for her experiments as well as the after-school science supplies). She also consistently shifted back and forth between any prescribed activity in after-school science—such as making microscopes, carrying out plant experiments, building plant boxes, and collecting samples from the community—to her own experiments. She often did this shifting smoothly and unproblematically. Latisha, like Jason and Claudia, intentionally and purposefully enacted a process in which she made new things that had meaning in her material life. Their social context gave their action meaning, and brought together margin and center. Their inventions—their deviations from the prescribed curriculum—were physical artifacts of their enacted relationship between context and action in science.

If anything, these questions about Jason, Latisha, and Claudia and the making of edible paper, purses, and a desk highlight just how complicated scientific literacy is. Seriously considering these questions forces us to embrace scientific literacy as highly political and activist. It also forces us to move beyond the generalized statements about scientific literacy, such as it is about deep and conceptual understandings or using science to engage in public discourse and debate. Although such ideas are important, the questions about these three children ought to move us into uncertain and always unfinished terrain where culture, community, knowledge, and power remain unsettled, leaving it to teachers and students to recreate a science, self, and community that continuously disrupt multiple and contextual margins and centers.

For example, Claudia's efforts hardly went unnoticed. As alluded to earlier, Claudia's desk building led many of the youth to ask, "How come Claudia is building a desk?" These questions generated conversations about the kinds of things, which, bounded by science, were done collectively after school. Why was it okay for Claudia to build a desk? Is building a desk science? Was building the planters considered science because the planters were intended to hold a garden full of flowers for the butterflies, or could the actual building process be science too? Do kids really have the authority to decide the direction of the after-school science program? The youth possessed authority before the desk-building incident—they wanted to care for pets and decided themselves that they wanted to build a butterfly garden—but was this the same kind of authority as Claudia's to make the decision to build the desk? Some of these conversations occurred individually, one-on-one between the youth and me as they came to ask me questions. Others happened in larger groups as one of the teachers tried to use the desk-building incident to generate conversations about what else the youth might want to learn about or do.

Ultimately it was the youth's conversation around Claudia's authority to decide to build a desk instead of the planter that was most powerful among the youth, for it changed how science was defined, produced, and used in their lives. For example, it was after these conversations that Ruben, a twelve-year-old Mexican American boy, single-handedly led a crusade for the next big project to be "building a club house." Citing Claudia's desk, he lobbied the other youth to think about the benefits of designing and building a clubhouse for youth on the shelter property. Ultimately, Ruben's efforts led the youth to design and build a picnic table and benches for their own use as outdoor furniture, and also possibly in a future clubhouse. Thus, Claudia's decision to build a desk transformed how others thought about what constituted science and radically changed the next two months of after-school science, during which they made conceptual pictures, blueprints, small models, then finally a full-scale picnic table.[9]

## SCIENTIFIC LITERACY FOR ALL, OR NOT

The reform efforts that mark the past fifteen years of science education hold as central the belief that schools must work to educate all students in science, not just those who demonstrate promise in scientific careers or those who easily fit into and succeed within the normative practice of schooling. Supported by both the National Research Council and the American Association for the Advancement of Science, these reform initiatives view scientific literacy for all as the educational solution to four problems prevalent among the general population: low levels of scientific knowledge, a lack of preparation to use scientific knowledge to make decisions that affect personal lives and communities, continued low numbers of women and minorities in the sciences, and inadequate school science practices.[10]

Indeed, because of its egalitarian stance, the science-for-all reform efforts have been hailed by science education researchers as crucial to those groups of people who have been underrepresented in the sciences: women, minorities, and students from high-poverty circumstances. Yet, it seems to us, as teachers and researchers in high-poverty urban settings and as former homeless persons ourselves that the science-for-all campaign fails to provide a useful paradigm for understanding the science education needs and experiences of youth living and learning in urban poverty. Indeed, the very assumptions on which these proposals are predicated actively work to marginalize high-poverty urban youth rather than build upon the knowledge and experience of the margin. For example, documents like the American Association for the Advancement of Science's *Project 2061* or the National Research Council's *National Standards* describing science for all—what it is and how it might be implemented—assume a universalist vision of science. Even though the reforms acknowledge the social and cultural dimensions of scientific practice, they also proclaim, in clear and certain terms, a set knowledge base that marks the scientifically literate person. The reforms also draw strength from a belief that schools are meritocratic in nature without considering how schools have played a historic and social role in reproducing race, ethnicity, class, and gender inequalities. Documents like *Project 2061* perpetuate the illusion that if all students learn science, all students will be equal. The reforms also maintain a deficit model of minority students. By favoring traditional scientific practices, behaviors, and habits of mind, for example, these reforms assume that students will choose to adopt these values when their own differ. When students do not do so, it is assumed that they, rather than the instruction or the content of instruction, are at fault.

These assumptions neglect to acknowledge that science and its practices reflect power differentials in our society. Without acknowledging these assumptions, the reforms require students in the margins to silence their cultural and linguistic heritage and to embrace a way of knowing that has effectively defined minorities and women as socially and intellectually inferior. The U.S. science education reform initiative *Project 2061* states that "teachers should . . . make it clear to female and minority students that they are expected to study the same subjects at the same level as everyone else and to perform as well."[11] This message implies that minority and female students need to work and act like their white male counterparts and that neither science nor instruction will be modified to accommodate them. Although it can be argued that this is a call for teachers to engage all students, not just white middle-class males, in the academic rigors of science, it can also be read as a call for teachers to encourage, if not require, acculturation. In the very effort to create inclusive science, education communities, policy, practice, and curriculum have become connected in the politics of assimilation with schools and teachers as agents. More deeply, those who do not succeed in this process of acculturation are shaken out of trajectories that lead into science and science-related (technological) disciplines.

It seems that despite the progressive goal of science for all, science educators, as a whole, have been reluctant to embrace the greater implications of what scientific literacy might mean. Indeed, school science continues to reflect a very narrow slice of the most positivist stance on science and as a result science is taught as an independent body of knowledge to be learned. Further, such initiatives have all but ignored the political and cultural ramifications of such a stance. As Claudia's desk story suggests, we need a serious, rigorous interrogation of what we label as scientific, how we understand the purposes and goals of doing science in school, at home, or in any other location, and in how we dissect youths' lives into scientific and non-scientific activities. In short, what we need is a theoretical framework that places the experiences of urban youth (and, as the next two chapters show, those of youth in rural settings as well) centrally in our science education efforts. We must be concerned with knowledge about youth, about who generates understandings of their experiences and how this knowledge is legitimized.

These stories show us the power of using the knowledge of the margins to support one in learning to use and create science in their worlds. This is not a new idea. Indeed, if we examine the professional community of scientists, we see knowledge from the margins advancing science in particularly powerful and transformative ways. For instance, one clear example of transformative science in the borderlands involves the studies and findings directly resulting from the arduous work of AIDS activists. The gay community and other AIDS activists banded together to understand a disease ravaging their communities, learned the discourse of the scientific community, then worked hard to communicate their personal stories, experiences, and knowledge base to the larger scientific community.[12] The activists (at least some of them) learned the knowledge and discourse of the scientific community, and communicated with scientists using the scientists' language. As a direct result of AIDS activists learning the science and scientific discourse around HIV/AIDS and then communicating their own needs in the language of science, government agencies such as the National Institutes of Health have revised their guidelines for clinical trials, double-blind trials, and control groups. Additionally, doctors and researchers have revised their research plans not only to take into account the needs expressed by those with AIDS, but also to refine their methodologies to deal more compassionately and humanely with AIDS sufferers. As Michelle McGinn and Wolff-Michael Roth remind us, "All of this suggests that . . . scientific practice and scientific knowledge are not relegated solely to scientific laboratories or science classrooms and their production is not limited to scientists or scientific bodies."[13]

## LOOKING AHEAD: THE POLITICAL NATURE OF SCIENCE EDUCATION

Research in science education urges us to consider culture, language, and daily experience as a basis for constructing more inclusive and more empowering science education for youth. Fundamental to these studies is the claim that science itself is a cultural construct and that we, as science educators, must be open to how youth construct science in our presence in classrooms and other informal learning sites. The stories of Claudia, Jason, and Latisha, or of the youths building a garden in an abandoned lot, however, suggest that understanding science as a cultural practice is not enough. We must not only begin to learn how to see the science in the work that youth do (and to see the young people as scientific in their efforts), but we must also see how young peoples' lives—indeed youths' science—transform how we understand the nature and practice of science, the role of science in the lives of urban youth, and what this means for the purposes and goals of school science. We must see science education in the more political and consequential terms that mark life in the borderlands.

However, using the lens of margin and center to understand Claudia's, Latisha's, or Jason's participation in science leaves us with one final question: Will the youth gain access to the culture of power in science if all they do is enact their own science? Our answer is probably not, if that is all that they do. However, youth ought to have opportunities—official opportunities—to move from understandings of traditional science and the scientific community to places of critique and transformation so that they can construct more meaningful responses to their local needs and so that the kinds epistemological, social, and cultural assumptions about science can be uncovered and challenged. This is different from simply building bridges between the two worlds (the world of youth/home and the world of school science) where both worlds remain unchanged. These opportunities must lend themselves to the transformation of both worlds.

Let us return to the case of AIDS to better understand this point. The activists' scientific knowledge gave credibility and authority to the scientific community, while their activism gave allegiance to the gay community. The youth in our study might need to do the same—be competent in both the scientific community as defined by those in power and be competent in their borderlands. Yet, both sides of this tension are not, and never can be, mutually exclusive. Although the AIDS community had to enter the scientific community on the scientific community's terms in order to be heard and valued, their persistence ultimately transformed, in a small way, the scientific community. Youth may have to gain competence in the rules and discourses of the scientific community, but that does not mean their education in science cannot be transformed by their presence.

Indeed, given that over 20 percent of all children and youth in the United States attend school while living at or below the poverty level, and that nearly one million children experience homelessness, an extreme enactment of poverty, each year, it is our responsibility as science teachers and educational researchers to understand just how youths' lives shape the science they construct, why they construct it, and how they construct it. And, we must do so with lenses that focus on the power and legitimacy of their stories rather than their perceived failures. Many researchers have written about disempowerment of high-poverty urban youth. Youth advocate for their own empowerment on a daily basis, and, in the process, often run up against a vision of schooling and science dissected from their lives at the core. Understanding the power of the borderland helps us to avoid understanding Claudia and her peers through the cultural-deficit models assumed within our current reform frameworks in science education or the kinds of limiting and incorrect stereotypes perpetuated in the media, in text books, and in popular culture. It also helps us to locate the tools we need to understand how to craft science, personal experience, empowerment, and transformation differently. Youth lives and youth science—if we listen—give us a way to rethink the nature of science, schooling, and borderland communities and the ways in which they come together.

# 6

## CONSTRUCTING SCIENTIFIC DIS/ABILITY

*[The] deletion of students' work and voices is daily practice in today's schools. Their contributions to collective achievements are consistently DELETEd in the service of sorting individuals, by means of grading, into standard curricular trajectories. Institutionalized forms of accountability such as grades, take students out of the continuity and complexity of their activities and pass them through sorting devices that are intended to assess many things but say nothing about whether they should engage in particular career trajectories.[1]*
—Wolff-Michael Roth and Michelle K. McGinn

In the preceding two chapters, we encountered children and youths whose experiences in school science have often been negative. Despite extended efforts, Latisha continued to get unsatisfactory grades. Even if these youths were to receive top grades, few would have opportunities to engage in trajectories of upward mobility. The needs of these students, as the needs of diverse groups of people—except white middle-class males—are often not met, leading to, by and large, their exclusion from science. In school science, there are often differences in achievement along the lines of gender, race, and social class. Yet across many studies, there were no such differences in achievement (as shown by statistical tests) after students participated in innovative, hands-on, and discourse-focused curriculums that I (Michael) had designed with resident teachers to promote an agenda of science for all students. The tests in another recent teaching project of mine revealed that five of the seven students in the top achievement quartile had been students who were designated by the local school system, North Vancouver, Canada, as cognitively disadvantaged (learning disabled) or socially disadvantaged individuals. When fellow science educators asked me why the normally highest achieving students were not also the highest achieving students in my teaching experiment, I felt embarrassed because I did not have a clear answer. My subsequent analyses of the data showed that while normally "disabled" or "lower-ability" students sometimes had problems on written tests, but when a great variety of test formats were used, it allowed them to achieve as well or even above other students. Whereas these analyses provided partial answers to my colleagues' questions, we still do not have a model that explains *why* traditional orderings of students were altered in the curriculums that I was designing. It turns out that if we use a system-oriented perspective of the activities in which such students are involved, we come to understand why the "learning disabled" students have done so well.

In this chapter, we show how "ability" and "disability" are the result of a particular organization that prevents or prohibits students from making use of opportunities to know and learn. We also show how the same students who are constructed as learning disabled actually do many things that we normally associate with high ability, if only the contexts of their activities are appropriate. We show how situations mediate the assessment of disability and ability, which could subsequently be attributed to and turned into characteristics of these same students. If science knowing and understanding are conceptualized as features of situations rather than individual persons, there are then considerable implications for science teaching.

## ACTIVITY, AGENCY, AND IDENTITY

The stories in this chapter feature two students from Oceanside, the village that already featured in Chapters 2 and 3. Both were identified by their school and the local school system as learning disabled. They took part in an environmental science unit described in more detail in the next chapter. Based on other activities in the community, where different representational forms are legitimately used, the teachers (including me as co-teacher) began to encourage students to conduct investigations on their own terms, to choose and take control over their data collection and representational tools to best fit their interests and needs. Audio-recorded descriptions, videotaped records of the Henderson Creek watershed-related student activities, photographs, drawings, and other representations began to proliferate (see also Chapter 7). This provided contexts of knowing and learning that led to an increasing participation of female and aboriginal students often excluded by other forms of instruction. It also meant that a traditional conception of science and science education in the community had to be abandoned. Ultimately, the children presented the results of their work at an annual open house organized by environmentalists whose principal focus was the ecological health of the Henderson Creek watershed.

Throughout the iterations of the environmental unit with different classes, the community was involved in the teaching. This involvement of community members therefore integrated the 13-year-old children's work with activities in the community of Oceanside in two ways. First, community members including aboriginal elders, environmentalists, scientists, and parents came to the school, assisting students and teachers in the activities. Second, the student activities were concerned with a pressing issue of the community; the science lessons took children out of the school and into the community. That is, the children's activity system was motivated by the same concerns that impelled other activities in the community. The children participated in legitimate peripheral ways in community affairs because the motives that drive the different activity systems—school and community life—shared many elements. It is this overlap with the activity system of everyday life in the community (motive, subjects [community], and production means [tools, instruments]) that makes the children's work "authentic." Rather than preparing for a life after school or for future science courses, children participated in and contributed to social life in the community. It is in that process that learning—belonging to the various conversations of which individual persons are part—was occurring.

An important aspect of this approach is the endeavor to understand activity systems, such as those that focus on knowing and doing science as historically constituted systems. That is, activity systems require an understanding of their historically contingent nature and of the cultural context that allowed them to emerge. Similarly, the identity of the subject (individual or group) is a function of all mediated relations that operate in the activity system. Thus, the problem of environmental health that motivates the activities described in this chapter cannot really be understood without studying the historical changes that turned the area from tribal hunting and gathering grounds to a farming community that was increasingly under pressure from the expansion of the urban communities. Correspondingly, agency, knowing, and learning are not thought of in terms of properties of individuals but in terms of situated and distributed "engagement in changing processes of human activity."[2] Furthermore, individual agency, knowing, and learning are subsets of generalized agency, knowing, and learning available to society at large. Human activities, such as conversing, farming, or engaging in environmentalism, are therefore irreducibly social phenomena that cannot be understood as the sum of the contributions of individuals; they are analogous to threads made of a variety of fibers.

In this chapter, we show that at least some students, far from being disabled or learning disabled, participate in historically ongoing systems of activity with others, who are differently located socially and have different subjective possibilities, to improvise struggles with each other over reaching the momentary, situated goal that motivates their current actions. We show that when students are isolated from their goals, intentions, tools, and certain social relations, they in fact look as if they were disabled. Teachers, school, and the institutional relations that they contribute to actively produce this disability. However, when such students are in a position to contribute in ways that most appropriately sustain their own efforts, their disability disappears.

Focusing on enabling collective rather than individual productivity radically changes what education is about. These implications can be made intelligible in the analogy of the different fibers and the thread that they constitute, which we already introduced and used in Chapters 2 and 3. Although made up of fibers, the properties of the thread cannot be derived from the properties of an individual fiber. Furthermore, the properties of a fiber cannot be derived from the thread. There is therefore a dialectic tension between the natures of fiber and thread—and by analogy, between individual human beings and the society of which they are part. A collective activity is analogous to the thread, and individual contributions are no more than the individual fibers. Thus, scientific literacy and illiteracy are *achieved collectively in specific contexts* rather than properties of individuals or states of individual minds. It makes no less sense to think of a thread independently of the fibers (individuals, tools, etc.) that constitute it than it makes sense to think the fibers independent of the thread that sustains them and gives them direction and shape.

In the following two sections we show how one type of school context produces disability (in mathematics) whereas another school context produces ability (in science). We do not have qualms with the fact that some situations can be recognized as enabling, whereas others turn out to be disabling. But we need to raise questions about translating enabling and disabling situations into attributes that individuals end up with as a result; students get stuck with these labels and develop identities accordingly. Thus, schools and school systems constantly tag students with attributes such as "learning disabled," "having ADHD," "mentally challenged," "educationally mentally retarded," and many others that subsequently lead to "special services" and a separation of these students from situations that may in fact be enabling. Many well-known examples about enabling and disabling situations come from research in ethnomathematics. Thus, for example, Jean Lave showed that adults shopping in the supermarket were nearly perfect on best-buy problems, being error-free on 99 percent of the cases encountered.[3] The same adult shoppers were correct on only 50 percent of best-buy problems presented in a school-like paper-and-pencil format. That is, whereas the supermarket constituted an enabling situation, many paper-and-pencil problems were disabling situations. Similarly, Geoff Saxe showed that Brazilian youths who could not read numbers or do school-like money problems nevertheless were successful at earning their livings as candy buyers and salespersons.[4] Again, the wholesaler's office and the street markets constituted enabling situations in which the youths contributed to their families and to society by earning a living. The following two sections show how disability and ability are produced in school contexts, forcing us to reconsider how we think about scientific literacy (ability) and illiteracy (disability).

## THE PRODUCTION OF LEARNING DISABILITY

There are suggestions that learning disabilities are the result of situations rather than attributes of individuals across situations; assessments of science ability are socially constructed and therefore value-laden.[5] This was also the case at Oceanside Middle School—where I (Michael) have done much of my work on learning and teaching environmental science. In this school, children who are labeled as learning disabled (LD) or as having special needs (e.g., because of their status as aboriginals) often do not exhibit learning problems or learning disabilities when their activities are integrated into the larger concerns of the Oceanside community (for details about the community and its water-related problems, see Chapter 2).

The students come from working- and middle-class backgrounds; about 10 percent of the students are from aboriginal families who chose public over the tribal school.[6] A substantial number of students in this school are designated as having special needs (the school receives funds for special instruction). For example, in one of the classes we taught, there were 27 students (15 male, 12 female), 5 of whom designated as LD, and therefore "special needs students," and four additional students were from the local First Nations band. In the course of this work, I observed that a considerable number of aboriginal students appeared uninvolved in the school, resigned, and generally achieved low grades. However, when I was invited to conduct a workshop in a summer science camp for aboriginal children that was normally taught by aboriginal people, I was able to see a drastic difference in the involvement of the same children when activities were framed in their native context.

As in previous studies where I had designed innovative, hands-on curriculums focused on participation in practices rather than on getting knowledge into the head, there were no differences in achievement between the 13-year-old male and female students. Furthermore, two LD students, Steve and Davie, achieved the highest scores on a unit test designed by the resident teacher in the class. Davie in particular had become such an expert that he assisted in teaching another class of seventh-grade students to conduct research in and alongside the creek. He also participated with others in the open house organized by the environmental activist group in the community. At the same time, excerpts from Steve's and Davie's answers on a unit test (Figure 6.1) both exhibit their understandings but also, particularly in Davie's case (Figure 6.1, bottom), his "spelling and writing problems." That is, the very format of traditional assessments, conducted in settings that isolate students from the social and material resources characteristic of the other settings where they were observed as being highly literate, constructs disabilities with which students get subsequently stuck. The production of learning disability became clear when I observed Davie in his mathematics class.

The mathematics teacher, Cam, had agreed to cooperate with the science teacher, Nadine, to teach students a variety of graphing techniques. By cooperating with Nadine, Cam saw that her science unit could reinforce those skills that students were supposed to learn in mathematics. On this day, Cam had prepared a sheet containing several columns of data that students could choose from, which they would then work with. He explained the task as one of finding relationships. He reminded the students of the lessons where he had taught them a variety of graphing techniques, including pie charting, bar graphing, and scatterplotting. Cam distributed sheets of graphing paper and the sheet containing task descriptions and data . He encouraged students to use pencils so that they could easily correct any errors that they might make.

As the students settle down, they reach for their pencils, rulers, and erasers. On this day, Jamie was paired with Davie. Jamie was a quiet student, always task oriented and doing what the teachers asked. He was classified as "one of the better students," not the best, but "always producing reliable results." Davie does not seem to know what they had been asked to do and queries the teacher, who is passing his desk.

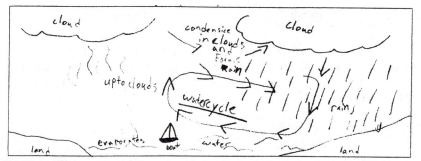

Healthy lake has good clean seethrough water. No sewage running in it and it has a good PH level of 7 or 8. It should also have rocks and rapids to get air back into the water and best of all it should have fish and bugs live in it.

In an unhealthy lake the water would be murky and dead. Sewage running in from all over. The PH level would be 1 or 2. Their would be no rocks so their would be no air to breath and all the fish and bugs would be dead.

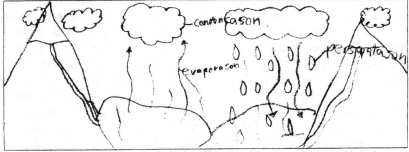

Healthy lakes have lowe pH levels and lake (nice?) have and ther tempernture is coldeder has not very much corbon dioxide and dissolved oxygn

Unhelthy laks have lots of roting weds a hi ph level and a hie temperature lots of corbon dioxide and dissolved oxygen.

---

**Fig. 6.1** These excerpts from a unit test by Steve (top) and Davie (bottom) provide evidence of their understanding and, in Davie's case, of his "disability," which does not show up in other situations.

Davie: What are we supposed to do? Like what is a bar graph? (*Points to an example of a bar graph in the book in front of him.*)

Cam: A scatterplot graph and choose the speed and one of these other categories.

Davie: We are comparing this (*He points to one column on the task sheet.*) and this (*Points to a second column.*) and this (*Points to a third column.*).

Cam: So make a scatterplot that compares two things.

Davie: But how do I make a scatterplot? (*He restlessly gets out of his seat and appears to move away from it.*)

Cam: You are not going to do it? (*He gently pushes Davie back into his seat.*)

> Davie: Jamie is going to do it.
> Cam: And you are going to do the rest of it? OK!

Despite the teacher's encouragement, Davie gets up again after the teacher has moved on to another pair of students. He returns about one minute later. Jamie, though usually a good student, does not know what to do.

> Jamie: What do we have to do?
> Davie: I thought you knew what to do.

Davie does not turn out to be of great help. Rather than answering, he puts the responsibility for knowing what to do on Jamie. He had relied on Jamie to know what they needed to do, and perhaps trusted that Jamie would do the work.

As Jamie begins to draw axes on his graph paper, Davie orients himself toward another group and throws some paper. He gets up and walks around, goes first to one group, then another, talking about the lemonade in the bottle from which he is constantly sipping. He returns and watches Jamie for a while, then talks to the students to the left of him, then to those on the right. Jamie does not look up but sedulously works on the task assigned by his math teacher. During one of the brief moments when Davie is watching, Jamie asks him to look for the largest number in the data table, which Davie finds and reads out. Davie then turns his attention to other things and people, and at one point, even whistles.

When Cam passes nearby, Davie says, "We don't get this," but the teacher continues moving toward another group. Davie watches the students on his left and begins to talk, but turns his attention to Jamie when the teacher comes back to their table. Brad, a student sitting at the next desk also joins in.

> Cam: (*To Davie.*) Are you contributing?
> Davie: Some.
> Brad: What kind of graph are you using?
> Davie: I don't know how to do it.

By answering "some" to the teacher's request, Davie keeps himself out of trouble. "Some" constitutes an appropriate description should the teacher have observed him in off-task behavior, but at the same time indicates a certain level of participation, which, because still unspecified, could be negotiated should the need arise. The teacher seems to be satisfied with the response and moves on. But it is clear that Davie does not know what to do when his neighbor, Brad, asks him about the kind of graph that he and Jamie are using. Davie never focuses again on the task for the remainder of the dedicated time. He walks about the classroom, shares his drink with other students, and sometimes watches what his peers in other groups are doing. He does not attend to the task or listen to the teacher, who returned once more to Davie's desk.

In the end, Davie spent less than two minutes of the twenty-six minutes allotted interacting with Jamie, talking to the teacher, or engaging in other ways. The science and mathematics teachers of this class, after viewing this and other videotapes, suggested that Davie always behaved in this way, that he had ADHD and severe writing problems. For all of these reasons, in addition to the test results from the school psychologist, he had been classified as "learning disabled." Davie was regularly pulled out of the classroom to receive the "special services" to which a student in these categories "has a right." Few if any in the school seems to ask whether pulling Davie out of the regular context with his peers would be more harmful than good. The ideology of teachers and principals in the school held that Davie had problems, which "needed to be fixed," before he could benefit from regular instruction. Nobody seemed to wonder whether the "special services" might actually be disservices, earning Davie similarly unchanging grades that Latitia, the girl in Chapter 5 experienced, despite extended engagement in "extra activities."

To understand and explain the production of failure to do school mathematics, let us look at the activity as a whole. (The motive of activity is located at the level of the society and therefore goes beyond the tasks that students complete; rather than hands-on activity, we should be talking about hands-on tasks.) Davie faces a task that he has not chosen; the object of this task is different for him than for the teacher, so there is a contradiction inherent in the task. He does not know the origin of the data and is unfamiliar with the context that created them. Furthermore, the teacher controls the means of production. Rather than allowing students to use the six computers in the classroom or the twenty-four computers in the neighboring, connected computer room, the teacher has them use paper and pencil. There is therefore a contradiction between the tools children are allowed to use and the more advanced tools actually available in the setting, and therefore also between this activity and an activity more advanced culturally and historically. The teacher allowed students to work with a partner, so that, drawing on the division of labor, "weaker" students could partake in successfully completing the task. However, Davie let Jamie do all the work. That is, there is a contradiction in the teacher's intention for the group work and the way in which Davie contributes.

In the context of these contradictions, Davie does not produce the graph or contribute to producing it in the way that the teacher had intended. There was no outcome. Associated with production is *consumption* in and by the community, which also means production of the individual subject within the community. That is, Davie's failure to produce something on the task is reattributed to him and becomes a label. Davie not only fails to produce the graph but also is produced (constructed) as a failure in the process. Now, whereas "the production of failure is as much part of routine collective activity as the production of average, ordinary knowledgeability,"[7] the present situation differs because the production of failure coproduces learning disability, which becomes a resource for others to construct Davie in ways that are a liability to him. As shown in the next section, this image of Davie as a failure and an LD student stands in stark contrast to other situations that produced a highly literate individual. We will use this contrast as a ground for suggesting that teachers (as well as psychologists) evaluate situations (characterized by all the entities that enter an activity-theoretic framework) rather than individuals.

## PRODUCING KNOWLEDGEABILITY

In their regular curriculum, both Davie and Steve experienced learning problems. Throughout the unit I (Michael) designed, however, Davie and Steve participated in knowledgeable ways, not only learning about science but also assisting peers and adults alike in learning science. Davie and Steve participated in an activity system and produced knowledgeability in such a way that, if one wanted to focus on individuals, (science) "ability" would have been attributed to these students. Four situations are described to show how it was possible for Davie and/or Steve to emerge from this unit as an expert rather than as learning disabled students. That is, this science unit, which essentially consisted of contributing knowledge to the community by working on a community-relevant problem, set up situations in which Davie and Steve turn out to be functionally and scientifically literate individuals. In the resulting activity system, the community mediated the relation between the subject (Davie and Steve) and the motive of the activity in enabling them to move along a trajectory of legitimate peripheral participation.

### Davie and Steve in the Field

This is the second day out in the field for the seventh-grade class. The teacher has asked the students to familiarize themselves with the different instruments and tools available for collecting data. Davie, Steve, and Jamie form a group. The video shows them deciding to investigate whether soil temperature is different in different surroundings. In contrast to the previous day, they have obtained a regular alcohol-based thermometer mounted in a rigid casing so that they can measure soil temperatures. Jamie has a notepad to record observations, the type of setting where they measure the temperature.

Steve: Usually it goes down, that is what I observed last time. The ground is usually colder when it is outside.

Davie: (*Closely observes thermometer and falling temperature.*) It's going down.

Steve: Observe the spot. Like, write down where it is.

Jamie: High stump and grass.

Steve: Let's pull it [thermometer] out.

Davie: No, because it hasn't gone completely down.

Steve: Thirteen. Well, I am going to stick it back in. (*Jamie is still writing.*) It doesn't take very long. Yesterday we measured about five or six or seven, all of them. (*Closely observes thermometer.*) It's gone to about. . . . (*Pause.*) Do you want to see how sensitive it is? (*Pulls out thermometer.*) Watch!

Davie: But we want to measure—

Steve: Watch! (*Holds thermometer tip in hand. Liquid column doesn't seem to move.*) Maybe because of all the dirt. Maybe it takes a bit longer.

Davie: It is not as sensitive.

Steve: The other one, when we just touched it, whoop. (*Indicates an up-down movement along the thermometer.*)

Davie: It is probably not as sensitive as the other is.

Steve: Yeah, it doesn't look as sensitive. I guess this is all that we have to do here.

Davie: We still didn't finish it.

Steve: Yeah, we did.

Davie: It was still going down when you took it out, because it's going slow.

Steve: See, it went up past fifteen. Jamie, it's your turn.

Davie: I think it will be lower. (*Looks up at canopy.*) That one (*Points toward the opening in the canopy.*) wasn't covered; it will make a difference.

In this episode, Steve and Davie construct sensitivity differences between soil thermometers. Arising from their observation that the indicator column had fallen only slowly, Steve pulls the thermometer from the ground to show Davie, who argues that the temperature reading "hasn't gone completely down." Demonstrating thermometer sensitivity, Steve holds the measuring tip in his hands but the liquid column does not seem to move. Steve uses this information to argue that the thermometer is not as sensitive as the one they had used on the previous day; Davie supports this conclusion by reiterating the statement about the lower sensitivity. Based on this conclusion, Davie subsequently argues that they needed to measure the temperature again, for Steve had pulled it before they "finished it." He suggests that the temperature should be lower than in the previous spot, which was not covered by the canopy and therefore was more exposed to the sun.

In this situation, Steve and Davie did not just use the tool in a rote manner to read the temperature. From the differences in responsiveness to warming, they constructed the thermometer as less sensitive than the one used on the previous day. Therefore, as is evident from Davie's statement, they needed to measure for a longer time to get the temperature. He used the previous measurement, taken in a presumably warmer spot, as an additional referent in making his point. This moment therefore shows considerable knowledgeability rather than the rote collection of data that students in "cookbook" activities often seem to engage in.

Davie and Steve were very much invested in this unit. They had many ideas for different investigations that they could conduct and found that the teacher did not plan sufficient time for going to Henderson Creek, where they were going to investigate. Davie and Steve, in the same way as their classmates, collected data and constructed representations of the creek that ultimately made it into the community, through the community newspaper and the Website of the environmentalist group described in Chapter 2 that sponsored the unit. In some instances, the children constructed visual representations that were not unlike those constructed by the environmental activists and their volunteers. As Figure 6.2 shows, Davie and Steve produced a creek profile that had striking resemblance with that produced within the environmentalist group (see also Figure 2.3)— differences, of course, arise from the different means of production employed to produce the respective diagrams (pencil vs. computer software).

Davie and Steve eagerly participated throughout the unit and developed considerable expertise. Working, among others, with Jamie, an environmental activist, or a class parent who accompanied the class into the field, Davie and Steve could not be perceived as learning disabled students. To the contrary, teachers observing the videotapes were taken by the tremendous level of knowledgeability that both exhibited and the leadership roles that they had taken with respect to peers. Viewing both students through the disability lens, the teachers had not seen either student in this light. When the science teacher asked students for volunteers to present their research and results in another seventh-grade class, which was slated to do a similar unit, both Davie and Steve volunteered.

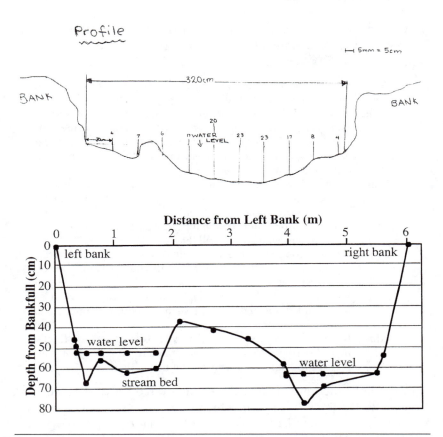

**Fig. 6.2** Cross sections of Henderson Creek produced by Davie and Steve as part of their investigations (top) and, in a different part of the creek, by the members of an environmental group (bottom).

### Presenting Research in Other Science Classes

Davie and Steve were central participants regardless which role they were taking in the project. Thus, when they accompanied their teacher (Nadine) and four peers (including Danielle and Niels, who appear in the transcript below) to another class to talk about their research and results, they did not simply tag along and thereby get out of their responsibility toward another course. Rather, they were active and knowledgeable participants throughout the presentation. The following is an excerpt from the presentation, during which the students and science teacher (Laura) of the other class asked questions in an ongoing way.

After other students and Nadine finished talking about the invertebrate study they had conducted, Steve comments that they completed other investigations as well.

Steve: We didn't just look at the invertebrates; we did like, everything, temperature and D-O [dissolved oxygen] stuff.

Danielle: Also, we've been—the water temperatures, because, well, if there are trees covering over top of the creek, then the water would be colder, because of the shade over the creek. So if there is less oxygen at higher temperature, it is very difficult for the critters in the water to survive.

Laura: So they survive more in colder water than in warmer water?

Niels: Yep, because the dissolved oxygen level, or D-O, is way higher.

Laura: So colder water has more oxygen?

Steve: Yeah. We also found that the different parts of the creek are at different temperatures and all that.

Davie: We were also measuring, like Danielle was saying. She was talking about the overhang about how the bushes came over. We measured that. And we also measured, as they were saying, the D-O, or dissolved oxygen, and how much oxygen is in the water, and it was higher in the shade—because the oxygen affects the organisms.

Nadine: It is important to have high levels of oxygen, because the fish need the oxygen to breathe and if there is not enough in there, there is probably not a whole lot of fish in there.

Danielle links the lower temperatures in covered areas of Henderson Creek with the levels of oxygen, which were lower when the temperature was higher. When Laura asks about the relationship between survival and water temperature, Niels provides an explanation for it. When Laura expands her question about the relationship between temperature and oxygen, Steve and then Davie provide an elaborate answer in which they relate the levels of dissolved oxygen (which they had measured with a dissolved-oxygen meter obtained from the environmental activists) to temperature. They also mention tree and bush coverage as affecting the temperature, an issue that had already emerged early in the unit (see previous episode). Nadine links the levels of oxygen to respiration and low survival if there is not sufficient oxygen.

In this situation, the students and Nadine speak about their work without prompts or props. The discourse is highly informative and scientifically literate. The students had not just obtained dissolved-oxygen levels from someone else, but measured them on their own. They learned to competently operate a variety of instruments (i.e., tools) and use them for their purposes. More importantly, the students did not just assemble their collected data in some required way but constructed meaningful relations between different types of observations (variables). When asked, they speak about these relations in a knowledgeable way, appropriately responding to questions from Laura, who learned, as subsequent debriefings and interviews showed, from these exchanges with the students from another class. Here, a teacher (Laura) learns science, among other things, from Davie and Steve, who supposedly are learning disabled students.

Presenting their work to another class was not the only way in which Davie and Steve contributed to the learning of others. They were among the first volunteers when asked whether there was someone interested in helping Laura and Michael to introduce this other class to doing research in and along Henderson Creek on their own. By participating in supporting the activities of their peers from another class, Davie and Steve both expanded the learning opportunities of others and the possibilities for their own participation in and learning of science. By participating with and supporting others, they increased their own knowledgeability of the subject, which we understand in terms of levels of participation in ongoing, community-based, and relevant meaningful activity.

### Expanding the Learning Opportunities of Others

As peer teachers and coaches, Davie and Steve contributed in varied ways to the successful science unit in Laura's class. Both students participated in whole-class presentations, where they illustrated, for example, the use of instruments, and led small groups of students in and along the creek. In the following excerpt, Davie and the teachers (Laura and Michael) introduce Laura's class to some fundamentals of working with Serber samplers and D-nets, used for capturing invertebrates.

> Davie: See, and you only do it in there [within metal square of Serber sampler] to find out in that one area how much bugs there are. And you have to do it really good when you use this one, because you want to find out exactly how many bugs there are. This one [D-net] you can just try and estimate the area in front, but because it is not accurate, you are just trying to get much bugs in there.
> Laura: Davie, how long do you get your hands in there and rub?
> Davie: I don't know exactly. I just move around in there, about a minute or two, just to get everything.
> Michael: With the D-net, you should take about one square foot, because otherwise we won't be able to compare the counts across sites.

In this episode, Davie demonstrates to his peers how to use the Serber sampler and the D-net, the two tools students used for sampling the invertebrates. But students are not the only ones to learn from this situation. Laura, who had not used these tools before, finds out about the procedure for collecting samples. This situation, like many others involving Davie that are recorded on video, does not produce the public appearance of a learning disability. Being both an individual subject and an aspect of the context for others, he contributes to the learning in the situation involving students and adults (e.g., teacher, parents) alike. In this, Davie is one of several knowledgeable participants that make science knowing and learning possible for the students in Laura's class.

Later during the same lesson, the video shows Davie simultaneously assisting two groups of students. One group of three boys had decided to measure the speed of the stream. A group of girls working next to them collected invertebrate samples.

> Davie: OK, you guys [boys' group] choose a spot. Maybe go along there [shore]. Then you have to measure how deep it is. And then make a breakdown [into upstream and down-steam].
> John: Is this exactly five meters?
> Davie: Yes, it is. You guys, put this [Styrofoam] in the middle of the stream, where the water is flowing a bit. And then you just throw it in there and measure how long it takes. (*Moves to girls' group, headed by Lisa.*) And you put the net in like this, and you move around like this (*Washes rocks with his in front of Serber sampler.*) and you will get lots of bugs in there.
> Lisa: And they will go into the net?
> Davie: Yes, the water flow will take them in. You also will probably have lots of sand.
> John: We could have the string, and then multiply the time by two.
> Davie: Yeah, that would work. Just pull the string. Who has the stopwatch?
> John: I do.
> Davie: You put the hand on zero, and when you let the ball go, you press the start.
> Len: Will we check for the bugs?
> Davie: Later, first we measure how fast the water goes.

In this situation, Davie accomplishes multiple tasks. He organizes John and his group into setting up their investigation, getting their tools, and he shows and explains how to sample a spot in the creek for invertebrate organisms. In stark contrast to the mathematics lesson described earlier, Davie is not only on task but also and simultaneously manages to knowledgeably assist two groups of students, who are engaged in and accomplish different investigations. He provides directions on how to note the results of measurements—an *outcome* of his actions—by showing, for example, how John and his group ought to use tables for recording stream speed and stream width (Figure 6.3, top). He subsequently helps them, finding additional assistance from a teacher, to produce a visual representation of the data. (The graph in Figure 6.3 features circles drawn by a biologist who assisted students in interpreting the plot.) Davie is frequently so eager that he often takes over from the students he is supposed to assist. The adult teachers have to remind him that he is to scaffold the inquiries of his peers rather than taking the inquiry away from them.

Even if one attributes knowing and learning to individual students, the present episode supports the contention that Davie contributes to the enactment of scientific literacy rather than of learning disability. Again, the situation supported the emergence of scientific literacy and did not create and make visible any learning disability. All we see are children in the pursuit of their investigations, assisted by another child who has had more experience participating in such investigations than the others.

### Exhibiting at the Open House

Visitors of all ages, adults and children who were younger than they were, came to the open house that took place in a community hall. Steve and Davie spoke to many visitors. Again, the situation did not contribute to bring disability and learning problems to the foreground. Rather, both students were experts in their own right duly recognized by their peers and by visitors. That is, the analysis of Davie-in-the-open-house-event-among-visitors-and-artifacts revealed high levels of expertise that, in the tradition of conventional psychology, can be attributed to Davie.

For example, the video shows Steve tending to a poster featuring a map and photographs of his research sites, a list of tools, drawings of different invertebrates, and a bar graph of the frequencies of different organisms. An adult approaches the poster and asks what he is presenting. As Steve begins to talk about the project, Davie joins into the interaction.

> Steve: We have gone out to three different sites, Centennial Park, Malcolm Road, which is right by Oceanside School, and Oceanside Farms. You know where this is at?
>
> Adult: (*Nods.*) Yeah.
>
> Steve: And we counted them. (*Points to histogram they had constructed, Figure 6.4.*) Like, we collected all these samples (*points to invertebrate drawings*) and counted them and we plotted them (*points to graph*). And we found these sorts of bugs. (*Adult looks at drawings of organisms.*)

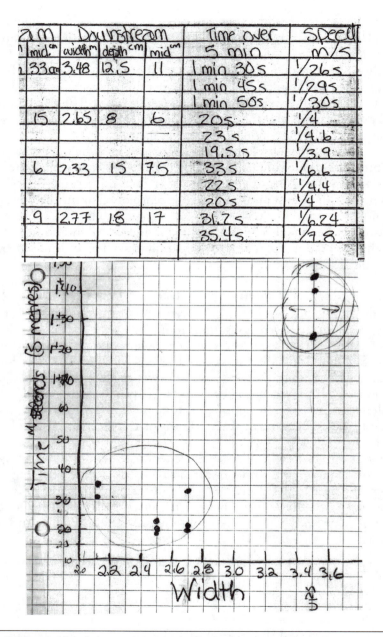

| a m | | | | Time over | Speed |
|---|---|---|---|---|---|
| mid.^cm | width^m | depth^cm | mid^cm | 5 min | m/s |
| 33cm | 3.48 | 12.5 | 11 | 1 min 30 s | 1/26 s |
| | | | | 1 min 45 s | 1/29 s |
| | | | | 1 min 50 s | 1/30 s |
| 15 | 2.65 | 8 | 6 | 20 s | 1/4 |
| | | | — | 23 s | 1/4.6 |
| | | | | 19.5 s | 1/3.9 |
| 6 | 2.33 | 15 | 7.5 | 33 s | 1/6.6 |
| | | | | 22 s | 1/4.4 |
| | | | | 20 s | 1/4 |
| 9 | 2.77 | 18 | 17 | 31.2 s | 1/6.24 |
| | | | | 35.4 s | 1/7.8 |

**Fig. 6.3** Data table and plot correlating stream speed and the width of Henderson Creek at different places (upstream, downstream).

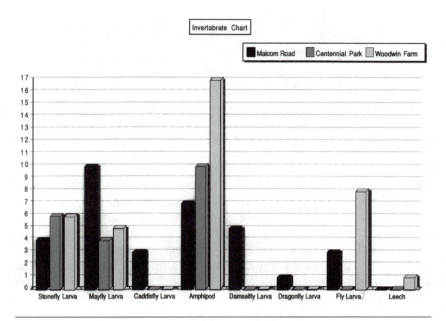

**Fig. 6.4** Histogram constructed by Steve and Davie, showing the number of invertebrates per square foot at three sampling sites along Henderson Creek.

Adult: Are those (*Points to stone fly larva drawing.*) around now? Are those fly larvas?

Davie: We might have one of those right now. I am not sure. But I know that we have lots of these, lots of mayflies and amphipods.

Steve: And worms.

Davie: And we also got crayfish.

Steve: And the ones that are called bloodworms.

Davie: These are very common in some spots. Some spots there are, like, lots of worms, and at other spots there are none. Usually, we don't get very many mayflies at that time of the year.

Adult: How did you catch all of them?

Steve: Like that (*Points to photograph showing student with Serber sampler.*) or with D-nets. Like see, we have tools there (*Points to displayed list of tools.*), and a D-net is a net that looks like a D. It has a flat side that sits on the bottom. And we just brush the rocks in front of it (*Waves with hand.*), and the bugs fall in. And then we just pick up the net (*Points to photo.*) and throw it into the bucket. Then we take it back to school and look at it.

Davie: (*To adult*) Come over here, I put one under [the microscope], so you can take a look at it. (*Goes to microscope, focuses it for the adult.*)

In the first part of this situation, Steve and Davie knowledgeably talk about their research, where it had been conducted, the type and frequency of the organisms that they had found. Davie points out that some of the organisms cannot be found at the particular time of the year during which they had sampled. Subsequently, the adult asks the two students how they had caught the organisms. In an extended fashion, Davie and Steve explain by drawing on resources immediately available in the situation. They point to photographs or describe tools in words. They articulate key features of the procedure by means of which the specimens were detached from the bottom of the creek, how these enter the net, and how to empty the net into a bucket, subsequently used to transport the organisms back to school. Steve's final statement segues Davie into an explanation of the microscope work he had done with the invertebrates. He places a tray under the microscope and allows the adult to observe it. Together, Davie and the adult then attempt to classify the organism, engaging in a comparison of the specimen under the microscope and a set of drawings used for classification purposes.

In the context of this open house, where community activists presented posters from their own work, and where visitors of all ages moved from exhibition to exhibition, Steve and Davie were legitimate contributors to a public event. Whereas the videotape that features Davie in his mathematics class and his written statements on the unit test (see Figure 6.1, bottom) lend themselves to make traditional assessments of a learning disabled student, the present data show Davie-at-the-open-house as highly knowledgeable. Evidently, the conditions that produced learning problems and disability become visible in the conventional school contexts did not exist here. Rather, Steve and Davie's participation contributed in important ways to the very emergence of the phenomenon in which we are interested here—scientific literacy.

## KNOWLEDGEABILITY IN EVERYDAY ACTIVITY

In the preceding section, we provide descriptions of several situations, transcripts from videotapes, and examples of the visual representations Davie and Steve produced or helped others to produce outcomes with the means at hand and given the social relations enacted. Davie and Steve came out of this unit feeling very successful. Every part of their involvement, as investigators, presenters to others, peer tutors, and open-house exhibitors, had provided them with opportunities to participate in legitimate ways not only at school but also, and more importantly, in the community. They interacted with environment, peers, activists, parent helpers, teachers, and open-house visitors about Henderson Creek and the environmental health of the associated watershed (motive of their inquiry). The outcomes of the interactions included visual scientific representations (inscriptions) of and scientific discourse about Henderson Creek. But, as a result of these productions, Davie and Steve were themselves produced as able, legitimate peripheral participants in community science. That is, based on these situations (and my videotapes), one is tempted to construct and re-attribute scientific literacy to both students, as something that they carry around in their heads. Here, then, we have a contradiction: How do Davie and Steve come to be both learning disabled and highly literate students at the same time? How is it possible that Davie fails to contribute to the construction of a data analysis in his mathematics class and yet be so astute in assisting his peers to construct a graph from their data? How is it possible that Davie (frequently) and Steve (sometimes) are jerked out of their regular classes to "fix" their learning disability when it is possible to design situations where they turn out to be highly able?

In the context of this science unit, Davie and Steve chose, together with their classmates, to conduct investigations in the creek and they chose the particular investigations that they wanted to conduct. Thus, there is no contradiction between the teacher's and the students' goal for individual investigations. Furthermore, the students chose the tools and instruments with which to conduct their inquiry, that is, they owned the means of production. Again, the corresponding contradiction that appeared in the mathematics class no longer existed. In ordinary schooling, teachers represent the community; students produce tasks for teachers who are the sole evaluators of learning outcomes, and who assign grades that become markers of students' qualities as learners and human beings. In the situation presented here, the community included students in other classes, their teacher, and the community at large. The representations of Henderson Creek produced by Steve and Davie became part of the knowledge in this community through communications and exchanges during the open house, in a newspaper article, and on the Website of the activists. The visual and verbal representations that they had produced were distributed across the community.

We do not claim that schools are the only setting that produce failure. Rather, failures and successes are produced in everyday activity in an ongoing way—though, in different amounts and of different quality than they are produced in schools. The production of failure is not our contention. Rather, the problem with school tasks is that they lead many students to fail. This failure, as shown in Figure 6.1, subsequently becomes an attribute of students noted in qualitative (anecdotal) form ("good student," "poor student," etc.) or in the form of grades, which in turn bias the (career) trajectories of the labeled individual. Thus, for Davie and Steve, the contradictions continued even as this science unit was under way. In other classes, they still failed to produce the teacher-determined standards, which added to the reification of the LD label and further jerking out of the regular classroom settings to "fix" the learning disability.

## RETHINKING SCIENTIFIC DIS/ABILITY

Science educators need to find and build alternative activity systems in which the mediational entities that influence learning in and of diverse student populations. We need activity systems that sustain a broader vision of scientific literacy than the narrow view currently enacted in schools and policy alike. We presented evidence from a three-year ethnographic project within a middle school where we (students, teachers, parents, activists, and researcher) enacted a curriculum consistent with the motivation of other activities in their community. In the process, learning was made possible as students exchanged knowledge and tools with others and produced knowledge for the community, which the community consumed. Our analyses showed that in this unit, the activity system focusing on the students shared many similarities with the activity system that focuses on other individuals in their community. Thus, in everyday water- and watershed-related activities, adults defined purposes, goals, tools, division of labor, rules of interaction, and so forth (see Chapter 2). Similarly, we found that the motivation for the children's actions integrated well to other immediate life-world aspects; these are indications of an empowered citizenship. We showed that this focus eliminated many contradictions characterizing ordinary schooling.

The considerations and findings presented here now allow us to view "ability" and "disability" in a different way. Because the unit of analysis in this study is the whole activity, the subject of activity never exists outside of its relation to the other elements in the activity system and the mediated relations that they give rise to. What we ought to consider (taking into account something that is already embodied in evaluative practices) are situations such as Davie-in-the-mathematics-class-required-to-do-data-analysis or Davie-in-another-seventh-grade-class-as-teacher-scaffolding-inquiry-in-and-about-the-creek. These hybrid entities involve all those entities and meditated relations that are salient in a systemic perspective of activity. It is these situations that are scientifically literate or mathematically illiterate; "good," "learning disabled," or "obnoxious" students are always good, learning-disabled, or obnoxious *situations* rather than properties of the students. (We take it for a given that attributions such as "poor" or "highly able" may be used for the same student in different situations.) As an activity system (here schooling) develops in time, so does the subject, whose lived experience and biography arise from activity as a thread woven from the fibers of the elements. Whether the resulting thread (i.e., the individual student who is the subject) is best characterized by the terms "learning disability" or "ability" is a function of the varied situations (constituted by motive, tools, rules, community, and division of labor) in which students find themselves.

Readers may have noticed that a subject both participates in producing and is itself the outcome of activity. This is an aspect of the dialectical constitution of the subject: we are always participating in activity, but who we are is determined from the outcomes of activity including interactions with others. We see that "ability" was produced as Davie and Steve participated, with other children, in an activity that was similarly motivated as those in which adult members of the community engaged (see Chapter 2). During the open house, Steve and Davie were accepted alongside the activists as legitimate participants in the community. The resulting conversations therefore broke the mold of normal modes of schooling, opening up the possibility for lifelong participation in such activities and therefore the possibility for lifelong learning without the discontinuities that characterize the transition from formal schooling to other aspects of life. More importantly, for students such as Davie and Steve, the unit provided a context from which they arose as able contributors to community life more generally than as learning disabled individuals.

If the motivation underlying school science and environmental activism, stewardship, or volunteerism are similar, based on the nature of tools, rules, divisions of labor, and community, we can expect individuals (subject) to move along trajectories that do not construct them as learning disabled. Students who participate in activities that contribute to the knowledge available in their community will develop into adolescents and adults, continuing to participate in the activities relating to environmental health. The possibility for such transitions is clearly indicated by a variety of situations that foster the participation of students and non-students alike.

## THE PRODUCTION OF SCIENTIFIC LITERACY
## AS CONVERSATION

We can think of Steve and Davie as being involved in a variety of conversations—which are always irreducible, semantically and syntactically, to individual characteristics. Conversations can be understood as activities in which differently located individuals participate. The interacting individuals constitute the subjects focusing on some topic, such as Steve, Davie, and the adult talking about the students' research results. In the process, the conversationalists draw on (the same or different) discursive repertoires, diagrams, drawings, and graphs (their means of production). Division of labor refers to the different roles of listener and speaker, which the individuals repeatedly exchange in the course of the conversation. Their interactions are mediated by the rules that mediate turn-taking or the rules of respect for one another. Finally, participants themselves are participants in the open house, which itself is part of Oceanside. In this activity system, learning dis/ability is neither a property of the individual participants nor something a priori available in the activity system as a resource. Rather, dis/ability is the contingently achieved outcome emerging from local organization of the different conversations. In the same way, dis/ability is produced in conversations that take place in other school situations.

It is apparent that one can think of situations as setting up "zones of proximal development," that is, zones in which students achieve more than if they work on their own, isolated from the resources normally accessible in out-of-school situations.[8] Our perspective allows us to rethink the notion of zone of proximal development as it relates to conversation as activity and dis/ability. In activity-centered theory, the community (society), among others, mediates subject-object relations. Individual (restricted) actions are only a subset of all (generalized) actions within society. Therefore, the difference between the everyday actions of individuals and the collectively generated, historically new form of activity constitutes a zone of potential learning. Conversations (e.g., during the open house or a public meeting) can therefore be constituted as zones of learning and development that allow collective bodies to produce and further develop ability.

Our way of thinking about learning as changing participation in collective activity addresses another problem. Traditional educators are concerned that unless individuals carry knowledge (internalized in one situation) around, it cannot be found in other situations in which these individuals take part. Such analyses are problematic in that they break holistic situations apart into things (individual subject) and the boxes (contexts) that contain them, attributing aspects to either things or boxes. However, from the perspective of activity, it does not matter whether some means of knowledge and artifact production (e.g., a graph) is available on a computer or has been internalized by the individual subject. Once the tool is available in the system, it contributes to the activity. The only difference is that, internalized, the use of tools can shift to the level of automatic (tacit), routine operations, whereas as knowledge residing in tools it may remain at the level of conscious actions.

We take knowing and learning as aspects of culturally and historically situated activity. Learning is discernable by noticing our and others' changing participation in changing social practices. Because interaction and participation cannot be understood as the sum total of an individual acting toward a stable environment, learning cannot be understood in terms of what happens to individuals. Rather, if learning is situated and distributed, educators must focus on enabling changing participation, that is, enabling new forms of collective activity that is generated at a level beyond the classroom. As critical science educators, we are particularly interested in forms of participation that are continuous with out-of-school experiences and therefore have the potential to lead to lifelong learning rather than to discontinuities between formal and informal learning settings. As critical science educators, we are also interested in conversations that allow individual students to be successful and able participants rather than disabled, marginalized, and forgotten individuals. As the examples provided here show, this is likely to mean that we have to give up the traditional controls over the means of production, the motive generating activity, and who the activity-defining community is.

## CODA

In other activity systems (e.g., penal and psychiatric), it has been recognized that locking subjects up in institutions (prison, psychiatric clinic) does frequently not contribute to the solution of problems but, in fact, contributes to their reproduction. (In *Discipline and Punish: The Birth of the Prison*, Michel Foucault explicitly shows the similarities in emergence, structure, and practices of schools and those of prisons and mental wards.) In some penal and psychiatric systems, structures have been elaborated that allow individuals to participate (in limited ways, sometimes under supervision) in the everyday affairs of their community. In Italy, a 1978 law sanctioned the end of the psychiatric hospital and established semi-residential structures in the community to provide opportunities for daytime re-socialization. Much like Jean Lave's adult shoppers or Geoffrey Saxe's Brazilian child street vendors, the former residents of psychiatric hospitals found support in the community that diminished, if not made disappear, the problem that the institutions had constructed, named, and used as attributes for the individuals.

In the learning situation described here, too, students are no longer contained in school buildings to keep them off the streets, to babysit them, or to discipline their bodies and minds. Rather, students' actions take place in the community more broadly. They are not relegated to particular locations (schools) with local and temporal effects. The outcomes of students' work has relevance and contributes to the broader life world that they inhabit together with their parents, siblings, elders, town council members, and others in the community. The same is true for the New York City youths that we encountered in Chapter 4, engaged in designing and constructing a community garden from an abandoned lot. Here, too, the youths' work had relevance and contributed to the community at large, both drawing it into the activity and giving back to it in terms of a finished product. If science is to be for *all* as the reform rhetoric has it, then there must be opportunities to participate in ways that emphasize students' strengths and address their interests. Rather than setting up situations that bring out disability or inability and thereby contribute to the reproduction of inequities, we may conceive of science education as an activity that produces knowledgeability by focusing on achievements of collectivities.

Such a view implies that (science) educators organize enabling situations characterized by a collective ability rather than disabling situations sorting students for career-selection purposes. In the same way, science educators might think of science as but one fiber next to many other fibers in thread of life (including local, aboriginal, and common-sense knowledge with all their so-called misconceptions and alternative frameworks). Science educators would then focus on learning as participating in solving everyday (and societally relevant) problems rather than on the question whether to teach "the nucleus contains protons and neutrons" before "an atom has shells filled with electrons" or the other way around. As critical science educators, we advocate that we not break individuals out of the societal contexts and material settings in which they normally conduct their activities. We advocate not severing the mediating relations of means of production, community, division of labor, and situated rules characteristic of ordinary circumstances. Thus, learning problems and learning disabilities, which are made visible when students such as Davie and Steve work in regular (traditional) classrooms, are virtually non-existent in settings such as those that we featured here. We deliberately say *virtually* non-existent because, as we pointed out, the studies in ethnomathematics showed that people who had a mean of 99 percent of correct solutions in the supermarket dropped to a mean of 50 percent correct solutions on supermarket-based word problems.

To date, aboriginal, female, and poverty-stricken students are still too frequently sorted out of science rather than supported so that they can emerge as able individuals, perhaps in a science that is changing its face. When educators focus on creating situations that enable rather than disable students, new possibilities of participation arise. Documenting these possibilities and difficulties, as well as the knowing and learning that emerge from them, remains virtually uncharted terrain. Much research remains to be done to study the forms that distributed and situated cognition take in the approach we propose.

# 7

## SCIENCE EDUCATION AS AND FOR CITIZEN SCIENCE

*The means of pursuing scientific literacy suggested by current reforms do not seem to anticipate diverse groups of people who put science to use in broader, different, or socially responsible ways.*[1]

Margaret Eisenhart, Elizabeth Finkel, and Scott F. Marion

*Do we teach biology, chemistry, physics, mathematics or do we teach young people to cope with their own world?*[2]

Gérard Fourez

One of the fathers of modern science education, Paul deHart Hurd, suggested that "a valid interpretation of scientific literacy must be consistent with the prevailing image of science and the revolutionary changes taking place in our society."[3] For many, this has meant using laboratory science as a template for what science is, independent of the epistemological paradigm brought to science education reform. Science courses often remain means of pushing students into the world of scientists rather than a way of helping them cope with their own life worlds. The needs of diverse groups of people—except white middle-class males—have not been met, leading to, by and large, their exclusion from science. Despite tremendous efforts expended, so the tenor often goes, educational reforms have for the most part failed to produce scientifically literate citizens.

Scholarly discussions of scientific literacy are often based on three (generally unstated and perhaps unfounded) assumptions: scientific literacy is an attribute of individuals, science is the paradigmatic mode for rational human conduct, and school knowledge is transportable to life after school. These assumptions lead science educators to ponder

(a) how individuals can be made to appropriate (internalize) or construct specific scientific concepts; (b) what science content to teach; and (c) how to make students transfer science to out-of-school situations. In this chapter, we want to push the rethinking of scientific literacy further. In the previous chapters we have made two suggestions: first, scientific literacy is a property of collective situations and characterizes interactions irreducible to characteristics of individuals; second, science is not a single normative framework for rationality but merely one of many resources (fibers) that people can draw on in everyday collective decision-making processes. We now suggest that scientific literacy is promoted when we view science education as and for participation in the necessarily political life of the community. By contributing in concrete ways to community life—that is, the collective control over societal conditions—individuals gain control over their personal conditions, because these are always individually relevant societal conditions. Students come to enact knowledge and, with it, power; and they take new positions in the dynamic of margin and center, which has traditionally constructed them as lesser beings. That is, students develop increasing control over (increasing levels of agency in) their life world by participating in activities that are meaningful because they contribute to their community as a whole.

We think of agency, knowing, and learning not as properties of individuals but in terms of situated and distributed "engagement in changing processes of human activity."[4] Individual agency, knowing, and learning are concrete realizations of agency, knowing, and learning generally possible within society. That is, human activities (including conversations) are irreducibly social phenomena that cannot be understood as the sum of the contributions of individuals. Society is analogous to a thread and each human being is a fiber (or multiple fibers) interacting with all the other fibers. From this interaction arise new properties that cannot be derived from the properties of each fiber. There is therefore a dialectic tension between the fiber and thread—and by analogy, between individual human beings and the society of which they are part. Subjectivity is first and foremost a characteristic of society as a whole; individual subjectivity constitutes the concrete, personal realization of collective subjectivity.

### Citizen Science

Studies in public understanding of science construct an image of the interaction between scientists and non-scientists that is much more complex, dynamic, and interactive than the traditional opposition between scientific expertise and ignorance and rejection of scientific knowledge may lead us to believe. In the everyday world of a community, science emerges not as a coherent, objective, and unproblematic body of knowledge and practices (see Chapters 2 and 3). Rather, science often turns out to be uncertain and contentious, and unable to answer important questions pertaining to the specific (local) issues at hand. In everyday situations, citizen thinking may offer a more comprehensive and effective basis for action than scientific thinking.

It makes sense to conceive of scientific literacy in terms of "citizen science," which is "a form of science that relates in reflexive ways to the concerns, interests and activities of citizens as they go about their everyday business."[5] In our own research, citizen science is related to a variety of contexts, ranging from personal matters (e.g., accessibility to safe drinking water), livelihood (e.g., best farming practices), leisure (e.g., gardening in sustainable, organic ways), to activism and organized protest. In contrast to the current ideology of scientific literacy as a property of individuals, we further propose to think about it as a characteristic of certain everyday *situations* in which citizen science occurs. In such a context, the "term *learning* simply glosses that some persons have achieved a particular relationship with each other, and it is in terms of these relations that information necessary to everyone's participation gets made available in ways that give people enough time on task to get good at what they do."[6] This implies that science educators no longer seek to stack educational environments to coax individuals into certain performances, but that they set up situations that allow a variety of participatory modes, more consistent with democratic ideals and praxis, in which people make decisions about their own lives and interests (see the three case studies in Chapter 5). If we wish science education to be relevant to people's everyday lives and citizenship, we do well to allow the learners to participate in a diversity of these relations. For expecting one set of relations (institutional school) to prepare students for a world of many relations does not make sense.

## COMMUNITY WATER PROBLEMS AS CURRICULAR TOPIC

Educators need to find and build alternative activity systems in which the mediational entities that influence learning in and of diverse student populations differ from "normal" science. Appropriate activity systems would sustain a broader vision of scientific literacy than the narrow view currently enacted in schools and policy alike. One goal for a critical science education would be to foster students' development of keen appreciations of the places where science and technology intertwine smoothly with one's experience of life. The emergence of broader visions is supported when school children focus on issues and problems that are of immediate concern to their own lives and community. Over a period of three years, we recorded and documented many events featuring adult citizens and school students who deal with the water-related problems of one community, Oceanside, in the Pacific Northwest.

Given Oceanside's water-related problems in (see Chapters 2 and 3), it was not difficult to convince teachers to participate in a study where students would learn science by investigating the town's Henderson Creek watershed. Over a two-year period, we have also assisted in the teaching of science to three seventh-grade classes over two- to four-month periods. In these classes, students design and conduct their own research in and along Henderson Creek with the intent to report their findings at an open house organized annually by the Henderson Creek Project (see Figure 7.1 for one of the research sites chosen by the students). The idea underlying these science classes was to get students become active citizens and contribute to the knowledge available in and to the community. Other students at the middle and high school also conducted research in the watershed as part of their involvement in regionally funded Streamkeepers program or in science fair competitions. In this way, students already participated in producing knowledge that was subsequently distributed in (and consumed by) their community and the activists. Members of the Henderson Creek Project, the authors, parents, and First Nations elders contributed in various ways to the teaching of the children by providing workshops, talks, and assisting them in framing research and collecting data.

Influenced by these considerations and by results of our own work over the past decade documenting and theorizing the situated nature of knowing, we assisted teachers in designing units that provided seventh-grade students a process for learning science while generating knowledge for their community. The science units began with articles from the community newspaper that described aspects of the environmental and water-related problems in and around Oceanside. For example, the following excerpt from one of these articles highlights that a revitalization of the ocean surrounding the peninsula where Oceanside is located needs to begin with improving the health of Henderson Creek and its tributary:

> **"Group is a bridge over troubled waters"**
> If the waters of the Pat Bay and Georgia Straight are to be revitalized, the streams and creeks that feed them must be save. A group at [Oceanside] wants to begin the process by breathing life back into [Henderson and . . .] Creeks.

**Fig. 7.1** One of the creek sections where students did their research. In the summer, the water was stagnant, and putrid, with low levels of oxygen and high temperatures.

The damage [. . .] was caused by channeling the creeks and removing gravel from the area. Straightening the creeks (ditching) not only makes the water move through the remaining culvert too quickly to support rearing beds, but removes the surrounding vegetation. That, in turn, erodes the environment on which birds and other species depend for survival.

Chief [. . .] spoke about the abundance of fish, shellfish, and other wildlife in the area during his youth. . . .

But for the long-term work, project coordinators said the wider community must be involved. . . .

The teachers read the article with the students and asked questions about the need for revitalizing the ocean (children have no difficulties in answering, given that some of their parents fish as a hobby or for livelihood). The discussions of the article ended with the teacher asking how the particular class should become involved, because the class is in fact one part of the "wider community." The students began generating ideas, often related to cleaning up the creek and to finding out more about Henderson Creek and its problems. After a field trip to different sites along the creek, the students began framing initial investigations and even entire programs of research.

When this project in school science classrooms began, we (Michael, his students, and the teachers they worked with) still believed that all students should engage in their activities in ways that would foster scientific practices conceived in a traditional way—designing experiments, graphing results, and so forth. That is, our model for school science was influenced by the science of scientists. However, we soon realized that requiring all students to measure series of variables, and to represent correlations in the form of Cartesian graphs or histograms excluded particular groups of students such as some girls and indigenous students. While these students still participated in the data collection, the subsequent data analyses and activities that focused on mathematical representations generally turned them off. In subsequent classes, we changed our approach. Taking our lead from other activities in the community, where different representational forms were legitimately used, we began to encourage students to investigate on their own terms (Figure 7.2), choosing their data collection and representational tools that best fit their interests and needs. Audio-recorded descriptions, videotaped records of the watershed and student activities, photographs, drawings, and other representations began to proliferate. This change provided forms of knowing and learning that led to an increasing participation of previously excluded students. It also meant that we had to abandon our traditional conception of what science and science education might look like in the community. Ultimately, the children presented the results of their work at a yearly open house organized by the activists focusing on the environmental health of the Henderson Creek watershed.

Parents, activists, aboriginal elders, scientists, graduate students, and other community members were an integral part of the science units. For example, every other week the classes spent one entire afternoon (noon–2:30 P.M.) in and around the creek. Parents both assisted in driving children to the different sites along the creek and participated in teaching by asking productive questions, scaffolding, and supervising children. Members from the environmentalist group also contributed, giving presentations, assisting in teaching kids how to use particular tools and how to do research in the creek, and analyzing data and organisms brought back to the classroom. Students from classes that had already completed or were near completion of their unit talked about

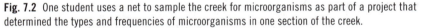

**Fig. 7.2** One student uses a net to sample the creek for microorganisms as part of a project that determined the types and frequencies of microorganisms in one section of the creek.

their work in another class that was just beginning, and assisted their peers during fieldwork and data analysis (see Chapter 6).

This involvement of community members therefore integrated the children's activities with activities in the community in two ways. First, the community came to the school, assisting students and teachers in their activities. Second, the student activities were concerned with a pressing issue of the community; the science lessons took children out of the school and into the community. That is, the children's activities were motivated by the same concerns that drove the activities of other community members. In terms of our systems model of activity, there is therefore legitimate (peripheral) participation because the motives that drives both activity systems share many elements. (It is true that students also enjoyed the science unit because it broke them out of the strict routine and control imposed upon them within the school building. This is one of the contradictions when teachers attempt to do something outside the norm.) It is this overlap with the activity system characterizing everyday life in the community (motivation, subjects [community], and tools) that makes the children's work "authentic." Rather than preparing for a life after school or for future science courses, children immediately participated in and contributed to social life in the community. It is in that process that learning (which belongs to the various conversations of which individual persons are part) was occurring.

## SCHOOL SCIENCE IN THE COMMUNITY

School science is often conceived as propaedeutic—preparatory study for subsequent science courses and for life. The project *Scope, Sequence, and Coordination* by the National Science Teachers' Association is explicitly based on breaking down and properly aligning curriculum content across grade levels. Despite research in other fields, such as mathematics, which shows that there are considerable discontinuities between school on the one hand and everyday activities and knowing on the other, science educators have yet to critically examine the assumption that school learning actually relates to everyday out-of-school activity. This question is paramount if science education is to contribute at all to a more general project of lifelong learning in science, which appears to imply continuous forms of learning across the boundaries of schooling.

In this section, we present evidence from our research within school science classes that enacted a curriculum consistent with the motivation of other activities in their community. In the process, learning was made possible as students exchanged knowledge and tools with others and produced knowledge for the community, where this knowledge was distributed and who "consumed" the knowledge. Furthermore, the activity system focusing on the students shared many similarities with the activity system that focuses on other individuals in their community (see Chapter 2). Thus, in everyday water- and watershed-related activities, adults defined purposes, goals, tools, division of labor, rules of interaction, and so forth. Similarly, we found that the motivation behind children's activity integrated well to other immediate life-world aspects; this is an indication of empowered citizenship.

### *Diversity of Projects and Representational Forms*

In designing the unit, we took our cues from the activities of others in the community concerned with the health of the local watershed and its main water-carrying body, Henderson Creek, and allowed students

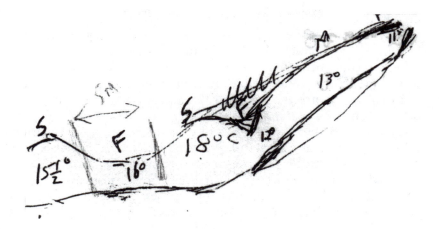

**Fig. 7.3** Map of one research site including temperatures of the creek and levels of shading. It was produced by a group of three "learning disabled" students with the scaffolding of a visiting graduate student/research scientist.

to pursue investigations of their own interests. Because people in the community created and used various representations of the watershed, creek, and the pressing issues, we changed from an initial focus on "scientific representations" (e.g., graphs) to encouraging students to create representations that best met their needs of expressive forms (Figure 7.3).

Although the object that defined the activity systems—Henderson Creek and the watershed it drains—was the same in most instances for all student groups, different tools and rules mediated the relations in different ways leading to very different outcomes. Nevertheless, the various outcomes ultimately contributed in their own ways to the totality of the findings generated by one or more classes. We understand the students' activities as authentic in the sense that their activities were motivated in the same way and by the same concerns that other activities in the community were motivated. Different members of the community in general and the environmentalist group in particular participated in the student-centered activity system. Other similarities with the activity systems in the community were some of the tools (colorimeter, rules). Not surprisingly, some of the *outcomes* of the student-centered activity system were therefore similar to those in the activity systems in the community. For example, the use of colorimeter, pH meter, or dissolved-oxygen meter all led to numeric representations of stream health. Middle school students and college students working on the Henderson Creek Project as a summer job produced very similar graphical representations (e.g., Fig. 6.2). Also, forms designed by scientists (water quality assessment, physical assessment) assisted students in their summer job and middle school students in producing representations that could be used by the environmental activists to pursue other goals (e.g., getting grants, proposing restoration work).

In our experience as teachers, if the science curriculum allows students to pursue questions of their interest and to use means for producing representations (instruments, camera, discourse) of their own choice, disinterest and exclusion, which are characteristic of traditional science courses, seldom become an issue. Framing their research agendas, having control over their research questions and the form of the representations, students articulated what they have learned in a great variety of ways. One student, Magda, described the project as follows:

> We are studying Henderson Creek to find out about what water and creatures are like at the different sites. One of the things we are trying to find out is the quality of the water. The water quality determines what creatures live there. The quality depends on the depth, the width, the bottom (whether it is sandy, rocky, or gravelly), the temperature and the speed of the current. We will take samples of the creatures and then the next day count them and look at them under a microscope. We will make graphs displaying all the different information we got. There will be professors there with us to help us and tell us how to do it.

Another student, Kathy, and her teammates conducted a series of interviews to find out "what the community thinks." They interviewed the mayor of Oceanside; the coordinator of Henderson Creek Project Meagan McDonald; a WSÁNEC' elder; and other community members. They transcribed and analyzed the interviews, and the transcriptions were subsequently made public at the open house.

> Kathy: Has it been just the last ten years that the fish have been dying off?
> Meagan: Actually, it has been the last fifty years that the cutthroat trout have declined in size, in range, and in numbers. So there is still a dwindling population of fish, but they are not as healthy as they were or should be.
> Kathy: Did people ever fish in Henderson Creek?
> Meagan: Yes, they did. We know that because of the anecdotal information and first-nation history. The last time people really fished there was around thirty to forty years ago. It was the settlers and First Nations people who fished there.
> Kathy: What polluted Henderson Creek?
> Meagan: There used to be a large wetland area in the middle of the Henderson Creek watershed that was drained in the late 1800s, then converted to ditches. So in that loss of the habitat from the draining, the gradual decline in water quality from things like

losing the tree cover, the water temperatures would increase because there was not enough shade for the water.

We do not think of scientific literacy as not something that is taught
to Kathy by Meagan. Rather, in this instance scientific literacy arises
from the order of interaction, the relation between questions and answers. Such participation allows change, over the course of the interview and in subsequent moments of interviews involving other
people. Here, Meagan's answers, which allowed a historical perspective
on the problems of Henderson Creek to emerge, were occasioned by
Kathy's informed questions. It is the interview situation, in the context
of the children's Henderson Creek projects, that allowed a scientifically
literate conversation to appear rather than chitchat about some other
topic.

Gabe, an aboriginal student from the local W̱SÁNEC' reservation,
who hardly engaged in any school-related task in his other classes, did
not want to work within a peer group. He was not interested in conducting investigations as others did. However, he was interested in
working with a video camera to document the activities of others and
to interview them about their investigations while they were actually
collecting or analyzing data.

> Gabe: Can you talk about your observations?
> Nicole: Right now, we are taking the moisture and pH of the soil in dif-
> ferent locations.
> Liza: And we are trying to find out whether it is any different when we
> are going through the plants.
> Nicole: Yeah, and we are looking at the bugs and stuff as well. We are hav-
> ing a good time.

Mr. Goulet, the parent of a female student enjoyed the project activities and requested to come along on every field trip. He did not consider his task as one of supervising and watching out for children but
one of scaffolding student investigations. We talked to him about the
importance of letting students frame goals and of asking productive
questions that led to further inquiry rather than to definite answers.
Subsequently, he took every possible occasion as a starting point for
allowing students to learn. For example, he worked with a group of
boys who had decided that they would find out the relationship between the cross-section and speed of the water. He questioned the
boys, attempting to assist them in coming up with creative means for
measuring the depth and width of the creek because it was too deep to
step into it, let alone cross it. He actively participated in measuring the
depth of the stream, swollen by the recent winter storms. Ultimately,
the group decided to measure the width of the creek by tying a piece of

wood at the end of a string and launching it to the other side of the creek. By pulling, they brought the piece of wood to lie on the bank, which allowed them to mark the string at their own side. They measured the length of string between the mark and the end of the string after the wood had been pulled across. The fact that the wood had floated gave rise to a "teachable moment" about the topic of density.

> Goulet: Why did it float instead of sinking?
> John: Like, this one is too big but if it was smaller . . .
> Goulet: It would have sunk?
> John: Yeah, but if it was heavier, then it would have sunk.
> Goulet: Right, so how would you figure out whether that would sink or not?
> Tim: We'll say, this will generally sink.
> Goulet: What would be a way to find out? Why would this [hammer] sink?
> Tim: Because this is more compact in weight.
> Goulet: So, if I compare this to the same amount of water, it would be heavier. So?
> John: It would sink.

Here, in the context of Mr. Goulet's questions to John and Tim, a conversation about sinking and floating emerged. The transcript shows that a qualitative theory involving the notions of "compactness" in weight and relative weight to water came to explain sinking and floating. Here again, scientific literacy characterizes the situation and might not have been observable if aspects of the situation had been changed (e.g., written test about density).

### Reporting to the Community

Given the different tools that the children had used to conduct investigations and construct their representations, the variety of the displays came as no surprise. There were maps, photographs, drawings of invertebrate organisms, instruments, tools, live invertebrates and microscopes to view them, larger organisms in a glass tank, interview transcripts, and a variety of scientific representations (graphs, histograms [e.g., Figure 7.4]). The type of representations used was little different from those used in the various exhibits by the environmental activists. That is, the children's representations were a reflection of those that are characteristically used in a community-based science. We provide several brief descriptions and transcripts to articulate scientific literacy in the community involving children.

Michelle and her three (female) teammates had been interested more in qualitative than in quantitative representations of the creek. For example, one of their projects involved a tape recorder, used to re-

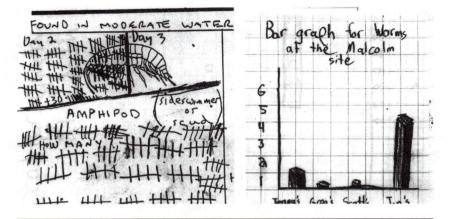

**Fig. 7.4** Records kept by one student group on the number of amphipods at one research site (left); comparison, made by one student group, of the number of worms based on the measurements collected by their own and three other groups.

cord verbal descriptions of several sites along the creek (including the ones represented in Figures 2.5, 7.1), and a camera for saliently depicting some issue identified by the girls. Accordingly, their exhibit contained many photographs, exemplifying, for example, the differences between where the creek had been turned into a ditch and where it was in a natural state. The work they had conducted in the field was represented in narrative form. The following explanation is characteristic of the information provided as results from her research, depicted in Figure 7.1.

> There were no fish in the ditches, just some little bugs, but no fish. But in the creek, in Centennial Park, there were cutthroat trout and stickleback. And the creek is much cleaner, because the ditch is next to the road. And people who are driving by are dumping garbage into the ditch, out of their cars and as they are walking by. So we found much more garbage, like we found pop cans, drinking things from McDonalds', French-fry cases, and things like that.

An important aspect of the open house was that students came to interact with visitors of all ages. The interactions between the seventh-grade students and children younger than themselves were as involved as interactions with adult visitors. In every situation, aspects of scientific literacy emerged in often unexpected and surprising ways. Thus, in his regular classes, Chris interacted very little with his peers. They saw in him a "computer nerd." Teachers often found it difficult to work with him, to get and keep Chris on task, or to get him to achieve to his potential. Chris thrived in the science unit, where he built a web site using his own and other's photos and texts.

During the open house, there were many interactions involving Chris that allowed scientific literacy to become visible. It is in and through the interaction that the adult in the following exchange comes to use the stereo microscope properly and to see an entity as arthropod rather than as a mosquito larvae.

> Adult: Have you got any insects?
> Chris: Yeah, yeah. But don't move it [glass container under microscope] around so much because I got it focused.
> Adult: (*Approaches microscope.*) You got it focused?
> Chris: Yeah. (*Adult only views through one lens of the two-lens stereomicroscope.*) You can look through both. Then you can see them better.
> Adult: What's these little ones in here? Are these mosquito larvae?
> Chris: No, there are no mosquito larvae in there.
> Adult: You see the little ones? (*Points toward glass.*)
> Chris: Yeah, the little ones that are swimming around, those are arthropods. They like to swim on the side first. They are neat critters.
> Adult: Yeah, and that is what the trout feed on?
> Chris: Well, I guess.
> Adult: (*Looks at drawings on display [similar to Figure 7.4, left], points to one.*) Oh, this is what fly larvae look like. Thanks.

This transcript exhibits the choreography of an interaction in which Chris contributed in a significant way to produce the appearance of scientific literacy rather than its opposite, the scientific ignorance others seem to detect in the general population. In this situation, Chris's participation in a community-based event provided opportunities for others to learn, and therefore to enter knowledge and representations produced in the school context into the community. At the outset, it is Chris who is more familiar with the creek and the animal life that can be found there. Then, the adult comes to understand increasingly not only what the students had done but also learns to distinguish different organisms. In this interaction, the adult found out that the students had not found the mosquito larvae that he thought to exist in the creek. In this finding out, a small fact produced by the actions of seventh-grade students had found its way back into the community.

In another situation, Jodie came to interact with Miles Magee, one of the co-founders of the Henderson Creek Project and one of the protagonists that readers already encountered in Chapter 3. Unbeknownst to Jodie, Miles Magee is a political scientist living in the community interested in assisting local people in empowering themselves concerning the environmental health of their community. Miles was very interested in the outcomes of the students' investigations and interacted with a number of them. In one instance, he asked Jodie about the colorimeter on exhibition, the same type of instrument that the summer work-study students have been using in order to conduct and produce water quality assessments (Chapter 2). In the course of their interaction, knowledgeability relating to a particular instrument and its operation was being produced.

> Miles: What is this?
>
> Jodie: A colorimeter. It measures the clarity of the water.
>
> Miles: Ah! A colorimeter?
>
> Jodie: You take the clear water and you put it in this glass and then, here, (*Puts it into instrument. Then pushes a few buttons.*) you take the standard, which is, like, the best there is. And then you switch this (*Takes different bottle.*) and put the one with the water from the creek. (*Covers sample.*) And then you scan the sample. And then you see what the things floating in the water are.
>
> Miles: Over-range, what does that mean?
>
> Jodie: (*Pushes a number of buttons.*)
>
> Miles: Oh, it is when it is over the range, I see.
>
> Jodie: First I have to do the standard again. (*Does standard.*) Then I take the creek water. (*Enters bottle into instrument. Pushes buttons.*)
>
> Miles: Oh, I see. This is really neat.

This interaction did not lead to a contrast between an all-knowing adult (expert) and a child; there was no belittling. Rather, the conversation involving Miles and Jodie allowed the articulation of an honest request for understanding and an illustration of the operation of the device. Scientific and technological literacy emerged from the dialectic tension between a request for information and the production of an answer in the form of a demonstration.

### *"Measures" of "Success"*

Enacting science in the community presents severe problems for assessment, especially when task orientation is replaced by a non-Western social orientation. For example, one group of Austrian students regarded the formal school assessment as a devaluation of the environmental work that they had done. Their own assessment criteria were based on real-life (rather than school-oriented) evaluation, as they had encountered them while dealing with the people in the community. The interactions at the open house involving students, activists, and community members not only led to the emergence of scientific literacy but also to the emergence of the legitimacy of the children's activities. From the perspective of the environmental activists, the children had contributed in a significant way to the success of the open house by contributing to its content and by being a drawing factor—the children's presence encouraged the participation of many parents and relatives alike. That is, the activists recognized the contributions of the seventh-grade students as the outcome of a legitimate activity of the type that they had called for in the (earlier quoted) newspaper article. The results of the students' investigations were mentioned in a Web publication and in a community newspaper article.

> The goal of the [Oceanside School] study was to determine the health of the benthic invertebrate community at three different sites, provide information to the community about the health of [Henderson] Creek, and provide students from [Oceanside] School a focus for ecological research and hands-on exposure to stream ecosystems. Preliminary data loosely suggests the site just below Centennial Park . . . was the healthiest. Further studies are required for more quantitative data than was gathered on these days. Overall, the study was highly successful in terms of the education and experience it provided to the school children and their parents. It also provided a general indication of the health of the various sites. The class also participated in the Henderson Creek Open House held in April and has set up a web site on their work in Henderson Creek. Other classes at [Oceanside] School, as well as other schools, are keen to begin similar initiatives or activities around Henderson Creek. (Web site)

> When it comes to the [Henderson] Creek-KENNES watershed Project, [Meagan McDonald] says, it's the people who will have to make the difference. . . . The open houses will have numerous exhibits including . . . a display by [Oceanside] Middle School Grade 7s on their invertebrae work done in [Henderson] Creek. . . . "What we want to see happen is that the community embraces the concept of a healthy watershed and takes it on themselves," she said Sunday from the banks of [Henderson] Creek, adding that water quality decline and habitat loss in local streams has severely influenced the range, numbers, and size of trout over the past several years. . . . For the past two months, [McDonald] has been working with students at [Oceanside] Middle School in an ambitious attempt to identify and count invertebrae—another barometer of water quality—at various sites on the Peninsula. Early results show the section of stream below [name] Park in Oceanside is in the best shape. (Community newspaper)

These publications, which emphasized the contribution of the children's work to the overall project of environmental health in the Henderson Creek watershed, further underscored the legitimacy of the activity. When considered in terms of "legitimate peripheral participation," the children contributed in more than marginal ways to knowing and learning available in their community about environmental health.

In the experiences of the children, the interactions in and with the community played an important role. When asked to reflect about what they had done and learned, many children spontaneously talked and wrote about the relation between community and their own activities.

> I worked very hard on the map and proceedings. During this course I learned about fieldwork: I learned how to collect samples of the creek and take temperatures and speed. I also did some work with the community. It taught me about working with others and working in the community. I noticed that ever since our Henderson Creek article was published in the . . . *News Review* that the public has begun to notice the creek. (Sally)

> In the Henderson Creek group the work that I have done and helped with includes: Worked on the model of the creek, typed out the descriptions of the sites with help from Davie, Brandon, and Steve cut them out. I was at the cultural center. What I've learned from all this is about the problem of the creek, how to work with the public [community]. The thing I learned was how much other people knew about Henderson Creek. Like Mr. Herbert as the Mayor of Oceanside he knew lots about it. How to work productively and still have fun with your friends. How to use special equipment like "D" nets, microscopes, colorimeter and all sorts of things. (Jodie)

Sally had noticed that the above-mentioned newspaper article had led community members ("the public") to notice the creek which some (including teachers) did not even know to exist. Sally's comment may also imply how important the newspaper article was to the gratification she (and her peers) received from being acknowledged in a public forum and therefore a legitimate contributor to the social life of the community. Jamie's comment also addresses his emergent awareness of existing knowledge and expresses a certain amount of pride in being able to participate in the use of scientific equipment.

## BEYOND PROPAEDEUTICS: SCIENTIFIC EDUCATION AS/FOR COMMUNITY-ORIENTED PRAXIS

A central fallacy of traditional science education is its focus on laboratory science as the touchstone against which science teaching and learning should be compared. Such approaches teach students to see the world with the eyes of science rather than to build their own view of the world; it encourages students to become conformist rather than autonomous. Research among community and health activists overwhelmingly shows that other forms of knowing and relating to the world can contribute to the resolution of urgent problems. Thus, it was through the interactions with and contributions by AIDS activists that the traditional scientific protocols for testing new drugs, double-blind treatment control studies, were changed into new, previously unacceptable forms of testing drugs.

### From School- to Community-Based Science

In the present chapter, we have described how students pursued investigations of their interest, drawing on those tools that best responded to their (intellectual, motivational) needs, and produced a large variety of representations of stream and watershed health. Our systems view focuses on *motivations, objects, tools,* and *subjects* in different activity systems, our research results highlights similarities between some everyday out-of-school activities and those of schoolchildren who constructed knowledge about the health of a stream. By contributing to an open house, dutifully reported in the local newspaper, and by displaying the results of their investigations, the children became legitimate participants in the (adult-oriented) social life of their community. In turn, community members—including activists, biologists, aboriginal elders, peer coaches, teachers, parents, and ourselves—participated in children's activities creating situations that led to the emergence of scientific literacy as outcomes of collective activity systems.

The work in the middle school shows that children can participate in activities with similar motivations as those of adults, and they can participate in a variety of forms of conversations with adults other than the regular teachers. These conversations therefore broke the mold of normal modes of schooling, opening up the possibility for lifelong participation in such activities and therefore the possibility for lifelong learning without the discontinuities that characterize the transition from formal schooling to other aspects of life. If the motivation underlying school science and environmental activism, stewardship, or volunteerism are similar, based on the nature of tools, rules, divisions of labor, and community, we can expect individuals (subjects) to move along trajectories that do not exhibit discontinuities characteristic of other transitions. Children who participate in activities that contribute to the knowledge available in their community will develop into adolescents and adults, continuing to participate in the activities relating to environmental health. The possibility for such transitions is clearly indicated by different situational organization that foster the participation of students and non-students alike. For example, as a result of our work in the schools, middle and high school students conducted investigations related to science fairs. As part of their career preparation some local high school students choose to participate in Streamkeepers, a program fostering the recovery and restoration of ecosystems, and open to any individual or group. Three national youth teams worked together one summer to help the Henderson Creek Project to improve the watershed by moving native plants before clearing

11,000 square meters for a pond and wetlands that will help improve the water quality in the area. High school and university students contribute to the data collection as part of funded summer work projects. Masters students at the local university become key people in constructing community surveys to yield multilayered (Geographical Information System) representations, involving maps that display groundcover (vegetation), surficial geology, soil, aquifers, topological, and present land-use (housing, zoning, or cadastral) information.

Redefining science education as citizen science, which involves participation in the political life of the community, and redefining scientific literacy as process and outcome of collective praxis may come with considerable political consequences. Thus, when students construct facts not only about environmental pollution but also begin naming and publishing the names of individuals, groups, and companies that perpetuate it, communities will begin to change. For example, one middle school student, Graeme, not directly participating but interested in our project researched the amount of coliform bacteria, a biological contaminant, in various parts of the stream. Facilitated by our research team, he accessed a variety of university laboratories that allowed him to test the water samples he had collected in different parts of the stream. He presented his results not only at the school and regional science fairs but also during the open house organized by the Henderson Creek Project. His report specifies particular sites of pollution and names the farms that contributed significantly to the contaminant levels.

> There is the chicken farm. It [375 coliform count] shows that because of agricultural use right above the test site, there is a lot of coliform in the water. But you are not allowed to do a test. But at the Geoffrey farm, I found 500 coliform per mil, which was way above what it should have been, compared to what happened at the mouth of Graham. So what I am guessing is that somewhere between the mouth of Graham and the farm of the Geoffrey's, there is a lot of extra coliform that gets into the waters that causes the high numbers.

Graeme concluded that the chicken farm and Geoffrey's farm were major contributors to coliform counts. Whereas we have no indication that the farmers objected (we do not know what Graeme meant by "you are not allowed to do a test"), the contribution of children to a community's knowledge resources, and the potential implications for political pressure on farmers and industrialists to change their current practices is evident. His research has become part of a political struggle for changing some farming-related practices in the community that have, in the past, resulted in contaminating Henderson Creek. But

Graeme's participation in community affairs shows the potential of young citizens to make contributions to the community with political and even economic implications. We know from one colleague, Jacques Désautels, that there are science teachers in the city of Québec, for example, whose eleventh-grade (16- and 17-year-old) students sample rivers and creeks to determine the levels of contaminants and then publicize the names of polluters; the same teachers have students who develop expertise related to reproduction, genetics, and health and then teach young women (mothers) living "across the track" about birth control and reproductive health. Again, these are political acts by students that already contribute to making this a better society.

Rather than direct participation, some science educators propose school-based mock activities, such as the consensus project model designed to empower student to deal with science and scientific experts on emerging socio-scientific issues by providing students with experiences, knowledge, skills, and attitudes. Such projects are laudable because the point of departure is not a scientific topic but some controversial real-world socio-scientific issue. Furthermore, this model highlights the search for collectively achieved solutions and the potential contributions of science in the face of controversial problems. However, we see two major problems with this approach. First, enacting consensus projects in school classrooms reproduces existing separations between school and everyday society; the processes and outcomes of the consensus projects are evaluated in terms of school objectives rather than in terms of their contribution to community life. The students have to *play* the roles of scientists, environmental activists, or local residents in a pretend activity rather than taking a place in community life more generally. Second, such models assume that what is learned during school-oriented pretend activity is somehow transferred to everyday knowing, which is a highly questionable assumption.

Teachers are often held to connect or to assist students in connecting school science to their everyday lives; but teachers experience difficulties in assisting students to make such connections. Even if such connections exist (e.g., in simulated problem contexts), the problem-solving activity may still be unrelated. The solution to build bridges (connect) between formal academic discourse and everyday life remains fraught by the presence of the gap between in- and after-school experiences. Rather than pursuing the making of connections, educators could involve students in the real thing. There is no gap if the students' activities already constitute an aspect of everyday out-of-school activity. That is, this new science education transcends traditional propaedeutic approaches that attempted to *prepare* students for subsequent levels of schooling and life after school, and provides students with opportunities to engage in everyday (relevant) activities that shape community and their own identities alike. The point is one of going about engaging in and contributing to the solutions of everyday-life contentious issues rather than making connections to bridge an artificial divide.

Based on our research of science in and for the community, we propose a different way of approaching science and science education, a way that acknowledges the limitations of science—which does not mean that scientific efforts become undervalued. Acknowledging the nature of science as it is and can be practiced in the community opens the door to richer understandings of science as a creative and perhaps imaginative activity, mediated by honesty in the face of agreed-upon evidence. It also allows us to see the role of power, knowledge, and position; and it allows us to understand the dynamic of margin and center. Such an approach permits groups and communities to enact different relations between scientific and other forms of knowledge, including various forms of situated knowing (e.g., traditional, relational). Rather than privileging disciplinary science, we ought to foster situations that allow the negotiation of different forms of knowledge geared to particular (controversial) problems as these arise in the daily life of a community.

### *Learning in Community-Based Activity*

Research falling under the umbrella of "situated cognition" generally shows that school knowledge has little if any bearing on everyday practice; performance of everyday mathematics, for example, is often unrelated to the amount or quality of school mathematics an individual was exposed to. It should not come as a surprise, then, that for many students, the knowledge taught in school—used as a commodity to be traded for grades and for getting ahead—is not very compelling. Teaching a small set of key scientific concepts and theories—often incompatible with everyday knowing and common sense—in better ways does not significantly change the situation.[7] When students begin to participate in "citizen science," they enter multiple relations, situations through which science is enacted in the community. This is a better science education as it familiarizes students with science practice and allows them to participate in the many relations that science is actually involved in. A systems view is a good way of articulating learning situations because it is both structured and allows for historicity and fluctuation.

We view knowing and learning as aspects of culturally and historically situated, collective activity, including the dimensions of power/

knowledge and margin/center. Learning is discernable by noticing self and others' changing participation in changing social practices. It is discernable from the particular relationships that they have achieved with others in their community at large. Because interaction and participation cannot be understood as the sum total of an individual acting toward a stable environment, learning cannot be understood in terms of what happens to individuals. Rather, if learning is situated and distributed, educators must focus on enabling changing participation, that is, enabling new forms of societal activity that is collectively generated. We are therefore particularly interested in forms of participation that are continuous with out-of-school experiences and have the potential to lead to lifelong learning rather than to discontinuities between formal and informal learning settings.

Participation in community life provides new opportunities for changing participation, that is, learning. These opportunities arise from the engagement in collective activities, which are more advanced than activities engaged in individually. Participation in collective activity therefore means participation in activity more advanced than what the individual could achieve. But participation in something that is beyond what we could do individually provides an opportunity to learn. The difference between what an individual can do on his or her own has come to be known as the "zone of proximal development." Our work allows us to rethink the "zone of proximal development" as it relates to conversation as activity and scientific literacy. Subject-object relations are understood as being, among others, mediated by society. Concrete individual actions are a subset of actions generally available to society. The zone of proximal development, then, describes the difference between everyday individual actions and collectively created historically new forms of societal activity. That is, the different conversations in which our students engage (e.g., during open house or public meeting) constitute zones of proximal development that allow collective bodies to produce and further develop scientific literacy. Students, whether they attend middle or high school, or work in the community as part of their summer jobs, can already participate in these conversations. Such participation could continue, without experienced discontinuities, when they move on to different levels of schooling, take on jobs in the community, or participate as laypersons in a variety of environmental issues at the local, national, or global level (e.g., as members of Greenpeace or Doctors without Borders).

In the approach outlined here, science and scientific literacy for the students constitute the praxis and outcome of a lived curriculum. Rather than studying to be admitted to higher levels of learning (science as propaedeutic) students actively participated in the social life of their community by contributing to the available database on the health of one local stream. For these students, science was a lived curriculum, in which students, as Paul deHart Hurd ones expressed it, "have a feeling that they are involved in their own development and recognize that they can use what they learn. This venture in science curriculum development recognizes the socialization of science and its relevance to how science impacts our culture, our lives, and the course of our democracy."[8] A lived science curriculum requires a collective endeavor involving not only science but also disciplinary knowledge in the social sciences, humanities, ethics, law, and political science. However, an interdisciplinary approach, which gives science an epistemologically equal place among rather than an epistemologically exceptional status, does not necessarily lead to a different science education. Hurd continued by listing specific social, cognitive, and personal concepts that each individual has to acquire. We disagree with this approach because it goes against our commitment to truly democratic forms of education (not in the sense of serving capitalist interests) that allow individual members to develop their own representations of salient issues.

# 8

## DANGEROUS TEACHING

### *Using Science as Tool and Context to Work for Social Justice*

Shagufta looked around the dark, quiet room as if to ensure that no one else was listening, then turned to us and began to describe her route to becoming a teacher. Her story, told partly in Urdu and partly in English, was offered in a hushed voice. She spoke quickly but deliberately about growing up in poverty in urban Pakistan. With no money or social support to further her education beyond tenth grade, Shagufta enrolled in night courses to become a teacher. Pausing as other teachers and students walked down the hallway outside the room, Shagufta talked about how her attendance at night school led her to be ostracized by her community for being a "woman of the night."

Shagufta, twenty-three, unmarried, and a daughter of working poor parents, is part of an extremely small percentage of Pakistani women who move from working poor families into professional or semiprofessional occupations. As we detail later in this chapter, Shagufta's move into teaching was a lonely, difficult experience, but one that she believed was important for herself and her community. She believes it is her responsibility to help other poor children in her country gain the kind of education they will need to challenge the social and economic norms that shape their lives. Since completing her teaching coursework, Shagufta has taken a full-time position teaching fifth grade in an impoverished community. Shagufta cherishes her role as teacher. She believes that she has a responsibility—indeed, a moral obligation—to help her own working class, orphaned and impoverished students use schooling as a road out of poverty. However, she also believes that she must help her students to improve their lives (and the conditions which frame those lives), regardless of whether they move out of poverty or not. Shagufta is required by her school's administration to prepare her students for national exams that most will never take (because they will leave school before the grade in which exams are administered), but which are required for students to move on to high school. Shagufta, however, teaches with much broader goals in mind. She works to cover the national curriculum, while at the same time foregrounding health, environmental issues, and literacy skills. Engaging students in critically examining and acting upon these issues is the core of her teaching practice.

We begin this chapter with a short introduction to Shagufta's experiences as a teacher because they raise questions about the purposes and goals of science education in communities where forms of scientific literacy are literally issues of life and death. There is no room in the lives of Shagufta's students for science teaching to be about only the acquisition of knowledge. Yet, as Shagufta's story about national exams suggests, there is no room for it to be otherwise. It is a catch-22 for students in poverty.

For the children living in shelters in the United States or the farmers and First Nations surrounding Henderson Creek, science is a highly political process, because it involves not simply engagement with subject matter (as policymakers would have us believe). It involves efforts to actively transform power relations that position people in poverty on the margins. In Chapters 4 and 5, we explored how power relations, science and individuals are transformed when youth engage in a science practice of their own making. In Chapters 6 and 7, we saw seventh-grade students participating in and contributing to their community by studying a creek and reporting results to the wider public during a two-day open-house event organized by environmentalists. In the example of Graeme in that instance and of the community garden created by homeless inner-city youth in a precious case, we saw the participation of youth was a political act. Such acts have ramifications for the teachers of such youth. In this chapter, we explore how such a radical political stance in science education is a dangerous, but wholly necessary, stance for teachers to take with their students.

### Dangerous Teaching
Derek Hodson makes the case that science education must be framed in sociopolitical terms if the science education community is to be successful in promoting a *critically* scientifically literate and socially

just global society.[1] A major component of this framing is viewing and enacting science teaching as a political act. That is, not only are the inner-city youth who are turning an empty lot into a garden, and students who research a creek to report their findings at an environmentalist event participating in the politics of science-related knowledge-power, but also their teachers engage in political acts. Science teaching must educate youths about the connection between sociocultural and scientific aspects of life, and it must provide opportunities for youth to participate in a practice of science in genuine social contexts:

> Those who translate concern into action are those who have a deep personal understanding of the issues (and their human and environmental implications) and feel a personal investment in addressing and solving the problems. Those who act are those who feel personally empowered to effect change, who feel that they can make a difference, and know how to do so. The school science curriculum has to play a much more overt role in assisting this transition. It is not enough for students to learn that science and technology are influenced by social, political, and economic forces; they also need to learn how to participate, and they need to experience participation. It is not enough for students to be armchair critics! What I am arguing here is that education for critical scientific literacy is inextricably linked with education for political literacy and with the ideology of education as social reconstruction.[2]

Not many researchers in science education have written about the consequences, both for good and for bad, of enacting a critical scientific literacy in school classrooms, where learning science is also a political endeavor oriented to bring about social change. However, those who have, by and large, report that this a difficult task for it raises a complex host of issues ranging from student, administrator, or parental resistance that emerges when such goals differ from the normative practices of schooling to the community empowerment and transformation that results when such a practice takes off![3] In the case of the lot transformation project, we saw how extended discourses with "outsiders" opened up questions about what was fair and real.

Margery Osborne, a teacher researcher of early elementary science, uses the phrase dangerous teaching to capture these and other consequences of enacting science teaching as a political act, for such practices often leave teachers and students in uncharted waters:

> I use the descriptor "dangerous" to capture the feelings that I have as I enact such teaching. . . . In effect to enact a "liberatory" or "democratic" education, the tension between the goals and the multiplicity of their manifestations must be maintained, the essence of a democratic education is to be dangerous if such an education is defined as enabling both

individual, group and societal reconstruction because this happens through constructing spaces where differences can be confronted. Maintaining the goals in a state of tension, living with the danger, falls to the teacher and defines much of the teacher's role in such a classroom. . . . I would argue that in order to serve my goals I must maintain this tension, generate these conflicts. And in my classes, I cannot act to resolve or suppress them.[4]

When science reform documents provide guidance only as to the content, process skills, and habits of mind that *must* be covered by the curriculum, how do teachers (or students, parents, and teacher educators) know what to do when the rest of the students' (and teacher's) worlds becomes a part of (rather than apart from) science? When science teaching moves away from singular constructions of understanding content and skills to a complex range of ways in which understanding intersects with ways of being in the world, new territory that is often difficult to navigate is opened up. Margery Osborne tells us that children, youth, and teachers use the disciplinary setting of science to construct not only scientific understandings, but also creative constructions of themselves, their voices, beliefs, goals, and ways of acting, without regard to established or "correct" ways of thinking in science; they witness others doing likewise in ways that diverge from their own; they learn the canon of a particular discipline; and, finally, they locate themselves in relation to that canon and the larger society. That is, as we pointed out in the previous two chapters, students not only produce material outcomes and knowledgeability but also, concurrently, their identities. Locating one's identity in relation to society potentially involves self- and societal critique. This territory is difficult to navigate because it relies on the unknown, or children's complete and complex set of lived experiences (not just those that tie neatly to science) for which teachers often cannot prepare. Likewise, it relies on self- and societal critique as a way of situating constructions of science alongside constructions of self (identity), a process that brings to relief the personal-subjective and political nature of science. Dangerous teaching is filled with tension among the many players in an educational setting: students, parents, teachers, administrators, schools, curricula, standardized tests, the local and national communities, the communities of practice of the various disciplines under study, and others.

Yet, dangerous teaching is what Shagufta feels compelled to do because the lives and worlds of her students and their communities are at stake. Indeed, science teaching as a political endeavor can be dangerous—for teachers and students as they construct new ways of being together and understanding each other, for schools and communities who have to reckon with teachers and youth who are empowered to use science for the better, and for policymakers and education leaders who may be asked, for example, to justify the importance of an end-of-year exam over a community-changing project.

We begin this chapter with a brief discussion of how enacting science teaching as a political act is both an opportunity to begin to build a more just society *and* a dangerous activity because this tension between opportunity and danger frames, quite vividly, the experiences of Shagufta and two of her colleagues, Haleema and Ms. Faizah. Indeed, our research with teachers in urban Pakistan reveals the opportunities for community transformation and empowerment at the core of their work with poor urban youth. Their experiences also demonstrate the dangers associated with challenging the political norms of women's work (teachers as keepers of traditions) and the place of poor urban youth in society (passively accepting unlivable conditions and thereby supporting the hegemony of the dominant [middle-class] culture). Yet, our work with these teachers reveals that the dangers associated with this practice seem to weigh greatly on these women. Teaching science as a political act traverses the borders of school. Doing science is stretched across people and contexts—it requires, as many of our chapters here show, both being in the community and the participation of the community. This stance on teaching entails quite a practical element of the dangerous work in which they engage. Taking such a radical, political stance places them at risk in their schools, their communities, and in their society—although the three women in our study feel compelled to take this stance. We have much to learn from these teachers: how they frame science teaching as a political act and how they negotiate such efforts in their own social, cultural, and political contexts.

## LEARNING FROM THREE DANGEROUS WOMEN THROUGH LIFE HISTORIES

The three teachers whose stories are told in this chapter taught in the same large urban area in eastern Pakistan. One of the teachers worked in a school that served poor children and with an overall curricular focus on human rights and children's whole lives, one was a headmistress in the same charity school system, and the third teacher taught in a teaching school that was not certified by the national government because of its progressive orientation. All three were female, spoke either Punjabi or Urdu as their first language, and selected teaching because it was one of the few career options open to women in their social class. The three women also believed they could make a difference in their community because of the strategic location of their position as teachers. One of the teachers came from an extremely impoverished background while the other two came from working class (but not extremely impoverished) backgrounds. The teachers ranged in teaching experience from two years to ten years and in age from their early twenties to their mid-forties.

We got to know all three of the teachers quite well over the course of two years, 1999–2001, through a narrative life history approach. We selected that approach for several important reasons. Narrative understandings of self—and the ways in which they allow us to understand the nature and meaning of individuals' knowledge, beliefs, and prior experiences—are important because such narratives are the form in which individuals understand themselves.[5] Narrative life history also allows us to understand beliefs, knowledge, and experiences as interconnected and interrelated systems, rather than as isolated fragments. This systemic view allows for a more accurate representation of the way in which individuals construct, maintain, evaluate, and change their understandings of themselves and their contexts. As a result, teachers' narratives about science teaching incorporate their knowledge, beliefs, and prior experience and frame and guide teachers' interpretations and implementations of what it means to teach science to children living in urban poverty.

Gathering the stories of these three remarkable women has been a thought-provoking and challenging experience as we have worked to generate better understandings of the teachers' lives; what they do with their students and their communities in the name of science; of education, and of empowerment; and why they are compelled to engage in such dangerous practices. It has also been a challenging experience research-wise, figuring out the best ways to communicate across language and cultures and finding ways to reach the teachers in their communities in a country with strict regulations regarding social relations and political action, and poor political relations with the United States (where Angie is a citizen). Although we are a purposefully diverse research team, we worked hard to overcome the obstacles that have framed our work. Our team consisted of: a white, female U.S. university researcher and teacher educator not fluent in Urdu (Angie), a Nepalese male who is a doctoral student at a U.S. institution and fluent in Urdu (Bhaskar), and a Pakistani female, teacher educator who is a member of the Pakistani professional class and fluent in Urdu and semi-fluent in Punjabi (Rubina). Though Angie and Bhaskar are not Pakistani, both were quite familiar with the customs and peoples, as they have both studied about and visited Pakistan before. Although we believe we built positive and trusting relationships with the women in our study, we knew at times, that we struggled with overcoming insti-tutionalized power relationships. At times, sharing with Angie was impeded by language and culture—although all of the teachers in our study spoke English as a second language (the national language of instruction in science in Pakistan), it was sometimes easier for one of the teachers in our study to communicate their experiences and ideas in Urdu or Punjabi. Additionally, Angie represented a wealthy country (U.S.), which had levied heavy sanctions on Pakistan during the time of the study. (Those sanctions were widely viewed in Pakistan as unfair and imperialistic.) Rubina, although Pakistani and sharing many of the customs with the women in our study, comes from a social class that has more control and power than the social classes where the three teachers come from. Rubina also was a teacher educator who provided support and guidance to some of the teachers in our study. Bhaskar, though fluent in Urdu and from a neighboring country, was male, and there were some things the women teachers just did not want to talk about with him. To build trust and to accommodate these differences in lived experiences, we spent time with the teachers together and alone, sharing and reflecting upon our experiences, as we understood them. We believe that our differences allowed us to see and understand the teachers' stories differently, strengthening our analysis of the stories.

## MS. FAIZAH: BUILDING A COMMUNITY AND A SCHOOL
### *Starting a School: Building a Relationship with the Community*
Ms. Faizah is in her mid-forties and is a headmistress at a charity school for orphans. In urban Pakistan, schooling is tiered. From the top down: elite private schools, government schools, schools run by non-government organization (NGOs), other private schools, and charity schools. As the name implies, charity schools are essentially welfare institutions, supported largely by Pakistan-based NGOs, philanthropic individuals, and foreign not-for-profit organizations. Charity schools are generally viewed favorably, as they are often the only kind of school available for children in very poor communities. Although government schools do exist in the poor communities, attendance fees are usually too steep for most high-poverty families.[6] Ms.

Faizah's school is home to roughly two hundred children from an orphan village plus another one hundred or so children from the immediate neighborhood. Her school is open only to very poor families, and families are required to show an affidavit from the magistrate to prove that they earn less than the set threshold. Her reasons for wanting the affidavit are to ensure that families with money do not take advantage of the school and to make parents show some motivation regarding their children's education. In Ms. Faizah's mind, acquiring that affidavit proves their motivation. However, Ms. Faizah makes exceptions to her own rule: she has allowed children to attend her school without the affidavit when she knows that they are extremely poor and their parents do not have either the financial resources or the cultural capital to acquire the affidavit.

Ms. Faizah (Figure 8.1) has been the headmistress at the school since 1996, ever since the school has been founded. When the school first opened, Ms. Faizah went from door to door telling the families about her school. Some people in the neighborhood and in her own community (she does not live in the school's neighborhood) thought that she was "crazy" because of the reputation of the neighborhood. However, Ms. Faizah felt it was worth the risk. In fact, she reported that the majority of the parents (of the neighborhood children in her

**Fig. 8.1** Ms. Faizah (middle) with Angie and Bhaskar (right).

school) walk their children to school because the neighborhood is not safe. She regrets that these are the circumstances, but believes that the school can help to improve the safety of the area.

Initially, Ms. Faizah had to work to find ways to foster stronger relationships with the community. She viewed the school as a gathering place for the community, where residents could come together to learn and to solve the needs of the neighborhood collectively. Yet Ms. Faizah found herself struggling in two ways. First, the people in the community did not trust her or the school to fairly respond to their needs. Families in the neighborhood were afraid of the school because it represented something that could have power over them. Additionally, because the school was also an orphan school, Ms. Faizah feared that some members of the community would not want to have anything to do with it. The school would bring orphaned children to an already resource-strapped neighborhood. She felt that she had to take many small steps to gain their trust. She wanted the families in the community to know that she desired their trust not so that she could tell them what to do or how their community could be, but rather so that she could better respond to their needs. To this end, Ms. Faizah worked tirelessly: she held meetings for parents to visit the school, to offer suggestions, complaints, or questions. This was a radical step, for school leaders especially in poor communities generally are seen as much more powerful than those in the community. Her openness to suggestions and critique, though intended to level the power dynamics between school and community, also made Ms. Faizah more vulnerable as a female leader. On several occasions, Ms. Faizah has had to fight against a small group of men who felt as though she was not an effective leader because she did not "command authority."

Ms. Faizah also held special activities in the afternoon for any parents in the neighborhood, regardless of whether their children attended school. Slowly, Ms. Faizah gained the trust and the confidence of the community. After five years, the school now serves as a central meeting place for the community and provides leadership and resources for dealing with community concerns.

Ms. Faizah's method of gaining community trust is a very different orientation than one normally finds in high-poverty neighborhoods in Pakistan because, historically, schooling has been a way to separate the educated from the non-educated. Opening her doors in a way that blurred boundaries between the educated and non-educated potentially lowered her status in the educated community. Opening her doors also suggested a different orientation to the purposes of schooling and the importance of knowledge. The school was not going to tell

**Fig. 8.2** Workers at Ms. Faizah's unheated school try to keep warm.

the community how to be; rather, Ms. Faizah wanted to build a partnership to help the community with whatever its needs are. She was willing to take the risk of having her status challenged to build the kind of relationship she felt was necessary for her school.

### A Generational Change

Ms. Faizah's school is strapped for resources. Her school is neither heated nor air-conditioned. In the winter, when evening temperatures hover below zero Celsius, daytime highs barely reach 7 °C, students, teachers, and school workers dress in layers and find creative ways to keep themselves warm (Figure 8.2). Because of the limited resources, Ms. Faizah does not allow school-based materials to be taken home. Additionally, because she knows that many children in her school have to engage in some sort of labor following the school day, she has instituted a policy that students are never given homework. Her school day extends from eight A.M. to one P.M. each day because she wants to keep attendance high and to respect her teachers' need to return home to care for their families or to work. She also suspects that many students could never afford to take the whole day for school. However, she does hold Saturday classes, from nine A.M. to one P.M., to ensure additional time in school. Her goal is for all students to complete tenth grade (the final grade of high school in Pakistan) and to have the opportunity to take advanced training in either sewing (girls) or woodworking (boys) to ensure some economic independence and competitiveness once they are "released" by the orphanage.

Ms. Faizah operates her school almost exclusively through donations. She is not embarrassed to take used books or supplies and she has even been able to gather a small number of old computers. The school runs on a rudimentary power system, so the computers are kept in one location where there are electrical outlets. She has also been able to enlist the support of a local teaching school's faculty to provide professional development for her teaching staff at no charge. She was quite careful in this selection, too, as she wanted to be supported by teachers who are not afraid to do things differently. In fact, this teaching school is not government-sanctioned because it does not offer or support the state-mandated curriculum. In Ms. Faizah's mind, this is an added benefit because it shows that those who work there are willing to take risks.

The slums that surround her school are home to the poorest families in urban Pakistan, and remain one of Ms. Faizah's primary concerns. Because there is little economic support of physical infrastructure, the slums generally are overburdened with overcrowding and poor sanitation. Sewer and water are handled together in open systems, and there is no official garbage disposal system. Families make due by burning trash or dumping it in abandoned lots. Children's spaces for play are often limited to the streets or to trash yards (see Figure 8.3). Though parks exist in nearby communities, most require entrance fees. Though Ms. Faizah blames the government for a lack of compassion toward those in poverty, she understands what

**Fig. 8.3** A local trash yard where children play.

happens in slums as transpiring along a viscious cycle: families are extremely poor, and mortality rates among infants and children are extremely high (due to water- and food-borne illnesses, malnutrition, and a lack of medical access). Families tend to have many children because they need them to work and bring home money, and they cannot count on all of their children making it to an age when they can then help to support the family. These families do not enroll their children in school because it would take away from their labor. But without any education, children will never have an opportunity to advance. Even though there is almost no chance that these children move into the professional class, she feels that if they could at least become literate and learn a trade, they would help their families that much more. Many of the orphan children from her school come from these circumstances, and she uses her school to try to stop this vicious cycle in its track, one child at a time. Indeed, Ms. Faizah believes that awareness is an important key—children, parents, and communities need to be aware of the power of education, and they all need to become aware of how power works within their community.

Ms. Faizah sees her country in the midst of what she calls a "generational change." The younger generation, like most of the teachers she employs, value education, and see education as a way to break down the caste system. She fully supports this idea and wants to help get the children in the community where she works into a good position to take advantage of this shifting mentality. Ms. Faizah is adamant that real change will take economic investment by the government and outsiders because in the very poor slums parents "discourage children from school" because they need the children for labor.

### Role as a Headmistress

Ms. Faizah's role as the headmistress is pivotal in making connections between the school and the community. In terms of science education, in particular, Ms. Faizah works closely with her teachers to help them gather the resources that they need to teach science in ways that will be useful to the students in her school. Ms. Faizah's view of resources is broad, including material items, almost all of which she gets for free because they are used or donated, and social and human resources, in terms of drawing on the ideas, creativities, and experiences of the teachers in her school and of the parents in the community. This is a radical stance in and of itself. As Ms. Faizah reports, "one hundred percent of the parents [in the community] are uneducated because they are from lower class." Valuing experiences that are not in the purview of a formal education potentially sets up a new kind of relationship between parents and the school. At the very least, it helps to remove some of the negative stigma and low expectation associated with the uneducated.

Ms. Faizah requires all teachers in her school to teach science from kindergarten through tenth grade in both direct and indirect ways. She believes in an interdisciplinary approach to science and all subject-area learning. Ms. Faizah admits that most of her science teachers do not take as strongly a political stance as she does regarding the connections between science and the community. Ms. Faizah does not see her role as converting her teachers to this view, for she knows this is a very delicate subject. Rather, she sees her role as leading by example. She wants to educate her teachers while educating her students. If she can raise questions about science or children's abilities and futures, then perhaps her teachers will question as well. One example that supports this vision of Ms. Faizah's was her work with human rights. Ms. Faizah has worked with her staff to enact a curriculum oriented to human rights across the school grades. Although the human rights curriculum focuses more on issues like peace (antiviolence and tolerance) and helping others, Ms. Faizah believes that at least it opens up the question of human rights. It is in what teachers and children do beyond the state-sanctioned program that the real power lies. She sees the emphasis on human rights as deeply connected to how teachers think about teaching subject matter knowledge. She is most concerned about how human rights intersect with both literacy levels and understandings of health.

Ms. Faizah also believes that traditional school success, although it looks quite different from the human rights program, is just as important for transforming poor children's experiences because so much social power rests in an individual's ability to claim a certain level of educational attainment. She knows that high attainment levels are difficult for the students in her school because of the families' lack of resources and because of social norms, and breaking these barriers, she feels, is also an act of empowerment. Ms. Faizah acknowledges that nearly 100 percent of the orphan students in her school graduate from high school but only about half of the neighborhood students graduate because there is greater familial and social pressure on the neighborhood children to leave school for the labor force. The orphan children, on the other hand, are cared for by school workers and are expected to learn a trade by age eighteen, at which point they are released from the school.

Furthermore, she also has her students complete more traditional assignments like writing essays and drawings because she wants to enter them in local contests. She wants other headmasters and headmistresses to know that the children in her school are just as capable as anyone else. She believes that another part of her role is to educate others about the capabilities of poor children. If the education system is to change in Pakistan, then she has to do more than simply teach the children. She must teach those in power.

## SHAGUFTA: CHALLENGING AUTHORITY
### *Gaining an Education*

Shagufta (Figure 8.4) was twenty-three and teaching fifth grade in a charity school in Lahore, Pakistan, when we first met her. Shagufta stands out from her teacher peers for many reasons. Although Shagufta is quite young, she is albino, leaving her long hair white and her skin very pale. This stands in sharp contrast to the vast majority of Pakistanis who possess richly deep brown hair and brown skin tones.

Most elementary teachers in Pakistan are female—the few exceptions being technology teachers—and most come from middle-class backgrounds. Unlike most of the other teachers at the school where she works, Shagufta grew up in an extremely poor family in the countryside of northern Pakistan and studied in a rural public school until fifth grade. At that time, her family moved to the city of Lahore. Shagufta feels lucky that her family moved to the city when they did. It was only by moving to Lahore that high school became a viable opportunity for Shagufta. The high school was easily accessible from her new home, and there were fewer family chores in their urban home. Shagufta is one of the few people in her community to have completed high school. Although she now believes that her education was not

**Fig. 8.4** Shagufta (center) with Angie and Bhaskar.

very good, it nevertheless enabled her to gain some credentials and move into a teaching career.

Shagufta received familial support to attend school only from her mother and grandmother. Her father and older brothers believed that a woman's education was wasted time. Shagufta desperately wanted a high school education and steadily managed to convince her parents to allow her to finish her degree. However, after completing high school, both parents opposed any further study. Even her mother, a primary supporter, was not interested in her continued education. Shagufta's mother believed that it was more important for her (and her sisters) to learn how to do household chores—cooking, cleaning, caring for children, and washing clothes—than to attend school. Shagufta's mother believed, as is the custom in Pakistan, that learning to manage the home would help the parents secure a good groom for the daughters more so than any formal education. On the contrary, Shagufta believed that education was of primary importance because a formal education would be the only way she could "stand on her own feet" and help her family's financial status. Shagufta also believed that in addition to learning about different topics like health or the environment, a formal education would allow her to gain social and political power, which would, by extension, help the family as well. If she could prove to her parents that her education was beneficial to the family (rather than to just herself), then her younger brother and sisters might have the chance of continuing their education beyond high school.

Shagufta spent one full year working to convince her mother that college was worthwhile. She knew that "if I had any chance of going to school then it was through convincing my mother." As she explains:

> First I convinced my eldest sister. And then, she also worked with me. Like she told my mother that if she wants to get an education then you [mother] should allow us. . . . Then with the passage of time my mother understood that if she wants then I should [be allowed]. But with this, my grandmother also . . . said to my mother, my grandmother is like eighty years old. She really wanted that I should get an education . . . and there was a teacher, Miss Namunasheesh, she also convinced my family. Very much that's why I joined college.

Finally, after a year she succeeded in convincing her mother that she should attend college, though her father and brothers remained strongly opposed to the idea.

> They always made fun of me like, with smile, "yay pani baraygee" (She will carry water.) (*Baskhar laughs.*) (*With laughter.*) "Pani baraygee, miss

banaygee ya, Ieeshay bayjayn college. . ." (Will carry water, will become a
teacher, let's send her to college.)

In Pakistan these remarks in Urdu are used satirically to insult or to
humiliate a person. What Shagufta is saying is that her brothers do not
believe that education, especially for women, can bring good things in
life. They strongly believe that women's role will always be to "carry
water," whether they are in their parents' home or their own. Her
brothers believe that sending a woman to college does not liberate
them from household duties, and thus they believe that allowing Shagufta to attend college was a waste of time and family resources.
Though her brothers do not have a high school education or hold
powerful positions in the labor force, they hold power in family's decision-making process.

Without the support of her father or brothers, Shagufta enrolled in
evening school, and completed a two-year college course in six
months:

> Even if I didn't join college, I joined an academy for six months like science
> academy, for two days in the evening and I paid three hundred rupees per
> month for that. It was difficult for my parents to pay three hundred ru-
> pees per month, but I said to them, "It's only for six months. After that
> you don't have to pay any money for me. Only for the six months." That's
> why they did it.

Shagufta's choice to attend evening school was pragmatic. The tuition was lower, admission was less competitive, and it allowed her to
work in the home during the day. Shagufta began to receive her father's support only when it became painfully obvious to Shagufta and
her entire family that the local community was strongly opposed to
her attendance at evening school. In fact, Shagufta's neighbors described her as a bad role model for other girls in the neighborhood because they might demand a college education as well. The community
also shunned Shagufta because she chose to attend night school, even
though it was the only way she could afford to go to college and to
continue to conduct women's work at home caring for her many siblings. The neighbors also feared that if their daughters engaged in this
kind of "night activity" they would be viewed by others as unsuitable
daughters-in-law or wives. The word spread in her neighborhood that
when Shagufta came home very late at night it was because she was
working as a prostitute. Her community could neither accept nor believe that her late arrival home was because she was attending courses:

> Shagufta: Community reaction was not good. They always say bad
> things, like "Your daughter is going in the night." (*Pause.*)

> Ah. (*Pointing toward Angie.*) "Aap ko pata hai jistaraha ki hamaray masaray mei batei hoti hain." (You know how people gossip in our society.)
>
> Researcher: Jee. [Term of acknowledgment.]
>
> Shagufta: You know very well.

Because of the lack of support, Shagufta felt that she was often alone in this struggle:

> It was difficult in the sense that no one was educated at my home. I had to do all the things by myself. . . . Like, who knows something about education? My focus was in education. My parents don't know a single thing about education. That is why it was very difficult.

Shagufta's college education has placed her in a new and relatively powerful position among her family and community. Although her relatives believe that she is now "too proud" because she has gained a teaching certificate, she has gained respect, and is the primary person her father consults whenever he makes major decisions.

> Definitely I feel that I am little bit changed rather than my family. Like my cousins, my brothers, my sisters, and also my father thinks that I am different from sisters and my brothers. He always talks, like whenever he has some problems, he always shares with me.

This is extremely important change in status because, in a way, Shagufta has risen above her ten siblings, including four brothers, in terms of authority in the household.

### *Gaining a Teaching Position: Working for Her Community*

By custom, but not by written law, women are not allowed to drive vehicles. Most professional workingwomen are driven to work either by family members or by private car service. Public buses are generally considered inappropriate forms of travel for professional working women (not of the poverty class). Shagufta takes the unusual step of taking the public bus to work. Although her father walks her to the bus stop, she commutes the rest of the way alone. She does this in part because she cannot afford car service. Her income is devoted to her parents' and siblings' day-to-day needs. She also does this in part because the bus is the form of transportation she grew up with and that the children in her school use, if they are lucky enough to have the opportunity.

Shagufta is a committed teacher of urban high-poverty students, and believes that a central aspect of her role as a teacher is enabling her students in gaining voice and power in their lives and in their communities. As an elementary school science teacher, Shagufta is very passionate about teaching children from poor families. In her own experiences growing up poor, she felt that she received a weak education. However, she also believes that she has a responsibility to pass on whatever she knows to other students from poor backgrounds:

> In those conditions, I got an education. I should—whatever I have learned, I have to pass it to others. And like these students are also from poor backgrounds, poor families, but they are coming to school, and they need an education. I have to teach them good, in a good way. . . . We have to teach them better because we have the same background.

Shagufta believes that despite her own best intentions, poor children, due to a set of compounding factors, are not receiving an adequate education. Schools lack material resources—in fact, at her own school, they have no real science equipment, and what they do have, she has made herself from materials she has gathered. The majority of the teachers in Shagufta's school have a negative attitude toward the children's futures. Although she believes that most of the teachers are good teachers, she stated that most teachers do not believe that the children will graduate from eighth grade, or even that these children are smart enough to do so because they are poor. Finally, because the school is poor it pays its teachers relatively low salaries. She feels that many of the teachers who work there only do so because they could not obtain more prestigious teaching positions. Shagufta, on the other hand, has chosen to teach at this school because she is committed to working closely with high-poverty populations.

To Shagufta, a key role of a teacher is to step outside the social boundaries, which define classes and take responsibility for educating high-poverty children. Shagufta reminds us that in Pakistan, children who grow up in families of low social status remain at a low economic status too: "If a person is a sweeper [a very low-status job], then his whole family is expected to be sweepers. They are not allowed to raise their social status because there are various social barriers, like not getting higher-paying job because of lack of educational opportunities for such families."

### The Political Domain of Science

Shagufta believes that science education needs to stem from the children's social and physical circumstances, such as teaching environmental and health issues that have a close proximity to her students' homes and surrounding areas. "First of all, we start from our homes. I will tell the children that, first of all, look at the environment at your homes. After that children should look at their streets and observe how those streets are. Are your streets clean? Are your alleys clean? The awareness toward environment starts from home." However, what is important about Shagufta's description of beginning science from the home is that it carries with it political overtones. She talks more about beginning science from the concerns that frame living in poverty than from generic home experiences that are devoid of context. For example, Shagufta described how a walk down a street in the neighborhoods of her students would reveal empty lots filled with garbage and sewer water pooled in alleys (see Figure 8.5).

These kinds of environmental issues are what she wants children to explore at home and at school. She asks these critical questions about the school's neighborhood not because she wants her students to feel bad about where they live, but rather because she wants to empower children to make healthy choices for themselves and their communities. She seeks to create learning activities that allow these very questions to come from the children rather than from her. From a learning standpoint, as we showed in the previous chapter, when science learning becomes contextual, students are more likely to become excited, enthusiastic, and eager to learn scientific concepts.

Shagufta's entire science curriculum is built around mini-projects that link fundamental health and environmental concerns with the children's neighborhood and with the state curriculum. She described a project that brought her students out in the neighborhood to survey the levels of air, water, and noise pollution. She wanted to work with them to build gauges to measure levels of noise and of air particulate, and intended to use the findings to help her students understand the health and environmental risks caused by those pollutants, and to devise practical steps they could take at home to improve their individual situations. She wanted to make these solutions community-wide, rather than individual, but each time Shagufta took her students off campus to study science, her headmistress reprimanded her for leaving campus. As a single women and a teacher of young children, this moved against the social norms. Shagufta also worked to connect her findings to the standard curriculum by engaging her students in conversation around some of the primary questions to emerge in their investigation, such as "We cannot live without water. If all the water is dirty what we will do?"

Yet, Shagufta's efforts to enact this kind of teaching have run up against many barriers. Although she did not have the scientific equipment typically used to conduct these studies, she believed that the students should only use those materials that they have access to anyway. This is a great barrier in and of itself, but it is not the only one; her teaching plans also bump up against the rules and customs of both her

**Fig. 8.5** This is an empty lot near Shagufta's school. Cleaning up such lots is one of Shagufta's priorities.

school and the community and this conflict greatly impedes her effort. In particular, she describes three such barriers.

First, Shagufta's administration supported science classrooms that were quiet and obedient, something she did not agree with. Perhaps more salient to Shagufta's political stance with respect to teaching was the belief that being educated in science means learning to ask questions of things that were normally not challenged, a theme that also describes Shagufta's life in general. Education should promote freedom to ask questions, express opinions and views, and choose what one wants to do both inside the classroom and outside of it.

> First, we should teach them and then we should give them the freedom to do what they want. We teach children, but we do not give them any freedom to do anything on their own. We always tell the children what they should not do, where they should sit, how they should ask questions. Salaahiyat (empowerment) is to let the child do what he or she has in his or her mind. A child should have lot of freedom in expressing his or her mind.

A second barrier is the national curriculum. Students in Pakistan are required to take end-of-year exams, which determine which high schools or colleges they are allowed to attend. Consequently, much attention is paid to the national curriculum. Shagufta felt a responsibility to this curriculum, for without mastering it her students would not be able to advance, if they so chose. However, the purposes of education are far broader. Although she hopes that her students will have opportunities to attend high school, she recognized that for economic and cultural reasons, most would not. Science education has to have pragmatic value. Though some of the topics in the state curriculum are related to various community issues, they are few and far between. Shagufta, however, centered her curriculum on community issues, even when her school administration was not very sympathetic about her deviation from usual curriculum.

Third, as a young teacher and a woman, Shagufta has run up against social limitations that she works hard to challenge as far as she can. Female teachers are not allowed to take students outside the classrooms because of social values and status that women have to adhere to, yet Shagufta has broken this rule on occasion.

As a result of these barriers, Shagufta felt as if she were being pulled into two worlds. One world involved using the community and the environment to teach the topics she knew she had to teach because they were on the end-of-year exam. The other world involved projects that actually made a difference in high-poverty communities. Many of Shagufta's neighbors as well as many of her students have been made ill from water-borne diseases, and she knows that she must play a role in reversing this trend. Her way of making sense of both worlds is to use her community-oriented perspective on science education to weave in the required concepts, and then to include additional ideas and concepts she feels are necessary for action. Thus, according to Shagufta, empowering a child from a poor family is not an easy task because first of all, they lack education and do not realize that they have the power to question the authority for their rights. Second, they lack political and financial means to influence or carry out their choices. Third, they are more pressed to get their day-to-day chores completed than to think about speaking for their rights. The didactic nature of instruction supported by the schooling system does not allow students to interact with the teacher and generates a hierarchy, and she sees the same thing happening in her community as well.

## HALEEMA: SCIENCE EDUCATION FOR EMPOWERMENT
### *Becoming a Teacher Educator*

Haleema entered science education through the sciences. She possesses both a bachelor's and a master's in botany and has engaged in laboratory research for several years. Since 1995, Haleema has served as a lecturer and later department chair in the science education program at an educational institution in urban Pakistan. It is at this educational institution that Haleema has been teaching in the pre-service and in-service programs, conducting study tours and collaborating with the schools to conduct different kinds of programs for teaching environmental science.

As a teacher educator in urban Pakistan, Haleema divides her time between teaching pre-service primary science methods courses, conducting in-service workshops with practicing teachers, and carrying out action-based research with children and teachers in urban areas of Pakistan. Nearly all of the primary school teachers with whom Haleema works are female. These women come to her programs from middle-class and lower middle-class backgrounds with little science education experience, and many of them openly acknowledge a fear of science. Haleema thus views her job as a teacher educator as a challenge to help these women learn science and learn how to use science in empowering ways in their own lives, to understand children better, and to realize that they, as teachers, can have a profound impact on the lives of children:

> The situation I am working in is with the pre-service teachers who come to our program after fourteen years of their education. Sometimes they come with science and sometimes without science. . . . For me, they are like primary school teachers who have never thought about the fact that they are important beings of the world. Especially the girls! We have 98 percent girls, from middle class and lower middle class. They can create a difference!

Haleema takes her job as a science teacher educator seriously. If schools are to improve, if poor, urban children are to gain a meaningful and relevant education, and if teachers are to feel empowered enough to make a difference in the lives of children, then she must work with teachers to help them feel confident and comfortable with science and the ways science may intersect in empowering ways with the lives of poor children and their communities.

The idea that schools are failing poor children drives Haleema's practice as a science teacher educator. It is imperative to her that she help uncover the reasons that schools are failing children, and that she help her pre-service and in-service teachers do the same. In particular, Haleema cites two main challenges facing poor schools and the children and teachers in poor urban schools: (a) the challenge of resources; and (b) the challenge of teacher preparation. Haleema described how poor children lack the kinds of home-based academic resources to which children from professional families have access, such as literacy instruction, books, and educational toys. She also described how schools that serve very poor children have extremely limited resources (i.e., no books or outdated books, no science equipment, no computers or other educational technology, limited blackboard space), and in some cases, the very poorest of schools even lack school buildings. According to Haleema it is important for teachers to really understand the child's background because poverty takes different forms and places children in different poverty classes. It is not enough just to know the child is poor: "In a poverty area, first of all, I will have to worry about their hunger, then their background, and what made them to be in that situation because there are again different classes of people living in poverty." What makes the task so difficult is the lack of qualified science teachers in the poor, urban schools:

> [We do not have] trained teachers, availability of resources, or even the knowledge of how to make use of available resources, or the knowledge to make connections between science and the children's everyday life. If a teacher does not know how to make use of local resources, that can create a serious problem. It is an issue for teachers to learn when, how, and where to make use of local resources or the immediate environment. School as a separate entity [separating children from their community] strengthens students' loneliness. Science [if taught appropriately] can help the children develop and have a relationship with their everyday life needs and experiences.

### Science Education for Self- and Community Empowerment

According to Haleema, science education for poor urban children must fundamentally be about self- and community-empowerment and it must also be about teaching for and promoting grassroots social change:

> Teachers should teach science to empower students to be more involved in social change because, for me, it should be the ultimate aim of education. I have seen parents and people around listen to children a lot. Even initiatives at home empower parents and enable them to feel proud of the fact that they are learning something from their children or that she or he is becoming so concerned about the environment. The same thing goes out in the community. The whole street and community would appreciate it and this political change will empower the whole community. A very important thing is that it is not that people do not want to do it. In Pakistan, and I think in many other countries, people just wait for initiatives sometimes because of lack of knowledge about how to do it and sometimes just because of their involvement in their daily life schedules. I have experienced it many times. Even children start taking care of the gardens by asking other children and people not to pluck the flowers from the garden. It is most of the time appreciated by parents, and children do listen to each other too. We did it with how garbage is dumped in a community and what should we do? No one was willing to care about it but once it was done by the children, every mother started doing it. They made compost with the help of gardeners of different homes and they shared it within the community.

Haleema first and foremost addresses the idea of science for empowerment and change in terms of the science content and process skills, which ought to be taught in school. Science must be taught and learned within relevant contexts, which have direct meaning and application in the lives of the children. Specifically, Haleema suggests that teaching students to be agents of change with and through science is important in two main areas—the environment and health—and therefore science education in poor urban settings ought to focus on these two themes. Haleema describes how her work with urban children brought her to this point in her thinking:

> [My experiences with urban children] convinced me more to deal with the issues of environment because like other Third World countries we are in real trouble because of environmental issues. Keeping in view what is happening in my city and surroundings, we lack basic education. We do not have any sense of responsibility and sense of ownership. I will clean my home and throw the garbage outside. I know I cannot change the whole Pakistan. It might not make any difference to the environment if one shopper bag is lying on the road, but it makes a lot of difference to the shopper bag if it reaches its destination.

As Haleema alludes to in the quote above, urban centers in Pakistan struggle with environmental issues. Although Haleema addresses the issue of recycling and pollution, she has shared numerous stories about how the environment and its intersections with health are key survival issues for families in urban poverty. Most children in poor neighborhoods in urban Pakistan live without adequate running water and proper sewage disposal facilities—indeed, much of the sewage drains into open irrigation systems mixing sometimes with potable water sources. From traffic and tropospheric ozone, carbon monoxide, and carbon particulate levels, to industrial as well as personal waste, urban communities struggle with air-quality issues as well.

For example, Haleema told us numerous stories about how the only access families in extreme poverty may have to bathing water may be through the *gandanalas*, the open irrigation canals that run along the roads in poorer neighborhoods (see Figure 8.6). These open systems, often containing high levels of industrial, agricultural, and human waste and farm runoff are unsuitable—indeed, dangerous—for human bathing. Yet because this is the only bathing water many extremely poor families have access to, they continue to use these sources. Access to cleaner water, however, is not the only issue here. As Haleema describes, part of the reason many poor families use these open irrigation systems for bathing is that they do not realize the health or environmental consequences of bathing in such polluted

**Fig. 8.6** Public bus stop in the neighborhood of Shagufta's school. It has an open irrigation canal, or *gandanala*, running next to it.

water. Haleema believes that an exploration of these open irrigation systems could help to educate children about a series of science, technology, society, and health issues. Such a study could incorporate environmental science through studying how the canals were created, where the water comes from and where it goes, how the water (in both quantity and quality) is influenced by weather patterns, and the kinds of pollutants (both visible and invisible) that may lurk in the water, and their sources (open sewerage systems, agricultural and industrial run off). Additionally, health science would emerge in such a study as well. Many of the diseases to which poor children are exposed (and some of which are the leading causes of death among poor children), such as typhoid, hepatitis, dysentery and various forms of food poisoning, are water borne. According to Haleema, a study of these systems could also lead into various epidemiological issues, like cancer and its causes.

Another example provided by Haleema relates to air quality. She told us many children in the poor neighborhoods suffer from respiratory problems as a result of poor ventilation systems in the home. Many poor Pakistani families heat and cook with wood and impure coal, both of which generate large amounts of smoke. Poor ventilation systems can cause the smoke to stay in the house, leading to respiratory problems. This issue should be explored with children, allowing them to understand why their homes are often filled with smoke and the impact this has on them. Such an exploration might provide children and their families with ideas for relatively inexpensive changes, which families could make to reduce the levels of smoke in their breathable air. Not only would this kind of exploration be helpful in teaching children useful science concepts such as air quality, convection, and respiratory systems to name just a few, but also it would draw heavily from students' prior knowledge about the key issues that frame daily life in poor, urban Pakistan. Haleema views this approach to science education as crucial for a number of reasons. Children would gain the needed knowledge and experiences to help bring about quality of life changes in their communities. This approach would also help improve the health of children living in poverty. In Pakistan, prevention is the key idea behind health education because poor people cannot afford treatment or do not have access to doctors and hospitals.

A third example involves gardening. During our stay in Pakistan, Haleema worked with her pre-service teachers to plant and tend a garden in an overgrown, littered public area. She wanted to teach her students about plants; after all, it was her own study of botany that drove her own interest in science. However, she wanted to weave learning about plants into a much larger sociopolitical and economic fabric. She selected a place for a garden that needed cleaning up. A garden would serve this purpose of beautifying the community while at the same time teach the students some things about recycling, reusing, and decomposition. Because she chose to grow common foods and flowers, a garden would connect to areas of science in which her students had some experience, or at least felt comfortable. This was important to her because her own students, pre-service teachers, overwhelmingly felt distanced and afraid of science. Needy families, which normally have little access to fresh fruits and vegetables, could use the produce from the garden. Finally, because the garden was in a community center, she felt it would provide sustained contact between science for change and the people in the neighborhood.

In short, Haleema believes that science curriculum and textbooks need to address the needs of the children from poor neighborhoods, and one way to do this would be to focus on environmental and health science. Not only can children be taught about how to grow food for their family or the dangers of bathing in dirty water, they can also learn about ways to help clean up the community or the water. They can even learn about the sources of pollution and engage in activities that might promote community awareness and action around the issue. Although Haleema does not want to spend educational time only on "negative" issues like water quality and air quality, she believes that children living in extreme poverty positions need concrete ways to improve their quality of life. Thus, the focus on health and environmental science not only has direct applications; it also focuses on self-empowerment.

Haleema often described both in words and in action the role and importance of self-empowerment for poor children. For example, in the following quote, Haleema describes in particular how self-empowerment in science education is tied to (a) learning to use the resources to which one has access to better one's life; and (b) having a positive outlook, by allowing one to focus on what one can do rather than on what one cannot. The quote also shows how Haleema is particularly keen on wanting poor children to realize that what nature offers is accessible to everyone, poor or rich, and that they take advantage of that. They also need to learn to be responsible for what they have because it is precious and should not be destroyed:

> Children in poverty lack resources, good food, clothes, and home. Once they look at themselves they start becoming sympathetic and remain caught in what they do not have. They do not pay any attention to what they have and I think sometimes they are never facilitated to see what they have. They are complete human beings, two eyes, two ears, two hands. They can walk the way they want to. They can run, and they can make a difference to what they have in their surroundings. I want them to start appreciating nature because at least this is what all of us on this globe share. Parks, grounds, deserts, animals, and water bodies. Why do we not start seeing who has created it and what for? For all of us human beings? Is there anyway we can contribute to these things? They should feel empowered and should have a sense of belonging.

In addition, Haleema believes that perhaps being an agent of change may be even more important for children in poverty than for other children because children in poverty often have fewer resources and fewer people and organizations working for them. Thus they must learn to not feel sorry about their lot in life but rather concentrate on working to improve it. Haleema ties the importance of self-empowerment not just to science education but also to the overall importance of schooling:

> I would say here we will have to worry about the purpose of education. What do we need: education or schooling? Do we want our children to be able to live a comfortable and happy life where they are able to critically analyze the situations? . . . So we need school as an entity that empowers people with skills and knowledge.

Haleema's ideal vision of education for poor children as about empowerment and social change also plays out in how she links science education for self-empowerment to community-empowerment. Community-empowerment is important to Haleema because it will hopefully lead to "grassroots movements to improve society for all." She describes this point in terms of environmental education:

> In order to be on the right track, we have to start working in science education at grassroots level. I think if I will be able to create a positive sense toward the environment, they will be able to play toward its betterment and improvement.

This is an important statement because it takes individual and social agency and extends its boundaries beyond the school and beyond learning for the sake of the self to the sake of the larger community. It suggests that what ought to be fundamental to urban science education are the sparks for social and environmental renewal.

According to Haleema, science educators in poor urban settings must realize that students have agency and that part of realizing that agency is learning to use local resources in positive, enhancing ways. One remedy to this situation would be to use the resources that a community already has, such as thinking about the city and all of its offerings as an active scientific laboratory. This would be an essential step in not just locating resources, but also in making science more situated and relevant. Haleema has many ideas for how the city can be used as an active laboratory in this situated approach to science teaching. Areas of study include industry, ecology, the environment, and health and how these areas interact. Further, when the city becomes an active laboratory it not only provides resources, but also it begins to build rich connections between the school and those who work in the community.

> The targets to be attained will be given in a way that one way or the other the community will have to contribute to it. It will be a study of an industry in the given area, ecology and environment of the area, birds and animals of an area and what are some of the issues in the community, how factory or industry is contributing to environmental issues.

For Haleema, science education for empowerment and social change embraces what she calls a "pragmatic and socioculturalism" framework. Knowledge and action are critically linked, and pre-service teachers must begin to make connections, especially around the needs of poor children. If teachers are going to learn to teach for empowerment and social change, then they must have, according to Haleema, a handle on the lives that students bring to the classroom and the ways in which the children and teachers can work together to improve those lives. Pre-service teachers must therefore begin to think about science emerging from everyday experiences such as cooking or tending a garden.

> We start from the kitchen and what you do there, in cooking and in disposing of things. What science is there? How do you bake a cake? What do you use there and why? Where do the wrappers and packings go? What can you do with them? Have you ever read the safety aspects of things you use in the kitchen? What is written on shampoo, vinegar, or oil, etc.?

## MANAGING DANGEROUS LIVES
### Working and Living within Tensions

Teaching for empowerment is dangerous because it exposes conflict. When normalized activities and beliefs are challenged, it brings to light the strain of different forces because students' whole lives are made a part of the classroom experience. Clearly the women in our study teach within multiple, intersecting tensions.

An overarching tension that cuts across Ms. Faizah's, Shagufta's, and Haleema's stories is how engaging in science teaching activities that challenge the purposes and goals of science education with high-poverty youth also means challenging their own roles as women and as teachers in society and challenging poor children's roles in society. This is an extremely complex dynamic. Shagufta wants to help her students to feel empowered and to gain a sense of agency; that is, she wants her students to be able to ask questions that challenge the way things are and she wants her students to feel confident and knowledgeable enough to ask those questions. She also wants her students to know where to go for resources to begin to explore solutions to those questions. She situates her work along these lines in science topics that are of immediate concern to the health and well-being of children. Thus, the most important areas of science to be explored, in Shagufta's mind, include the use and locations of *gandanalas* in poor communities, urban transportation systems in poor communities, food systems, garbage disposal, health care (personal and community), and children's play spaces. Each of these science topics intersects with students' lives through environmental issues, health issues, *and* socio-political issues.

Yet, while Shagufta attempts to make these concerns a valid part of the school experience for her students, she is restricted in her own actions because she is female, because she is a teacher, and because she teaches in a very poor school in a very poor community where education is highly regulated and highly unequal. Shagufta wants to use education to offer a better way of life to poor children but she has few resources available at school to allow her to do so. She wants to draw upon the resources of the community, because in her mind, this is a crucial element to empowering science, but as a female she is not allowed to take her students into the community in the way Michael has taken his students (Chapter 7). Though she disobeys that rule at times, she runs up against those in the community who feel that education belongs inside the school building. She is a teacher whose primary objective is to pass on values, culture, and knowledge, but she feels that some values and traditions ought to be questioned rather than simply passed on. She wants to draw on her own resources (i.e., her history of growing up in poverty and making it as a teacher) but she finds her own story is not valued in school because it is not acknowledged in the school curriculum.

Despite these contradictions, Shagufta and Haleema are working in schools, as teacher and teacher educator, to have community-based topics and experiences officially included in the school curriculum and policies because this will legitimize their teaching of these topics while also obscuring the political nature of their work from those in power who look unfavorably upon their efforts. The study of these topics is not officially promoted by the national curriculum, and deviation from the national curriculum is viewed unfavorably. Contemporary social relations within the country do not support (mainly female) teachers in working with students off school property, in engaging in political work, or in deviating from the national control. If the schools supported the study of these topics, the teachers believe they would have more protection while engaging their students in these activities.

The importance of engaging in community-empowerment and the danger in raising questions about sociopolitical issues or in engaging in physically visible community development efforts was seen when one teacher cut back on her work with students in the community outside the school following a severe reprimand. It is important to note that severe reprimands take many forms, including physical abuse and community isolation. The desire to help students become educated and politically involved must be balanced with the practical reality that society (both the local community and the larger society) will actively work to prevent most of these students (at some point, in some way) from realizing these goals, mainly through forcing them to enter the labor force at early ages to support the family.

### *Managing and Remaking Tensions: Science as Context and Tool*

The stories of the women in this chapter—just like the stories about Henderson Creek and Oceanside or the transformation of the abandoned inner-city lot in previous chapters—point toward the complexities and the dangers of teaching science as a political and socially just act. These dangers are individual and social and have affected these women in very real ways. Although in some very different ways, the women have risked their own livelihoods because they believe in the importance of working for youth empowerment in poor communities, they believe that they must use the little power they have to help make this so, or to, as Ms. Faizah would say, help to bring about a generational change. Their own personal journeys—getting to the places of power to help others—have also been fraught with similar challenges and dangers. Each of the women has defied social, economic, and cultural norms and expectations to work on behalf of poor children and their communities. Ms. Faizah risked her own safety and her reputation to make her school accessible to those in her community. Shagufta risked being ostracized by her community just to win the right to attend college. She continues to risk further alienation by independently taking the bus to work and resisting marriage and household duties. Haleema risks status both within teacher education and her community. Indeed, her entire school risks similar status because it supports practices not sanctioned by the government.

For us, these women's stories suggest just how much doing science, whether in the classroom or elsewhere, is always a political act, regardless of what political stance one takes or how explicit one makes it. Following the state-mandated curriculum or choosing not to teach poor children is just as political and just as consequential as the decisions made by these three women. However, the political decisions made by these women challenge what is normal and thus expose how their actions influence (and are influenced by) the schools in which they work, the communities and the society (both national and global) in which they live and work. Understanding their roles and actions this way helps to position the power of their work in greater terms and underscores how all science education is always bigger than what goes on behind closed classroom doors. It's bigger in the sense that what happens in classrooms is informed by larger social and political relations, those regarding how women must act, how poor children must act, and what women and poor children are entitled to. It is also bigger in the sense that the actual "doing" of science relies on the collective expertise of those involved in the process. As Shagufta aptly reminds us, her students can learn about air pollution because that is in the national syllabus and on the national exam. However, air pollution is not a real science experience until it is explored in the community alongside the very people who live and work with affected air quality on a daily basis. Embedded in Shagufta's expression is the notion that the experiences of the children in communities with low air quality can make significant contributions to the actual study of that science. Without them, air pollution is only a topic in a book. Likewise, Haleema's report of the recycling activities make a similar claim about how science education is bigger than what goes on behind classroom doors.

Science education for social justice repositions the learning and doing of science from an individual (or even classroom) activity to an interactivity, intimately a part of the contexts and the relationships in which it takes place. In other words, these teachers position the praxis of science with children such that it involves the collaboration of people and things and contexts. They position science within relationships and they position children who are viewed as powerless in the schooling system and in their communities as having the ability to act. Through the study of *gandanalas* or trash lots or personal hygiene, Shagufta helps children not only to use science to act on these things that affect their lives, but she also helps them to use the space of science to challenge authority and decision-making in their society. Such decisions define who these children are supposed to be and the places they are supposed to live.

The way these teachers do this is by positioning science as both context and tool rather than as a body of knowledge to be learned or a mandate to be followed. In other words, these teachers use the space of science to challenge particularly powerful social relations that work toward their oppression. By "space of science" we mean the overall situation, like the very context of studying water pollution through the pooled sewer water in the alleyways because these are the conditions in which the children live. Here, the act of learning science in a community context provides a space for challenging norms about participation and identity. It carries with it different rules and boundary conditions that may make some things more acceptable.

The teachers also use science as a means or an instrument for opening up contexts and relationships. Ms. Faizah talked about wanting the students in her school to feel empowered to ask questions, even if those questions challenge traditional authority or traditions. Science is a tool used by Ms. Faizah to allow some of those questions to be asked. Ms. Faizah was quite political about this too. She did so in very traditional ways—she had the students in her school compete in city-wide science contests, using her students' work in the science contest to challenge others' views on what poor children can do. More directly connected to the children's lives, however, she used science activities to engage parents in the goings-on of the school because science projects were "hands-on" and often involved ideas many of the parents knew something about their daily lives. Ms. Faizah may not have been as radical as either Shagufta or Haleema in her views of what science actually is, but she used science as an area of study that connected the world around her school and connected to the national curriculum as well to challenge the barriers setting up by economic inequality and schooling in urban Pakistan.

## LOOKING AHEAD

Teaching science as a political act is dangerous because it explicitly situates science across people, within power, and as part of social processes and institutions. Using science as a tool for change is an enactment of power and relationships; it is interactivity, pulling people and contexts together in particular ways. Situating working for change in the context of science gives the practice a power and validity that women's lives and poor children's lives might not have otherwise.

Yet because science emerges from interactivity, rather than being knowledge in books or in someone's mind, using science as a tool and context for change means that the dangers of engaging such work stretch far and deep as well. Ms. Faizah, Shagufta, and Haleema engaged in dangerous teaching, even when that practice was dangerous for them inside and outside the classroom because each one felt, in their own unique way, obligated to reframe teaching in poor urban settings in political terms of new social relations and environmental conditions built upon equity and social justice within urban Pakistan are to be realized. The three teachers uphold this obligation because they believe that current schooling practices in poor communities are not responsive to (and indeed purposefully ignore) a key set of issues that serve to perpetuate social, political, and economic inequalities. They live this obligation in ways that challenge their own safety and position within society. These three teachers' commitments run deep. They do much more than simply choose to teach in poor urban settings then return to the comforts of their home each night, as many good teachers do. Each of these women has taken public risks that create dangers for themselves at work and at home.

We provided glimpses into the practices of three educators, yet these glimpses are far too one-sided. We chose to focus on their work for social change because this issue was important to them and important to us. We chose to highlight examples of their teaching that demonstrated the risks they have taken. But, these teachers' lives are real; and with this concrete reality of their lives comes the challenge of infusing this belief system into everything they do. So, though Shagufta fought to bring her science teaching into the community, much of her time is also spent in the confines of the classroom weaving her way back and forth between the national curriculum and her goals for her students. Though Haleema passionately worked to engage her pre-service teachers in a teaching practice that would be empowering for poor children, she often found her students resisting her message and wanting a traditional methods experience. Ms. Faizah, though she embraced the needs of her community and the need for human rights, kept a mindful watch of the national exams and her students' performances on those exams, for in the end, she felt this was their best hope for success.

All three teachers talked about the challenge of political control in the very tension set up between "what schools are supposed to do" and "what science education is for" and the needs of the children in high poverty. Shagufta was particularly concerned that schooling is set up such that it appears that poor children have the same chance to succeed as all other children—they get the same curriculum and take the same tests. She worries, however, that without appropriate consideration for the needs of poor families (i.e., the need for income, the need for sanitary conditions, etc.), then schools cannot and never will be equal.

Teaching science as a political act is not something that should be necessary only in countries with repressive regimes or sociocultural value systems different from those of industrialized nations. Rather, we believe that industrialized nations subscribing to free global markets require concentrated dangerous teaching toward social justice. We can no longer continue exploiting our environment or exporting our problems by moving industries, tobacco production and consumption, and "modern" exploitative food production into Third World countries. But we must teach students to become aware of the social, political, and economic forces that shape the ways we know and live. Teaching is a political act when it promotes active participation in citizen science and engagement for social justice.

A practice for social justice is dangerous, for it challenges so many things at one time. Using science as a context and a tool for change opens up spaces (though they may be small in the larger scheme of the lives of these educators and their students) for those teachers who expose normative practices for what they are and offered their students a different view of the world.

# NOTES

## Acknowledgments

1. Wolff-Michael Roth and Stuart Lee, "Scientific Literacy as Collective Praxis," *Public Understanding of Science*, vol. 11, no. 1 (2002), 33–56.
2. Wolff-Michael Roth, "Scientific Literacy as an Emergent Feature of Human Practice," *Journal of Curriculum Studies*, vol. 35, no.1 (2003), 9–24.
3. Wolff-Michael Roth, "Constructing Dis/ability in Science," paper presented at the annual meeting of the National Association for Research in Science Teaching, New Orleans, LA (April 2002).
4. Wolff-Michael Roth and Stuart Lee, "School Science in and for the Community: An Activity Theoretical Perspective," paper presented at the annual meeting of the American Educational Research Association, Seattle, WA (April 2001).
5. Angela Calabrese Barton, "Margin and Center: Intersections of Urban, Homeless Children and a Pedagogy of Liberation," *Theory into Practice*, vol. 37, no. 4 (1998), 296–305.

## Chapter 1

1. This quote appears in a number of press releases. See, for example, the web site of the Office of Science of the U.S. Department of Energy, whose motto is "Science for America's Future." See http://www.er. doe.gov/feature_articles_2001/December/Homeland_Security/Homeland Security.htm).
2. *Project 2061* is available online at URL http://www.project2061.org/.
3. Norm Levitt, *Prometheus Bedeviled: Science and the Contradictions of Contemporary Culture* (New Brunswick, N.J.: Rutgers University Press, 1999), 4.
4. Morris H. Shamos, *The Myth of Scientific Literacy* (New Brunswick, N.J.: Rutgers University Press, 1995), 191.
5. Peter Fensham, "Changing the Drivers for Science Education," *Canadian Journal of Science, Mathematics and Technology Education*, vol. 2, no. 1 (2002), 9–24.
6. Wolff-Michael Roth and Michelle K. McGinn, "Deinstitutionalizing School Science: Implications of a Strong View of Situated Cognition," *Research in Science Education*, vol. 27, no. 4 (1997), 497–513.
7. Michelle K. McGinn and Wolff-Michael Roth, "Toward a New Science Education: Implications of Recent Research in Science and Technology Studies," *Educational Researcher*, vol. 28, no. 3 (1999), 14–24.

8. See, for example, Alan Irwin and Bryan Wynne, eds., *Misunderstanding Science? The Public Reconstruction of Science and Technology* (Cambridge: Cambridge University Press, 1996).

9. A study of the production of artifacts that become commodities exchanged for marks (grades) has yet to be conducted. Suffice to indicate the fundamental alienation many (non-middle-class) students experience in schooling is similar to that experienced by factory workers who exchange products of labor for wages.

10. Edgar Jenkins, "School Science, Citizenship and the Public Understanding of Science, *International Journal of Science Education*, vol. 21 (1999), 703–10, at 704.

11. Ray P. McDermott, "The Acquisition of a Child by a Learning Disability," in Seth Chaiklin and Jean Lave, eds., *Understanding Practice: Perspectives on Activity and Context* (Cambridge: Cambridge University Press, 1993), 269–305, at 277, emphasis in the original.

12. Derek Hodson, "Going Beyond Cultural Pluralism: Science Education for Sociopolitical Action," *Science Education*, vol. 83 (1999), 775–96, at 789.

## *Chapter 2*

1. Margaret Eisenhart, Elizabeth Finkel, and Scott F. Marion, "Creating the Conditions for Scientific Literacy: A Re-Examination," *American Educational Research Journal*, vol. 33, no. 2 (1996), 261–95, at 281.

2. The roots of activity theory as it is currently used lie in the work of Alexei N. Leont'ev. See Alexei N. Leont'ev, *Activity, Consciousness and Personality* (Englewood Cliffs, N.J.: Prentice Hall, 1978). More recent discussions and elaborations of activity theory can be found in Yrjö Engeström, Reijo Miettinen, and Raija-Leena Punamäki, eds., *Perspectives on Activity Theory* (Cambridge: Cambridge University Press, 1999).

3. Stuart H. Lee and Wolff-Michael Roth, "How Ditch and Drain Become a Healthy Creek: Representations, Translations and Agency During the Re/Design of a Watershed," *Social Studies of Science*, vol. 31, no. 4 (2001), 315–56.

4. Gene Rowe and Lynn J. Frewer, "Public Participation Methods: A Framework for Evaluation," *Science, Technology, and Human Values*, vol. 25, no. 1 (2000), 3–29. See also Alan Irwin, "Constructing the Scientific Citizen: Science and Democracy in the Biosciences," *Public Understanding of Science*, vol. 10, no. 1 (2001), 1–18.

5. See, for example, Wolff-Michael Roth et al., "Those Who Get Hurt Aren't Always Being Heard: Scientist-Resident Interactions Over Community Water," *Science, Technology, and Human Values* (in press). There are other reports that show that scientists often attempt to bludgeon the public. See, for example, Nick Brown and Mike Michael, "Switching between Science and Culture in Transpecies Transplantation," *Science, Technology, and Human Values*, vol. 26, no. 1 (2001), 3–22.

6. Kevin P. Paul, *The Care-Takers* (Sidney, B.C.: Institute of the Ocean Sciences, 1995), 2–3.

7. Dave Elliott Sr., *Saltwater People*, ed. Janet Poth (Central Saanich, B.C.: School District No. 63, 1983), 17.

8. Earl Claxton, *The Saanich Year* (Brentwood Bay, B.C.: Saanich Indian School Board, 1993), 27.

9. Elliott, *Saltwater People*, 18.

10. Gerard Fourez, "Scientific and Technological Literacy as a Social Practice," *Social Studies of Science*, vol. 27, no. 6 (1997), 903–36.

11. Edgar Jenkins, "School Science, Citizenship and the Public Understanding of Science," *International Journal of Science Education*, vol. 21, no. 7 (1999), 703–10, at 708.

# Chapter 3

1. For the documentary, see Matt H. Schneps and Philip M. Sadler, *A Private Universe* [Video] (Washington, D.C.: Annenberg/CPB, 1987/1992). Bruce Mateson was quoted by Jeff Foust, Boston NSS January Lecture Summary, *SpaceViews*, February 1997 (available at http://www.seds.org/spaceviews/9702/nss-news.html, August 19, 2002). Now, what is so wrong with saying that it is warmer when the source of heat (sun) is closer to the testing location (Earth)? It normally is—but planet temperatures are also functions of the diurnal cycle, presence and density of an atmosphere, and the orientation of the polar axis with respect to the plane constituted by the planet's trajectory. Additionally, in the Northern Hemisphere, the temperatures are not aligned with the tilt of Earth.
2. Jean Lave, "The Practice of Learning," in Seth Chaiklin and Jean Lave, eds., *Understanding Practice: Perspectives on Activity and Context* (Cambridge: Cambridge University Press, 1993), 3–32, at 15.
3. Emily Martin, "Anthropology and the Cultural Study of Science," *Science, Technology, and Human Values*, vol. 23, no. 1 (1998), 24–44, at 30.
4. Lave, "The Practice of Learning," 17.
5. Educated individuals can make out these rigid politics, as a recently completed study showed, which involved seven, very differently located individuals analyzing the Salina Drive controversy. See Wolff-Michael Roth et al., "Those Who Get Hurt Aren't Always Being Heard: Scientist-Resident Interactions over Community Water," *Science, Technology, and Human Values* (in press).
6. Ray P. McDermott, The acquisition of a child by a learning disability. In Seth Chaiklin and Jean Lave, eds., *Understanding Practice: Perspectives on Activity and Context* (Cambridge: Cambridge University Press, 1993), 269–305, at 292.

# Chapter 4

1. See David Dickson, "Science and its Public: The Need for a Third Way," *Social Studies of Science*, vol. 30, no. 6 (2000), 917–23.
2. Ibid., 920.
3. Ibid., 919.
4. Charles Daniels, *Lords of the Harvest: Biotech, Big Money and the Future of Food* (Cambridge, Mass.: Perseus Publishing, 2001).
5. Hugh Gusterson, "How Not to Construct a Radioactive Waste Incinerator," *Science, Technology, and Human Values*, vol. 25, no. 3 (2000), 332–51.
6. Ibid., 345.
7. The voice is that of Angie. In particular, we would like to mention Dana Fusco and Courtney St. Prix, who took the lead in planning the action research program with the youth.
8. See Phillip Carspecken, *Critical Ethnography in Educational Research: A Theoretical and Practical Guide* (New York: Routledge, 1996); Enrique Trueba, *Latinos Unidos: From Cultural Diversity to the Politics of Solidarity* (Lanham, Md.: Rowman and Littlefield, 1999).
9. Growing up in poverty, the other author (Michael), too, has repeatedly been homeless, living out of a sleeping bag, a tent pitched on wilderness campgrounds that charged no fees, or a car. Equally important, though, poverty meant limited means to purchase food, which led to eating only one meal a day for months on end. Michael also conducts, together with Ken Tobin, research in Philadelphia's inner-city schools predominantly attended by urban youths from poverty-stricken families.

10. See Angela Calabrese Barton and Darkside, "Autobiography in Science Education: Greater Objectivity through Local Knowledge," *Research in Science Education*, vol. 30, no. 1 (2000), 23–42.

11. See Rick Beard, *On Being Homeless: Historical Perspectives* (New York: Museum of the City of New York, 1987).

12. Homes for the Homeless, *Day to Day . . . Parent to Child: The Future of Violence among Homeless Children in America* (New York: Institute for Children and Poverty, 1998).

13. This word is used to refer to non-homeless.

14. National Center for Health Statistics, *Current Estimates from the National Health Interview Survey, 1994* (Washington, D.C.: U.S. Dept. of Health and Human Services, 1995).

15. These policies include such things as slashed public assistance, reduced food stamps, cuts in housing assistance, denied Earned Income Tax Credits, and cuts in welfare spending.

16. See Ralph de Costa Nunez, *The New Poverty: Homeless Families in America* (New York: Insight Books, 1996).

17. See Gene Rowe and Lynn J. Frewer, "Public Participation Methods: A Framework for Evaluation," *Science, Technology, and Human Values*, vol. 25, no. 1 (2000), 3–29, at 6.

18. This name and all names of the youth, shelters, and neighborhoods are pseudonyms used to protect the identity of the participants. All youth in this study selected their pseudonyms themselves. All youths' first choices for pseudonyms were accepted, even when those names were questionable.

19. Dickson, "Science and Its Public," 918.

20. See Sandra Harding, *Is Science Multicultural?: Postcolonialisms, Feminisms, and Epistemologies* (Bloomington: Indiana University Press, 1998).

## Chapter 5

1. All names in this chapter are pseudonyms. Latisha wrote this poem during an after-school science program at the shelter where she lives.

2. bell hooks, *Feminist Theory: From Margin to Center* (Boston, Mass.: South End Press, 1984), ix.

3. Gloria Anzaldua, *Borderlands/La Frontera: The New Mestiza* (San Francisco: Spinster/Aunt Lute Press, 1987); bell hooks, *Ain't I a Woman: Black Women and Feminism* (Boston, Mass.: South End Press, 1981).

4. One day a month, Angie baked with Latisha at her request. They used a cookbook Latisha found in the donations box at her shelter, and which prompted their baking meetings, and a small electric portable stove that Angie brought from home. Almost always, at Latisha's request, the pair cooked desserts.

5. hooks, *Feminist Theory*, ix.

6. The data about Claudia presented here were collected through interviews, observations, informal conversations, and review of school-based artifacts (report cards, written school work, etc.).

7. Hope Shelter is home to seventy homeless families in Well Springs, Texas, a large city. The shelter has been in existence for four years and serves only families in extreme poverty who come from domestic abuse situations. The shelter, which sits on the outskirts of the city, is home to over a hundred children, only one-third of whom are school-aged. The shelter is a "long-term" shelter or "supportive housing complex," providing shelter to families for, on average, twelve to fifteen months. The demographics of the residents at Hope are mixed. At any given time, about half the population is Hispanic (predominantly Mexican American), one quarter is African American, and one quarter is white.

9. Almost a year later, the picnic table remains central to the youth's after-school lives. It is the only piece of outdoor furniture in the fenced-off area by the children's building. They use it as an activities table, a place to eat, a platform for peering over the fence that marks the shelter boundary, and as home base in outdoor games.

10. See Margaret Eisenhart, Elizabeth Finkel, and Scott F. Marion, "Creating the Conditions for Scientific Literacy: A Re-Examination," *American Educational Research Journal*, vol. 33, no. 2 (1996), 261–95.

11. American Association for the Advancement of Science. *Science for all Americans: Project 2061* (Washington, D.C.: AAAS, 1989), 151.

12. See Steven Epstein, *Impure Science: AIDS, Activism, and the Politics of Knowledge* (Berkeley: University of California Press, 1997); Randy Shilts, *And the Band Played On* (New York: Penguin Books, 1987).

13. See Michelle K. McGinn and Wolff-Michael Roth, "Toward a New Science Education: Implications of Recent Research in Science and Technology Studies," *Educational Researcher*, vol. 28, no. 3 (1999), 14–24, at 15.

# Chapter 6

1. Wolff-Michael Roth and Michelle K. McGinn, ">unDELETE science education: /lives/work/voices," *Journal of Research in Science Teaching*, vol. 35, no. 4 (1998), 399–421, at 401.

2. Jean Lave, "The Practice of Learning," in Seth Chaiklin and Jean Lave, eds., *Understanding Practice: Perspectives on Activity and Context* (Cambridge: Cambridge University Press, 1993), 3–32, at 12.

3. Jean Lave, *Cognition in Practice* (Cambridge: Cambridge University Press, 1988).

4. Geoffrey B. Saxe, *Culture and Cognitive Development: Studies in Mathematical Understanding* (Hillsdale, N.J.: Lawrence Erlbaum Associates, 1991).

5. Hugh Mehan, "Beneath the Skin and Between the Ears: A Case Study in the Politics of Representation," in Seth Chaiklin and Jean Lave, eds., *Understanding Practice: Perspectives on Activity and Context* (Cambridge, England: Cambridge University Press, 1993), 241–68; Dana Fusco and Angela Barton Calabrese, "Representing Student Achievements in Science," *Journal of Research in Science Teaching*, vol. 38, no. 4 (2001), 337–54.

6. Aboriginal students have a choice to attend a local tribal school or to attend the public middle school. About 10 percent of the middle school student population has aboriginal status.

7. Lave, "The Practice of Learning," 12.

8. See also our discussion of the "zone of proximal development" in Chapter 3.

# Chapter 7

1. See Margaret Eisenhart, Elizabeth Finkel, and Scott F. Marion, "Creating the Conditions for Scientific Literacy: A Re-Examination," *American Educational Research Journal*, vol. 33, no. 2 (1996), 261–95, at 281.

2. Gerard Fourez, Scientific and technological literacy as a social practice," *Social Studies of Science*, vol. 27, no. 6 (1997), 903–36, at 907.

3. Paul deHart Hurd, "Scientific Literacy: New Minds for a Changing World," *Science Education*, vol. 82, no. 6 (1998), 407–16.

4. Jean Lave, "The Practice of Learning," in Seth Chaiklin and Jean Lave, eds., *Understanding Practice: Perspectives on Activity and Context* (Cambridge: Cambridge University Press, 1993), 3–32, at 12.

5. Edgar Jenkins, "School Science, Citizenship and the Public Understanding of Science," *International Journal of Science Education*, vol. 21, no. 7 (1999), 703–10, at 704.

6.  Ray P. McDermott, The acquisition of a child by a learning disability. In Seth Chaiklin and Jean Lave, eds., *Understanding Practice: Perspectives on Activity and Context* (Cambridge: Cambridge University Press, 1993), 269–305, at 277.
7.  Some argue that even if all students learned scientific concepts, they would not automatically use science in socially responsible ways; there is no evidence that trained scientists do so. Furthermore, it does not change the social costs often associated with doing well in school, where non-adherence to middle-class values and interactional patterns often leads to resistance and subsequent failure.
8.  Hurd, "Scientific Literacy," 411.

## *Chapter 8*

1.  Derek Hodson, "Going beyond Cultural Pluralism: Science Education for Sociopolitical Action," *Science Education*, vol. 83, no. 5 (1999), 775–96.
2.  Ibid., 789.
3.  For excellent examples, please see: Margery Osborne, "Responsive Science Pedagogy in a Democracy: Dangerous Teaching," *Theory into Practice*, vol. 37, no. 4 (1998), 289–96; Kenneth Tobin, Gale Seiler, and Ed Walls, "Reproduction of Social Class in the Teaching and Learning of Science in Urban High Schools," *Research in Science Education*, vol. 29, no. 2 (1998), 171–87; Lorie Hammond, "Notes from California: An Anthropological Approach to Urban Science Education for Language Minority Families," *Journal of Research in Science Teaching*, Vol. 38, No. 10 (2001), 983–99; 2001; Gale Seiler, "Reversing the 'Standard' Direction: Science Emerging from the Lives of African American Students," *Journal of Research in Science Teaching*, vol. 38, no. 9 (2001), 1000–15.
4.  Osborne, "Responsive Science Pedagogy," 290.
5.  See Kathleen Casey, *I Answer with My Life: Life Histories of Women Teachers Working for Social Change* (New York: Routledge, 1993); Jean D. Clandinin and F. Michael Connelly, *Narrative Inquiry: Experience and Story in Qualitative Research* (San Francisco: Jossey-Bass Publishers, 2000); Corey Drake, James P. Spillane and Kimberly Hufferd-Ackles, "Storied Identities: Teacher Learning and Subject-Matter Context," *Journal of Curriculum Studies*, vol. 33, no. 1 (2001), 1–24.
6.  Government schools are free, under the national law, in that they do not charge tuition. However, there are many other fees associated with schooling that make these schools unaffordable to some, such as attendance fees, book fees, lab fees, enrollment fees, and so on. Additionally, in some extremely impoverished neighborhoods, government schools exist only as ghost schools, meaning that the school exists on paper, and government money is passed on to individuals to run the school, but the money is distributed to individuals for personal profit, and no actual school exists.

# INDEX

*A Private Universe*, 49. *See also* Harvard
  graduates
aboriginal, children, 134; elders, 47,
  131, 162, 174; families, 133;
  knowledge, 154; people, 11, 74, 134;
  perspectives, 40–5; students, 130, 133,
  155, 167, 219
Abraham, Spencer, 2
accountability, 90, 101, 129
activist, 11, 23, 47, 81, 149, 150, 151, 160;
  AIDS, 126–7, 128; community, 14, 17,
  77, 96, 148; environmental, 13, 14, 25,
  27–9, 33, 36, 40, 41, 44, 47, 134, 140,
  142; science education as, 123
aesthetics, 3, 68, 74
Afghanistan, 1
agency, 6, 11, 14, 16–7, 50, 104, 108, 117,
  130–33, 158, 209, 216; expanded, 17;
  federal, 25; generalized, 131;
  individual, 108, 131, 158; social, 208.
  *See also* power to act
agendas, 6; alternative, 4; national, 5;
  reform, 3, 7–9, 47; research, 21, 166;
  science for all, 129
AIDS, 51, 78, 86, 92, 126–7, 128, 173,
  219n12
alienation, 56, 120, 211, 216n9
American Association for the
  Advancement of Science, 4, 125,
  219n11

Amnesty International, 1
Anzaldua, Gloria, 218n3
Attention Deficit Hyperactive Disorder
  (ADHD), 3, 132
authenticity, 96, 131, 164; authentic
  activity, 9, 73, 165; authentic science,
  21
authority, 5, 59, 110, 117, 124, 128, 189;
  challenging, 194–201, 212; collective,
  117; health, 39, 66, 70; from the
  margins, 119–22; scientific, 122
awareness, 73, 173, 192

Barton, Angela Calabrese, 82, 215n5,
  218n10, 219n5
Beard, Rick, 218n11
*Benchmarks*, 4
border, 40, 122, 126, 127, 128, 185;
  borderland, 109, 218n3; borderland
  community, 128; Doctors without
  Borders, 178; home-school, 109
boundary, 24, 219; conditions, 212;
  crossing, 9; work, 50
Brown, Nick, 216n5
bureaucracy, 84, 86

Carspecken, Phillip, 217n8
Casey, Kathleen, 220n5
Chaiklin, Seth, 216n11, 217n2, 217n6,
  219n2, 219n5, 219n4, 220n6

**221**

discrimination, 10
disempowerment, 128
division of labor, 10, 11, 26, 29, 32, 36, 45, 46, 48, 50, 137, 150, 151, 152, 154, 164
Doctors without Borders, 178
Drake, Corey, 220n5

economics, 3, 19, 32, 74
education, formal, 17, 21, 47, 49, 192, 195. *See also* formal learning setting, schooling
Eisenhart, Margaret, viii, 157, 216n1, 219n10, 219n1
Elliott, Dave, 216n7, 216n9
empowerment, 15, 113, 117, 128, 150, 170, 176, 185–6, 199, 200, 212, 213; act of, 193; community, 183, 203–8, 210; personal, 183; science (education) as/for, 102, 127, 201–8, 209; self-, 203–8; teaching for, 209; youth, 210; zone, 5. *See also* power, power-knowledge, knowledge as power
enculturation, 6
Engeström, Yrjö, 216n2
engineers, 1–2, 6, 11, 19, 38, 55–6, 57, 59, 64, 66, 69, 70, 77; environmental, 65–6; municipal, 55, 58; professional, 56; public health, 56, 57
Epstein, Steve, 219n12
equity, 103, 213
ethics, 2, 11, 19, 50, 74
ethnicity, 83, 109, 122, 125
exams, 8–9; end-of-year, 185, 200–201; high-stakes, 8, 102; national, 12, 182, 211, 213
exams, high-stakes, 8, 102. *See also* PISA, testing, TIMMS
experiment, 102, 113, 123, 162; double-blind, 51, 127; drugs, 51; evidence, 48; teaching, 130
expertise, 2, 13, 29–31, 40, 59, 62, 81, 89, 94, 95, 140, 176; collective, 211; different kind of, 62, 104; distributed, 27; levels of, 39, 47, 145; limits of, 65–71; local, 62; scientific, 7, 18, 38, 39, 63, 159; special, 54

experts, 18, 50, 56, 62, 80, 103–4, 145; engaging with, 95–99; outside, 6, 90; scientific, 8, 90, 176; social, 8

failure, 17, 128, 138, 161, 220n7; production of 17, 53, 137, 138, 149
farmers, 12, 17, 22, 25–6, 27, 31, 44, 70, 77, 175, 182; Third World, 79
Fensham, Peter, 6–7, 215
Finkel, Elizabeth, 157, 216n1, 219n10, 219n1
First Nations, 5, 40, 42, 43, 77, 133, 160, 166, 182
Fourez, Gerard, 157, 216n10, 219n2
Frewer, Lynn J., 216n4, 218n17

garbage, 84, 87, 88, 98, 169, 199, 203–4, 209; removal, 92, 96, 103, 191
garden, 10, 46, 124, 127, 159; butterfly, 117–9, 120, 124; community, 11, 14, 16, 77–106, 108, 154, 182
gender, 19, 109, 122, 125, 129
genetically modified organism (GMO), 2–3, 10, 15, 19, 78–79, 36; anti-GMO, 2; non-GMO, 11
genome, 3, 12
globalization, 2
government, 1, 25, 78, 90, 93, 95, 101–2, 127, 185, 187, 192, 220; non-government organization, 187; non-government sanctioned, 191, 211
grassroots, 192
Greenpeace, 178
Gusterson, Hugh, 217n5

habitat, 27–9, 40, 118, 166, 172; assessment, 32, 34–5
Hammond, Lorie, 220n3
Hardin, Sandra, 101, 218n20
Harvard graduates, 4, 49
hegemony, 15, 49–75, 185; counter-hegemony, 60, 62, 66, 71, 74; struggle for, 56, 57, 66, 71, 74
heterogeneity, 32, 37, 40, 47, 48, 50, 52, 53, 55–9, 86
Hodson, Derek, 11, 182, 216n12, 220n1
homogeneity, 8, 47, 50